1997

This book explores interconnections between voyage narratives and travel plays in a period of intense foreign relations and the incipient colonization of the New World.

Eminent Renaissance scholars from five countries use historical enquiry and textual analysis to offer new readings of narrative and dramatic texts, envisaged both in the context of the period and from the far-reaching perspective of Britain's cultural history.

Plays like *The Spanish Tragedy, Doctor Faustus, Eastward Ho!* or *The Tempest* – itself the subject of three chapters – are discussed alongside relatively obscure works like *The Travels of the Three English Brothers* by Day, Rowley and Wilkins, Daborne's *A Christian Turn'd Turk* or Fletcher and Massinger's *The Sea-Voyage*. The plays are never approached as mere cultural documents. The underlying assumption is that the theatre is not reducible to a medium for conflicting ideologies but should be viewed as a privileged site of various meanings, of roads leading in several directions.

Several chapters identify the various discourses which inform contemporary travel documents. The authors of these chapters clarify the cultural codes which travel narratives place between the reader and the supposed eyewitness. The readings of drama and travel literature are grounded firmly in the period for which they were written, and take into account the preconceptions and perceptions of their original public.

TRAVEL AND DRAMA IN
SHAKESPEARE'S TIME

TRAVEL AND DRAMA
IN SHAKESPEARE'S
TIME

EDITED BY

JEAN-PIERRE MAQUERLOT

AND

MICHÈLE WILLEMS

Centre d'études du théâtre anglo-saxon, Université de Rouen

CAMBRIDGE
UNIVERSITY PRESS

Published by the Press Syndicate of the University of Cambridge
The Pitt Building, Trumpington Street, Cambridge CB2 1RP
40 West 20th Street, New York, NY 10011-4211, USA
10 Stamford Road, Oakleigh, Melbourne 3166, Australia

© Cambridge University Press 1996

First published 1996

Printed in Great Britain at the University Press, Cambridge

A catalogue record for this book is available from the British Library

Library of Congress cataloguing in publication data

Travel and drama in Shakespeare's time / edited by Jean-Pierre
Maquerlot and Michèle Willems.
p.   cm.
Includes index.
ISBN 0 521 47500 7 (hardback)
1. English drama – Early modern and Elizabethan, 1500–1600 – History and criticism.
2. Travel in literature. 3. Shakespeare, William, 1564–1616 – Contemporary England.
4. Travellers' writings, English – History and criticism. 5. English drama – 17th
century – History and criticism. 6. Shakespeare, William, 1564–1616. *Tempest.* 7.
Renaissance – England. 8. Travellers in literature.
I. Maquerlot, Jean-Pierre. II. Willems, Michèle.
PR58. T75T73 1996
822'.309355 – dc20
95 – 46797   CIP

ISBN 0 521 47500 7 hardback

Contents

Contributors

JONATHAN BATE, *University of Liverpool*

PHILIP EDWARDS, *University of Liverpool*

BRIAN GIBBONS, *Westfälische Universität, Münster*

ANDREW GURR, *University of Reading*

ANDREW HADFIELD, *University of Wales, Aberystwyth*

MICHAEL HATTAWAY, *University of Sheffield*

PETER HOLLAND, *Trinity Hall, Cambridge*

JEAN-PIERRE MAQUERLOT, *Université de Rouen*

KENNETH MUIR, *University of Liverpool*

J. R. MULRYNE, *University of Warwick*

ANTHONY PARR, *University of the Western Cape*

YVES PEYRÉ, *Université de Toulouse*

LOIS POTTER, *University of Delaware*

LEO SALINGAR, *Trinity College, Cambridge*

GÜNTER WALCH, *Humboldt-Universität zu Berlin*

MICHÈLE WILLEMS, *Université de Rouen*

CHAPTER I

Introduction

Jean-Pierre Maquerlot and Michèle Willems

The theoretical question of how we read or receive the works of the past has been at the core of critical concerns in the last decades. One approach to the problem may be summed up by Antoine Vitez's comparison of the plays of the past ages with 'sunken galleons which we bring back to light in pieces, without ever putting them together, since, in any case, we no longer know how to use them'.[1] In this attempted salvage operation, it is increasingly recognized that one of the missing pieces is the set of cultural assumptions underlying the plays. The difficulty of recapturing the ideological frame of reference of the original audience is perhaps one reason why so many directors now practise substitution devices like the transposition of historical periods.

As its title indicates, the present collection of essays shares in the current curiosity about the interconnections between text and context. It is thus doubly apposite to begin our introduction with a quotation from a French director constantly interested in historicity, since *Travel and drama in Shakespeare's time* is largely the offspring of a fruitful international encounter held in 1992 at Rouen, during which critics reflected upon 'Idea and Form in Renaissance Theatre: European Crosscurrents and New World Perspectives'.[2] The crossing of boundaries, the attempt to reconstruct the past from historical, geographical, sociological as well as political angles, were thus part of the initial project, as was the concern with form as well as with content, with the text as an artistic artefact as well as document. The concepts of *travel and drama*, it became apparent in discussion, are essentially productive through their confrontation; a whole range of interconnections emerges from the exploration of the rarely visited domain of voyage accounts and

I

foreign relations in Shakespeare's England, on the one hand, and the more familiar ground of drama in Shakespeare's age, on the other.

Within this network of interacting texts, some of the essays (like Andrew Hadfield's) concentrate more on travel than on drama, while others (like Kenneth Muir's) are more concerned with drama than with travel, but they all cohere to explore, from adjacent and finally converging perspectives, the various negotiations between these two phenomena.

Anthony Parr's account of the exploits of the Sherley brothers in the late 1590s analyses how the mostly abortive endeavours of the three brothers paradoxically developed into a myth shaped by a series of publications and then dramatized by Day, Rowley and Wilkins. *The Travels of the Three English Brothers* (1607) provides an interesting example of drama inspired by actual travel and of interaction between myth and fiction as well as between narrative and drama, since the playwrights used Anthony Nixon's commissioned pamphlet, *The Three English Brothers* (written in the same year) as their immediate source.

In his documented study of 'Elizabethan perceptions of Ireland', Andrew Hadfield surveys the English representations of Ireland and Irishness provided by travel writing such as Campion's *History of Ireland* (c. 1571), Spenser's *A View of the Present State of Ireland* (c. 1596) or Fynes Moryson's *Itinerary* (1617). By analysing the discourse of English observers rather than that of official documents, he shows that Ireland was perceived in two fundamentally different ways: as a kingdom ruled by the English monarch and as a colony akin to those of the New World; so that rather than suggesting that 'Ireland was no more than a stepping-stone *en route* to the colonization of the Americas', he stresses 'the problematic and transgressional nature of the evidence'.

Jonathan Bate also focuses mainly on travel writing, some real, some fictional, starting from the actual experiences of Henry Wotton (through an examination of his *Letters* and of Walton's *Life* of the diplomat, first published in 1651), moving on to the record of Thomas Coryate's walk to Venice in his *Crudities* (1611) to finish with the Italian half of Nashe's fiction, *The Unfortunate Traveller* (1594). One type of interaction between travel and drama is here uncovered, as Bate analyses Coryate's sense of the theatricality of

Venice, and then proceeds to discuss Jonson's *Volpone* and the role of its English traveller, Sir Pol.

Philip Edwards' essay on 'Tragic form and the voyagers' suggests a further form of interpenetration of voyage accounts and drama. Approaching travel as drama, Edwards investigates the links between Elizabethan tragedy and the chronicles of Elizabethan voyages, grounding his argument on the tragic pattern of the final voyage of Sir Humphrey Gilbert in 1583, as it is narrated by Edward Hayes, as well as on other documents of disaster on the high seas, including those of Cavendish (1591–93) and Ralegh (1596), and John Nicholl's *Houre Glasse of Indian Newes*, published in 1607. He thus discovers in the narratives of real-life drama the same intertwined patterns of responsibility and causality as in tragedy.

In his re-evaluation of *The Spanish Tragedy* (1582–92) in the light of contemporary Spanish and Portuguese events, Ronnie Mulryne does not actually refer to travel but rather to foreign relations. Moving beyond the Hispanophobic prejudice established by Eugene Hill and Ronald Broude in their analyses of the play, Mulryne reveals undercurrents of allusion such as the English anxiety about Spanish annexation of Portugal and the interest in potential Portuguese opposition to Spain. He also shows that the concluding masque of *Soliman and Perseda* celebrates the triumph of Turkish anti-Christianity, in line with alleged Spanish perversion of Christian values, and he finally sets the play within a wider consideration of 'Elect nation' propagandist theatre.

Both Yves Peyré and Lois Potter, exploring the workings of Renaissance multilayered intertextuality, reconstruct the debts and cultural connections of the dramatists they study. In 'Marlowe's Argonauts', Peyré shows how Marlowe, appropriating the culture of Antiquity to explore the potentialities of his own present, uses the travels of the Argonauts as an image of desire. The quest of the Golden Fleece, often used at the time 'to lend mythic aura to the discoverers of America', provided the dramatist with an image of travel which encapsulates 'suggestions of conflicting quests for love, material riches, noble adventure and spiritual discovery', and Peyré analyses it to uncover some of the tensions that structure Marlowe's drama and poetry.

In 'Pirates and "turning Turk" in Renaissance drama', Lois

Potter examines some rarely studied sea plays as well as some better-known ones, in the light of the history of piracy under James I. Some semi-biographical plays such as Heywood and Rowley's *Fortune by Land and Sea* (1607–9), which stages the historical Purser and Clinton, or Daborne's *A Christian Turn'd Turk* (1612), defined by its subtitle, *The Tragical Lives and Deaths of the Two Famous Pirates, Ward and Dansiker*, pose the problem of how close fiction can remain to facts. They are also used as foils to Shakespeare's treatment of similar material in *Hamlet* or *Othello*.

In Brian Gibbons' essay 'The wrong end of the telescope', *Henry V* (1599) is shown to have spawned an interestingly odd assortment of plays (*The Shoemaker's Holiday*, written in the same year, *Eastward Ho!* (1605), *The Tempest* (1610) and *Bartholomew Fair* (1614)) which are all bound up by a sense of mutual parody and a common interest in the social and political notion of a commonwealth. Civil disruption, whether in the form of a military expedition abroad, a voyage-cum-shipwreck off the Bermuda coast or on the less exotic shores of the Isle of Dogs, or a fair, such as the one held annually in Smithfield, turns out to produce, as through a lens, a critical, defamiliarized image of the home-country.

In 'Travelling hopefully: the dramatic form of journeys in English Renaissance drama', Peter Holland concentrates more specifically on the dramaturgical difficulties of representing journeys on stage. Drawing upon a large corpus of plays (ranging from Marlowe's *Doctor Faustus* (*c.* 1588) to Brome's *The Antipodes* (1637)), Holland reviews various techniques used to shape travel material into dramatic form. Beside such staple devices as choruses, dumb shows, chance encounters and scenes of failed or delayed recognition, Holland discovers a more imaginative venture in *The Travels of the Three English Brothers*, its series of confrontations between different ethnic groups allowing a systematic exploration of cultural gaps between East and West.

The next essays are more specifically concerned with plays drawing upon the discovery of the New World, the prime example of which is *The Tempest*. The link between the two is provided by *The Sea-Voyage* which serves as the focal point of Michael Hattaway's essay, 'Seeing things: Amazons and cannibals'. Whereas *The Tempest* (which obviously inspired Fletcher and Massinger's play) confronts the fact of colonialism and its dour implications, *The Sea-Voyage*, like most of the minor travel plays elsewhere examined, is found to occlude cultural differences through its ethnocentric manipulation of conventional tropes pertaining to the New World (romantic space, fertile and infertile lands and savage peoples). Ideologically, the play's romantic plot with its constant demonization of women and its Amazons finally discovered to be Portuguese ladies in disguise, offers an interesting case of 'gendered racism'.

In his discussion of *The Tempest*, Andrew Gurr returns to London in order to recontextualize the play in terms of the Elizabethan and literary traditions of 'service'. Shakespeare's romance, Gurr argues, may be seen to derive as much from forms of domestic organization as from a vision of colonial power in action. Starting from the premise that much of the play's formal patterning develops out of the differentiated relations of Ariel and Caliban to their master, Gurr shows that Prospero's slave-servants, though subjected to the island's conditions of unpaid slavery, occupy different positions within the spectrum of service – Ariel being closer to the status of the bound apprentice and Caliban to that of the household servant.

Looking at the play from an aesthetic rather than a social viewpoint, Leo Salingar argues that what *The Tempest* owes to reports of voyages to the New World, and more particularly to the colonization of Virginia, is essentially an infusion of realism into the world of romance, an alchemy which, Salingar suggests, may account for the play's uniqueness. Like the travel accounts it draws upon, Shakespeare's *Tempest* evinces a 'critical sense of reality' entangling with a 'desire for wonders'. Citing Tasso's concern that what is true to life should coalesce with the marvellous in epic poetry, Salingar sees the play as Shakespeare's theatrical response to what seems to have been a major imaginative demand of his contemporaries.

In the last of the three essays concentrating on *The Tempest*, Günter Walch calls attention to several discourses embedded in the play and generated by its island location. Though the discourse of colonialism reflected notably in Prospero and Miranda's vision of a languageless Other, looms large in Walch's analysis, greater emphasis is laid on the discourse of memory and on the more frequently explored discourse of metatheatricality. In the island-shaped wooden O in which new meanings are produced, these two discourses are shown to be powerful agents of the play's deconstruction of its own text.

'Lope de Vega and Shakespeare', the concluding essay by Kenneth Muir, may be described as a journey in itself, which takes the reader from England to Spain and back and is made possible by its author's knowledge of Spanish and his critical expertise in both these dramatists. But the paper's relevance to the subject matter of this volume rests on more solid foundations than a mere metaphor. Basing his argument on four plays by Lope (*Peribañez* (1613), *The Dog in the Manger* (1618), *Fuenteovejuna* (1619) and *El Castigo sin Venganza* (1631)) dramatizing questions of honour in which 'social *mores* and Christian teaching were bound to conflict', Muir shows that both in Lope and Shakespeare a structurally built-in ambivalence or polysemy exists, despite cultural differences; hence the theoretical validity of multiple interpretations, a theme amply demonstrated throughout the volume but most noticeable, of course, regarding *The Tempest*.

One specific feature of this collection of essays is precisely the fact that its dramatic corpus receives fresh contextualization because it constantly interacts with a corpus of travel accounts. These texts which, as Philip Edwards complains, remain 'so little read by students of literature', are here mostly referred to and analysed through the voyage narratives gathered by Hakluyt and Purchas.[3] The object of many essays is to identify the various discourses which inform these contemporary documents. Whether they move to Italy, Ireland or follow the adventures of the Sherley brothers, Bate, Hadfield or Parr aim at clarifying the rhetorical and cultural codes which travel narratives place between the reader and the supposed eyewitness. Within their largely common frame of references to voyage narratives and travel-inspired drama, all the contributors combine historical enquiry and textual analysis to provide readings of drama and travel literature which ground them firmly in the period for which they were written and take into account the preconceptions and perceptions of their original public. Ronnie Mulryne uncovers a rich range of meanings in *The Spanish Tragedy* by reconstructing the political and religious prejudices of the audience of the 1580s and 1590s. Conversely, Parr explores the cultural significance of prose narratives and plays connected with the Sherley brothers and shows how they shaped the Jacobean public's attitude to the foreign. Textual analysis is strengthened by ideological interpretation and vice versa.

The basic concern for historical perspective as well as for contextual and intertextual investigation is further enhanced by forays into modern literature as a means to illuminate – through similitudes and contrasts – certain preoccupations and values of the Renaissance. Discussing the theme of disorientation in Utopian fiction, Gibbons sets up a powerful confrontation between Conrad's *Heart of Darkness* (1899) and More's seminal *Utopia* (1516). Hattaway also cuts across the centuries, calling up Seamus Heaney's recent collection of verse *Seeing Things* (1991), to suggest that Donne's perception of 'new Nature', acquired through trade, may be extended to other forms of social behaviour such as travelling and play-watching.

'It is our task to consider not just what was seen but how it was seen', Hattaway adds. All the essays in this collection constitute precisely this stimulating reflection on the intriguing concept of cultural otherness, on the problems of visualizing and defining the Other which are discovered to be, most of the time, another means of defining the Self. Indeed, whether voyagers or dramatists look towards Europe and the East (Turkey and Persia) for cultural differences (as in Bate, Holland, Mulryne, Potter and Parr) or towards the New World to substantiate Utopian or dystopian visions or to feed their expectations of marvels (as in Hattaway, Gurr and Salingar), whether they find strangeness at home (as in the Elizabethan social system described by Gurr) or just away from home (across the Irish Sea as in Hadfield's study, in Italy, as in Bate's essay or in Roman Catholic Spain and Portugal, as in Mulryne's analysis of *The Spanish Tragedy*), they all tend to view the Other as an inversion of the same, that is through the glass of an England-based culture. Carried to extremes, the Europeans' mutilated and mutilating vision obliterates cultural alterity, reducing it almost to invisibility. At the dawn of European colonial enterprise, it is not surprising to find the Other constructed into a culturally non-existent entity, in need, therefore, of European domination (Walch).

The New and the Old Worlds which we read about or discover on the stage look more like 'allegories of the forms and pressures of the time' (Hattaway), than like actual perceptions of 'remote otherness' (Gibbons); they give the image of an Other which provides at the same time a 'means of self-examination' (Bate). 'Persia was not so much Europe's Other as its opposite or foil', Parr writes; or again Hattaway: 'Geographic plays, like history plays, are not reflections of other cultures, but reflections upon the culture inhabited by their audience.'

Though pursuing their quest for the wonders promised by Mandeville and others, Renaissance explorers *and* writers must needs graft the old upon the new, mingle the strange and the familiar, thus relocating the myth of the Golden Age in America (Salingar), transferring to the New World the myth of the Amazons from its native Scythia or Libya (Hattaway), appropriating Antiquity to encapsulate in its legends some of the most disturbing contradictions of their own time (Peyré) or, in a more homely fashion, acclimatizing the native traditions of 'the idle or industrious apprentice' to Prospero's symbolic island (Gurr).

Another merit of the constantly interactive approach of travel and drama is the interest it nurtures for a wide range of travel plays which had so far received little attention but are here illuminated in their own right or by the connections established between them. It is not so common after all to find such plays as *A Christian Turn'd Turk*, *The English Traveller* (printed in 1633) or *The Sea-Voyage* looked at from more than one angle and drawn into meaningful, if sometimes unexpected, analyses. Several contributors note that plays concerned with the New World are rare and that most travel plays move east, dealing rather with Moorish and Turkish worlds. Thus the confrontation between East and West, between Persian and Christian practices is discovered to be an articulating force in *The Travels of the Three English Brothers*. Even a better-known play like *Eastward Ho!* benefits from being freshly contextualized. It is here successively approached as a dramatic parody of the ideal commonwealth, as an instance of comic non-travel, and as a specimen of an idle/industrious servant play to support by way of contrast Gurr's analysis of the Prospero/Ariel/Caliban triangular structure of *The Tempest*. This is a case where the various essays clearly augment each other's findings, providing glancing sidelights which both enrich the understanding of so-called 'minor' plays and converge to contextualize the new readings proposed for *The Tempest*.

When set against these lesser plays, Shakespeare's play unsurprisingly appears, like the rest of his drama, as much more sophisticated and ambivalent; one of the virtues of a confrontation between different plays is precisely that suggestions can be made to explain this hierarchy, as when Lois Potter concludes her study of various dramatic examples of 'turning Turk', including Shakespeare's, with this remark: 'Shakespeare [evoked], as Daborne and others could not do, not only what the renegade loses but the real attractions of what he gains.' One plausible explanation concerning *The Tempest* is that, like its simultaneously Mediterranean and Bermudan magic island, it is in itself a 'palimpsest in which a number of discrepant codes are laid across one another' (Gibbons). Among these, two are of special interest, as they seem to account for much of the play's elusive discourse and intriguing artistic form: the codes of 'romance and actuality, fantasy and tried experience', whose interplay, Salingar observes, gives *The Tempest* its peculiar 'shimmering' quality. But the play's ingrained polysemy, what Günter Walch aptly describes as its 'resistance to interpretative closure', calls for a broader reflection on Shakespearean art. It emblematizes the dramatist's gift or cultivation of 'negative capability', which Kenneth Muir also sees embodied in Lope de Vega, another 'poet for the defence', an expression coined by Muir to define Shakespeare's capacity for dramatizing both sides of a debate.

Most of the essays lay bare internal tensions of meaning in the texts they analyse: Hadfield's study reveals a discourse of inclusion/exclusion towards the Irish which he connects with the dichotomy savage/civilized and the perception of Ireland as both an exotic culture and part of domestic society. Both fascination *and* repulsion appear, from Bate's essay, to define the Elizabethans' perceptions of Italy. Lois Potter also insists on the equivocal reactions to piracy which contained both attraction and repulsion. This common and repeated interest in ambiguities and plurality of meaning often serves as a means of analysing the specificity of the literary text,[4] as when Peyré grounds his analysis of Marlowe's plays on the ironies and ambiguities derived by the dramatist from the myth of the Argonauts exploited both as extolling the spirit of adventure and enterprise and as containing powerful undercurrents of negative readings; or when Philip Edwards finds in the tension between human responsibility and supernatural intervention a structure which informs both travel narrative and tragedy as opposed to real life; or when Günter Walch turns to poiesis rather than mimesis to interpret the making of fictional worlds in *The Tempest* and compares the play to 'a theatrical laboratory in which to conduct a crucial test under isolated island conditions'.

The plays discussed here are never approached as mere cultural documents. Strongly historical as it is, Parr's essay analyses the playwrights' various manipulations of factual or reported detail, and several more theatre-oriented papers confront some of the questions raised by the difficulty of staging voyages, discussing some of the means through which travel writing is made to adjust (sometimes with mitigated success) to the demands of comedy and tragedy. A particularly innovative treatment of the voyage motif can be found, Holland argues, in those plays where anticipation, incompletion or mere imagination of travel constitute the principal structuring device of drama and, possibly, the surest therapy for would-be voyagers. Conversely, Philip Edwards' paper demonstrates how tragedy as a genre (with its stories of heroic disaster) has shaped the voyage narratives of Hayes, Cavendish and Ralegh. Theatre consciousness is again seen to emerge in *A True Declaration of the Estate of the Colonie of Virginia*, a pamphlet issued in 1610 by the London Virginia Company, in which the shipwreck of the expedition flagship on the coast of Shakespeare's 'still vex'd Bermoothes' is significantly described as a 'tragicall Comoedie' (quoted by Salingar). In their individual ways, most of the essays cohere to set off the ways in which playwriting more than other writing and Shakespearean drama more than other drama, expose and exploit the ambiguities and paradoxes present in the perceptions of other worlds and of Others.

The authors of *Travel and drama in Shakespeare's time* set their work in the context of current critical trends. The studies of *The Tempest* refer to a wide range of critical reactions and particularly of post-colonialist readings of the play,[5] though often to qualify them.

As he stresses the manner in which home-grown patriarchal relations inform the play, Gurr draws attention to features unduly neglected or obscured by a more one-sided approach; and Salingar concurs with Gurr on the reductiveness of such readings in that they tend to mask the play's basic kinship with contemporary romances, including Shakespeare's own previous work. Similarly, on the subject of Irishness, Hadfield regrets that 'too much colonial and post-colonial theory should consider the formation of identity as a product of the colonial scene alone'.

But on the whole, the contributors do not participate other than marginally in the current debate on the use and abuses of historical material. They do not propose to revolutionize critical thinking or break new theoretical ground, but they share in a tradition of starting from the text and of using sources, influences and intertexts (what James Smith, quoted by Leo Salingar, calls 'congeners') to illuminate the specificity of the text itself, envisaged as an autonomous, if historically and culturally determined, achievement. While the various essays implicitly recognize the *dependence* of the aesthetic material, they do not overlook the *autonomy* of the aesthetic object, to take up concepts commonly used in Marxist criticism. A play is never seen as the repository for a given, unchanging and universal meaning, but rather as an untiring generator of meanings. In that 'working-house of thought', to use Walch's Shakespearean description of the play's compound of meanings, one definitely discovers the documentary, the cultural, the historical; but in the 'quick forge', one also uncovers inherited images or archetypal imaginative demands, once *travel* has been transmuted into *drama*. And as Peyré remarks about Marlowe's tragedies, the end of the journey is always the same: 'the unexplored country is that of death'.

Underlying the emphasis on the polyphony of drama is the implicit assumption – never theorized but operating throughout – that the theatre cannot be reduced to a medium for conflicting ideologies and even less to one reading, political or other. In this respect, it is tempting to leave the last word to an avowed Marxist and to finish, as we started, with a quotation from Antoine Vitez, reflecting, this time, on his 1972 staging of Sophocles' *Electra*: 'In a performance of the tragedy where a political reading was privileged ... other readings would be silenced; and this would be a pity, because it seems to me *politically* useful for the reader to be placed in front of roads leading in several directions.'[6]

NOTES

1 '...Les œuvres du passé sont des architectures brisées, des galions engloutis, et nous les ramenons à la lumière par morceaux, sans jamais les reconstituer, car de toute façon l'usage en est perdu.' *Le théâtre des idées*, entretiens avec Danièle Sallenave et Georges Banu, Paris, 1991: quoted by Anne Ubersfeld in *Antoine Vitez, metteur en scène et poète* (Paris, 1994).

   Antoine Vitez was one of the most prominent directors in France in the 1980s, constantly concerned with the problems of staging the classics for a twentieth-century audience. He was the director of the *Comédie-Française* when he died in 1990 at the age of sixty.

2 Most of the essays in this collection started their lives as papers at this conference organized by our colleague Jean-Paul Pichardie, at which our own research group *(Centre d'études du théâtre anglo-saxon (CETAS))*, conducted a workshop on 'European Crosscurrents and New World Perspectives'. A number of essays were later commissioned to widen the scope, both historically and dramatically.

3 Hakluyt's *Principall Navigations, Voiages and Discoveries of the English Nation* was issued in 1589 and subsequently enlarged for the three-volume edition of 1598–1600 to include, notably, Ralegh's *Discoverie of the Empyre of Guiana* (1596) and Hayes' account of the last and fatal voyage to America of Sir Humphrey Gilbert, two narratives referred to several times in this volume. Samuel Purchas collected travel narratives in *Purchas His Pilgrimage, or Relations of the World and the Religions observed in All Ages* (1613) and *Hakluytes Posthumus, or Purchas His Pilgrimes, contayning a History of the World in Sea-Voyages and Land Travell by Englishmen and Others* (1625); the latter work, which was based on manuscripts left by Hakluyt and unpublished at the time of his death (1616), included the first issue of Thomas Cavendish's own account of his final voyage (1591–3) and an abbreviated reprint of John Nicholl's *Houre Glasse of Indian Newes*, two narratives also mentioned in this volume.

   On Cavendish and others, see Philip Edwards' superb study, *Last Voyages* (Oxford, 1988).

4 This by no means implies that ambivalence or polysemy only appear in the so-called 'literary texts', by which we designate texts whose primary – though not exclusive – function is to enhance the creativeness of language in a deliberate attempt to procure aesthetic pleasure, either in the playhouse or in the study. Polysemy (and

aesthetic pleasure as well) may be found in non-literary texts, most visibly perhaps among those which serve predominantly as vehicles for ideological discourse. What distinguishes literary texts however, is that in their case ambiguity of meaning seems to be constitutive of the very act of artistic writing, a social practice conveniently described as *écriture*, in France and elsewhere.

5 These include, to quote only a few seminal texts: Stephen J. Greenblatt, 'Learning to Curse: Aspects of Linguistic Colonialism in the Sixteenth Century', in *First Images of America: the Impact of the New World on the Old*, ed. Fredi Chiapelli (Berkeley, 1976), 1; Charles Frey, '*The Tempest* and the New World', *Shakespeare Quarterly* 30 (1979); Trevor R. Griffiths, '"This Island's Mine": Caliban and Colonialism', *Yearbook of English Studies. Colonial and Imperial Themes* 13 (1983); Paul Brown, '"This thing of Darkness I Acknowledge Mine": *The Tempest* and the Discourse of Colonialism', in *Political Shakespeare : New Ways in Cultural Materialism*, eds. Jonathan Dollimore and Alan Sinfield (Ithaca and London, 1985).

For a historical survey of the 'Americanist' readings of *The Tempest*, see Alden T. Vaughan's informative 'Shakespeare's Indians: the Americanization of Caliban' *Shakespeare Quarterly* 39 (1988).

6 Dans une représentation de la tragédie où serait privilégiée la lecture politique... les autres lectures seraient tuées; et ce serait dommage parce qu'il me semble **politiquement** utile que le lecteur soit placé en face de plusieurs chemins.' (Quoted in Ubersfeld's *Vitez*, p. 24.)

CHAPTER 2

Foreign relations in Jacobean England: the Sherley brothers and the 'voyage of Persia'

Anthony Parr

The foreign relations of my title are both diplomatic and textual. I am concerned with the ways in which some of the travel narratives or 'relations' of the period present intercultural contact and help to shape attitudes to the foreign, both in their own right and also through the literary and theatrical texts that are inspired by them. A large and varied body of such material grew up around the exploits of the Sherley brothers in the late 1590s and during the Jacobean era, and I shall begin with the most flamboyant piece of writing it has to offer, a fairly typical extract from *Purchas His Pilgrimes*, Samuel Purchas' huge collection of travel narratives, published in 1625 as a sequel to Hakluyt's *Principall Navigations*:

Amongst our English Travellers, I know not whether any have merited more respect than the Honorable, I had almost said Heroike Gentlemen, Sir Anthony & Sir Robert Sherleys. And if the Argonauts of old, and Graecian Worthies, were worthily reputed Heroicall for Europaean exploits in Asia: what may wee thinke of the Sherley-Brethren, which not from the neerer Graecian shoares, but from beyond the Europaean World, Et penitus toto divisus Orbe Britannia; have not coasted a little way (as did those) but pierced the very bowells of the Asian Seas and Lands, unto the Persian centre...[1]

Samuel Purchas' 'briefe Memoriall' of the travels of two of the three Sherley brothers is the last in a series of tributes strictly contemporary with their exploits, and it was to be particularly influential in shaping the subsequent myth of their achievements. By the nineteenth century these products of the English provincial gentry, whose father had held high office under Elizabeth I but whose fortunes were declining by the 1590s, had become figures of legendary glamour: as the *Gentleman's Magazine* put it in 1844,

'Those three brave Sherleys! Each separate history a romance!' And subsequent books about them, with titles like *The Sherleian Odyssey* and *Elizabethans Errant*, have continued to treat them, though not without qualification, as a happy band of brothers whose adventures taken together epitomize the Elizabethan spirit of derring-do. This romantic image had been created in the first place by upbeat accounts in Hakluyt and elsewhere of privateering voyages by Thomas and Anthony Sherley, expeditions which were in fact undistinguished and at times disastrous, and which also attracted some withering private commentary (by people like the letter-writer John Chamberlain).[2] Subsequently the Sherley myth was built up by a series of publications in the early seventeenth century, ranging from first-hand accounts of the brothers' later travels (including autobiography) to a stage play about their adventures.

Many of these accounts of the Sherleys seem to have been designed to improve the brothers' public standing in England, for despite their deeds on the high seas, which encouraged some to compare them with Drake and Cavendish, their exploits did not always endear them to those in authority. This is largely because the political and commercial imperatives of the period sat uneasily with the brothers' thoroughly conventional thirst for fame and honour, which led Anthony Sherley to make the Earl of Essex 'the patterne of my civill life, and from him to draw a worthy modell of all my actions',[3] and encouraged his elder brother Thomas to become a professional buccaneer, taking privateering commissions from the Grand Duke of Tuscany – a career that was notably unsuccessful but was halted only by his incarceration in a Turkish jail.[4] It is significant that Purchas does not mention Thomas who, as the only one of the brothers to return permanently to England, was probably behind some of the propaganda on behalf of the family, for – as Purchas' careful description of Anthony and Robert as 'Honorable, I had almost said Heroike Gentlemen' suggests – it seems to be evident to him in 1625, as arguably it wasn't to a later and more sentimental age, that swashbuckling alone is not a secure claim to national reputation. But all three brothers were somewhat out of place in the political climate of Jacobean England, despite the partial rehabilitation of Sir Anthony after James' accession because of his connection with Essex (Queen Elizabeth I had banned Sherley from returning to England after his unauthorized departure from the country in 1598). And while Lord Admiral Howard might confess that he was 'haunted with the spirit of the Sherleys',[5] statesmen like Sir Robert Cecil were more likely to express exasperation at the brothers' meddling in international affairs, and deplore the tendency of their actions to queer the pitch of English foreign policy.

As Purchas' encomium suggests, it is with Anthony and his younger brother Robert that we are concerned, and in particular with the way in which they 'pierced the very bowells of the Asian Seas and Lands, unto the Persian centre'. In 1598 the two were members of an Essex-inspired mission to frustrate the Pope's designs upon the duchy of Ferrara; and when this fell through they repaired to Venice, probably along with many other now-unemployed soldiers of fortune, and proceeded to spend the money that Essex had put up to fight the cause of the Ferrarese ruler Cesare d'Este. One member of the party claimed that Anthony Sherley turned his sights on Persia as a result of a chance encounter with a merchant of that country who told him 'of the royalty of the Sophi, his king, which pleased Sir Anthony very well';[6] but it seems clear that Sherley was casting about for a new cause and found it in another Essex initiative currently under way, which was to evaluate and if possible break the grip of the Iberian nations on oriental trade. The Venetians had a powerful interest in this, since their wealth had been built on the overland trade routes and was now threatened by the sea route to the Indies, and in particular by the Portuguese presence in the Persian Gulf, which shut off oriental traffic through the Euphrates valley to the Mediterranean. The English Levant Company had similar priorities, and the suggestion that Sherley and his men go to Persia with the purpose of undermining the Shah's agreement with the Portuguese, and if possible attack the latter's fortress at Ormuz on the Gulf, clearly proved irresistible.

Anthony Sherley later claimed in his memoirs that it was Essex who proposed the 'voyage of Persia', but by then the statement, though perhaps technically correct, was somewhat disingenuous, since in the interim his stated purpose in going there had changed.

In all the early published accounts of the Persian mission the goal of Sherley's journey is unambiguous: it is the creation of a Christian–Persian alliance against the Turks, and it was to advance this cause that he was sent by the Shah to the West in 1599. Essex would not have backed such a plan; yet it seems unlikely that Sherley came up with it on his own. He would have known that he could expect no official backing from an English government which for commercial reasons favoured friendly relations with Turkey – in fact the English ambassador at Constantinople had obtained a passport for the Sherleys through the Ottoman dominions; and he knew also that Venice would be as opposed to this new initiative as it was in favour of the original scheme of hitting the Portuguese. The popular version of events presented on stage and in pamphlets was that the Shah was 'animated by [Sherley's] forcible perswasions'[7] to seek an alliance with Christian Europe. But it seems much more likely that Abbas I, having secured his eastern frontier with victories against the Uzbeks just as the Sherleys arrived in Persia, saw his opportunity to mount a campaign against the Turks, with whom he had been forced into a humiliating treaty at the start of his reign. He was certainly ready to use Anthony Sherley to whip up support in European courts; and so a whirlwind diplomatic tour commenced in 1599, taking Sherley with his Persian colleague Husayn 'Ali Beg to Moscow, Prague and Rome, and then on his own to Venice, Morocco and Spain, in which last country he spent most of the rest of his life. Meanwhile Robert Sherley, who had been held hostage in Persia during his brother's mission, was entrusted with a second embassy, starting in 1609, which took him to Cracow, Prague, Florence, Rome, Madrid and London, returning to Persia via the Great Mogul's court in India. A protracted third embassy finally saw him in England once again in 1624, this time with commercial proposals for a sea trade with Persia via the Gulf (made feasible by the capture of Ormuz in 1622); he was frustrated in his designs both by the opposition of the Levant and East India Companies and by the death of James I, and when he returned to Persia he was repudiated by the Shah, and died there in 1628.

Purchas tells us that a dinner he had with Robert Sherley during this last visit to London is the source of his information; but we might wonder why Purchas, who was after all in the pay of the East

India Company, should speak so fulsomely about someone whose intentions were regarded with suspicion in both commercial and diplomatic circles. This is really part of a larger question or paradox about the Sherleys: that their exploits and endeavours were for the most part entirely abortive, and unpopular with people of influence in England, yet they attracted in the period a considerable literature, much of which is dedicated to enrolling them in the pantheon of the nation's worthies. What are we to make of this? Circumstantially, of course, all of the published panegyrics can be related to specific events: the first embassy yielded in 1600 a short pamphlet (*A True Report*) which was immediately suppressed, and in 1601 William Parry's *New and Large Discourse* of Anthony Sherley's travels. The release of Thomas Sherley from prison in Constantinople led (we may assume) to his commissioning Anthony Nixon to write *The Three English Brothers* in 1607, a piece of hackwork which was the main source for a stage play, *The Travels of the Three English Brothers*, printed in the same year. The play was on the stage before Nixon's pamphlet was published, suggesting a close co-operation between the writers – one which may have been commercially driven, cashing in on topical material, but could also reflect a concerted attempt to promote the family's interests.[8] Two years later, when Robert's first embassy was expected in London, Middleton published a fulsome account of his reception at Cracow earlier in the mission: it is based on a Polish original which Sherley probably sent over to be translated and put out as advance publicity.[9] And finally, as we have seen, Purchas wrote up the Sherleys under the stimulus of Robert's second embassy in 1625.

All this might suggest that there was an organized strain of dissident opinion working in favour of the Sherleys, though at this distance we are unlikely to be able to trace more than a piecemeal lobbying on their behalf – by friends of the family to restore Anthony and Robert to favour, or perhaps in support of Anglo-Persian trade proposals or to promote the anti-Turkish alliance. But even if we knew more about the politics of publication in this instance, to look only for narrowly polemical intent is to neglect the rhetorical character of these texts and probably to mistake their role in Jacobean cultural life. If some of them are initially designed as propaganda or public relations, they nonetheless function primarily as a free-floating discourse that celebrates the travels of the brothers as a species of fame, a source of honour and renown. The exploits of the Sherleys are perceived to have a value independent of policy; and by being treated in ways that locate them within a larger narrative of national enterprise – in his *Polyolbion*, for instance, Michael Drayton salutes Anthony Sherley as heir to the great Elizabethan explorers[10] – they become part of a process of shaping public attitudes to exotic experience and defining the challenge of empire.

We can see something of this process at work in Purchas' hectic 'briefe Memoriall'. When he first pauses to draw breath, the writer dutifully repeats a familiar homily on the purposes of travel:

Let mee admire such a Traveller, which travells not of and for some vaine discourse, or private gaine or skill, but still travelleth and is delivered of the public good...[11]

Nonetheless in what follows Purchas lays the emphasis on Robert's Ulyssean courage and stamina rather than on his diplomatic achievements. Of course, Purchas is compelled by the facts to do this, and he further supplies the gap in the positive record with a mischievous interpretation of the brothers' aims, which were he says to

kindle a fire betwixt the two most puissant of both Asian and Mahumetan Princes, that by their division and diversion of Turkish invasions, Christian Princes, Countries, and States might bee indebted to their private undertaking...

If Purchas was trying to boost Sherley's popularity in England by such statements, he must have known that they could also jeopardize the understanding with Persia on which new political and commercial initiatives depended. We might even infer that Purchas shared the opposition of his employers to fresh trade initiatives and so unconsciously phrases Anglo-Persian relations in these rather prejudicial terms. But we are still left with the fact that he chose in 1625 to apostrophize Robert Sherley and his piercing of 'the Persian centre', despite its meagre political harvest, and in the remainder of this paper I want to ask what part such encomia play in the formation of what we might broadly call the culture of foreign relations in the earlier seventeenth century. To do this I shall locate Purchas' account in a larger matrix of diplomatic history and ideas, and compare some of its assumptions with the first-hand perspectives of several members of the Sherley mission to Persia, as we find them in narrative accounts by Anthony Sherley, William Parry, George Manwaring, Abel Pincon and others.[12] I shall then look briefly at the secondary literature about the Sherleys created by professional writers in England, and ask what part it plays in the creation of cultural attitudes and beliefs.

To western eyes in the early modern period, and long after, the Persian court was an exotic symbol like those of India, China and Japan. It was Spenser's 'nurse of pompous pride', reputed to be a place of fantastic luxury and wealth. Such locations fell into the category neither of the primitive (the unlettered, semi-nomadic societies of the New World and Africa) nor of the 'enemy within' the Old World, usually represented by the infidel Turks, or by Jews or Jesuits. In this sense, Persia was not so much Europe's Other as its opposite or foil; and while the fascination with the glamorous East was later to become a disabling orientalism, arguably it was during the early modern period a positive alternative to views of Asia either as the home of barbarian hordes or of the hellish doctrine of Islam–Western conceptions described by Edward Said as 'a closed system' which 'no empirical material can either dislodge or alter'.[13] It is notable that when they want to counter the pejorative implications of Persian luxury, several writers evoke the country's ancient past and paint a picture of classical austerity and virtue.[14] And others agreed with Anthony Sherley that 'the fashion of [the Shah's] government differing so much from that which we call barbarousnesse,...it may justly serve for as great an *Idea* for a Principality, as *Platoes* Common-wealth did for a Government'.[15]

Persia was of course like Turkey an Islamic country, but just as European perceptions of global politics were fundamentally sectarian, pitting Catholic against Protestant in the early scramble for empire, so Christian thinking was quick to fasten on the division between the Sunni faith of the Turks and the Shia orthodoxy imposed by the Safavid Shahs in Iran. Anthony Sherley confidently interprets the religious policy of Shah Abbas I as one of using

Shi'ism to unite his countrymen against the Turk, and points out that where the Sunni faction within his own borders is concerned, he 'doth not onely strive to roote it out, but to defile it, and make it odious; having in use, once a yeare, with great solemnity, to burne publiquely, as maine Heretiques, the images of *Ussen* and *Omar*'[16] – the caliphs venerated by Sunni Muslims but rejected as false prophets by the Shi'ites. We are sometimes warned not to assume, from our modern secular standpoint, that religious motives must really be political ones (though Purchas in his reprint of Sherley's *Relation* readily glossed this passage with the words '*Kings care of Religion for Policie*');[17] and it seems to be true that, while Christian Europeans were certainly capable of cynically exploiting Muslim differences, they were also inclined to look for substantial points of contact with the culture that they found themselves courting. There were several aspects of Shia Islam to which Christians, and in particular Protestant Englishmen, might extend sympathy. The burning of false images already referred to is one such; more substantially, they could be expected to warm to Persia's dynastic and monarchical view of the succession from the Prophet, disallowing the elective caliphate which followed Mohammed's death and (on this view) barred his family from their rights. The consequent martyrdom of 'Ali and his son Husayn, regarded by Shias as the true successors to the Prophet, supplies a further link with Christianity;[18] and it is not surprising that stories about Persian respect for Christ's ministry were easily elaborated into rumours that the Shah was about to convert to Christianity and that he stood godfather to Robert Sherley's child – a detail that forms the climax of the 1607 play *The Travels of the Three English Brothers*.

But the essential point is perhaps more broadly political. James Boon has suggested that in the early seventeenth century, as first the Catholic and then Protestant visions of global unity disintegrate, imperial propaganda seeks a new universalism, and finds it in the development of an old idea. Since the fourteenth century, he points out, the known world had been mapped as a host of kings joined through 'a portolan system of co-ordinates'. Boon persuasively argues that Samuel Purchas' great collection is unified by its project of articulating 'a royal British order, to the exclusion of Catholics and Dutch Protestants alike, which tied exotic courts to the monarch'[19] – that is, tracing fundamental reciprocities between James' court and royal systems in (predominantly) India and the Far East, a sort of proto-commonwealth made possible by the navigational feats of Britain's sailors and the enterprise of its merchants, though commerce is not seen as the primary linkage. Something like this vision seems to lie behind Purchas' extravagant testimonial to Robert Sherley's travels:

Noble attempt to goe meet the Sunne! and from the West and North where he was borne, to visit the East and South, and that both in overland Diameter first, and Sea circumference after, coasting the Europaean and Asian, compassing the African shores, piercing the Persian Gulfe, and passing the Indus and Indian Continent, climbing the Candahar Hills, into, and over, and thorow and thorow Persia; passing the Caspian, and penetrating the Deserts more then Tartarian fortie two daies together...Quae regio in terris Sherlii non plena laboris? These have seene him, and hee hath seene them with Eyes more then of a Traveller, more then his owne, Himselfe being the Eyes of a mightie Monarch, which in his person visited so many Countries, Cities, and Courts.[20]

This passage is not really an itinerary, or a record of ambassadorial endeavour, but evokes an imperial mission whose meaning is disclosed in the last sentence, where the rhetorical antithesis ('These have seene him, and hee hath seene them') turns the act of seeing into one of diplomatic recognition, placing strange places and their rulers on the royal map; and from the Olympian perspective Purchas adopts at this point, such a process is seen as more significant than successful negotiation of specific issues. The failure of Sherley's mission is irrelevant, finally; what matters in the long run is the irradiating British perspective, controlled by 'the Eyes of a mightie Monarch', that will find out and harmonize everything. (The pronouncements of British envoys and negotiators today, in the afterglow of empire as in its beginnings, still tend to promote such a view.)

This is diplomacy conceived at a high level of abstraction, or as a scenario viewed from the unique vantage-point of the King in a Jacobean court masque. In this instance, it must be said, it also looks suspiciously like a rhetorical ploy to get round the awkward questions that the whole Sherley initiative raises. James I might take Purchas' hint and interpret an embassy from 'the remote

Persian' as a compliment, but he was also unhappy about one of his own subjects acting as envoy from a foreign prince. And as we have already seen, cracks appear in the smooth surface of Purchas' vision of East–West reciprocity when he talks about sowing discord among the heathen for Christian advantage. But for all that, such a vision is not simply the product of Purchas' extravagant musings. It could also emerge as a practical response to the challenge of cross-cultural encounter. Diplomats and other travellers confronted with the opulence and high ceremonial of oriental courts realized that they were looking at highly developed, strongly ethnocentric cultures which could not easily be belittled – indeed, Europeans often felt belittled *by* them; and they responded by digging into their own vocabulary of public gesture and conspicuous display. Accounts of the Sherleys' arrival at Qasvin and their first meeting with the Shah reveal a careful contriving of effect: making sure that they enter the city by night so as not to be first seen in their riding clothes, and calculated dressing for the big occasion – Anthony and Robert clad in 'such stuff as we brought with us' (as Parry says), gold and silver suits respectively, but adding rich turbans to their outfits, and giving the livery of their attendants a Persian touch. A 'very seemly show', says Parry, 'the fashion of our apparel somewhat differing from the Persian':[21] a nicely judged difference designed to promote dialogue and mutual respect.

This kind of dialogue is essentially theatrical in nature, executing diplomacy in terms of a pageant or masque; and this seems to provide those concerned with a framework for interpreting the more intractable moments of cross-cultural encounter. Take, for instance, the first encounter with the Shah outside the walls of Qasvin, as the European party witnesses the victorious Persian return from the wars. Abel Pincon, Anthony Sherley's French steward, is alert to the way Shah Abbas stages this event: 'In his triumphal entry he caused to be carried on the end of strong and heavy spears twenty thousand heads of Tartars whom he had defeated in Usbeg, which appeared to me a hideous spectacle.' Parry notes 'one thousand and two hundred heads of the conquered Tartars'; while Manwaring records 'a prospect as is not usually seen, which was, twelve hundred soldiers, horsemen, carrying twelve hundred heads of men on their lances', and adds the detail of some 'having the ears of men put on strings and hanged about their necks'.[22] The confusion about numbers perhaps indicates the overwhelming and disorienting effect of this display, especially as the evidence tends to suggest that the larger number may be the more accurate. Only Anthony Sherley in his *Relation* tries to explicate what he calls this 'strange demonstration', revealing that while Abbas waited outside Qasvin, 'there were 30000 men, sent out of the Towne on foote with horse-mens staves, upon which were fastened vizards of so many heads: All those in the morning. . .wee found marching in battell aray towards the Towne.'[23] Add to this the information (from the only Persian witness we have)[24] that after the decisive battle at Harat the Persians collected 24,000 cut-off Uzbeg heads to bring back, and the mechanics of stage management are clearly exposed: what appears to be the quasi-spontaneous triumph of the victorious soldier bearing a victim's head on his pike is actually effected with specially mustered props and walk-on extras to carry them. Sherley tells us that on the staves 'were fastned *vizards* of so many heads', and for a moment this inclines us to wonder if the heads themselves aren't replicas, masks, purely conventional images of death. In fact, he is using the word metaphorically, to signify that the heads, which are real enough, are also spectral, mask-*like* in their deathly torpor; and this usage is also his acknowledgement of the way the heads have been made into elements or (as it were) features of a theatrical design. In fact, what is striking about most of these responses is how readily they accept the grisly spectacle as a cultural sign, and are consequently insulated by this from the full shock of physical reality. Of course, severed heads were familiar enough in European contexts – those of traitors exhibited on Tower Bridge, for example – serving a political admonitory function and signalling the perfection of royal power and justice. But the Persian triumph is quite different in tone and scale, and while this kind of victory parade might have been familiar to the Sherley party from classical or exotic literature, it would be so as an image of how *others* – non-Europeans, the numberless hordes of Asia – conduct themselves in war. Yet at no point in the present accounts are the severed heads offered as an example of barbarism. The spectacle is a strange one – a 'prospect. . .not usually seen', as Manwaring rather primly tells us – but its meaning is controlled and disclosed by the occasion it serves. The Europeans are not free to interpret it as gratuitous or as an isolated piece of savagery, but are forced to read it in terms of the iconography of royal power. Contrast this with the moment in Conrad's *Heart of Darkness*, when Marlow first sees the heads surmounting the posts around Kurtz's dwelling in the jungle, and insists on separating the 'savage sight' (which has a 'right to exist...in the sunshine') from the 'intolerable' ceremonies of obeisance to Kurtz.[25] That kind of separation, arguably, is not possible in a Renaissance context.

In all these accounts, mass decapitation is accepted as part of what Stephen Orgel calls 'the illusion of power':[26] to reject it, as the Spaniards rejected Aztec practices of human sacrifice, is to refuse the possibility of dialogue with an alien political culture. This is not simply a question of practical diplomacy, playing along with foreign atrocities for the sake of larger political objectives; it is also a matter of bridging the gap between two different rhetorics of self-assertion, and thereby establishing a basis on which the awareness of cultural difference can generate *rapprochement* rather than incomprehension. As I have suggested, this was often accomplished on the ground by turning diplomacy into a theatrical rite, and many of the memoirs and first-hand accounts preserve details of this process. But the process doesn't stop there. We need to ask: what happens after the event, in what we might call the secondary literature – the prose narratives, plays and so on that feed off the travel reports, drawing out or rearranging their implications for a larger audience? This sort of writing shapes the attitudes to the foreign of the Jacobean public, often by moralizing or over-organizing the narrative. Both tendencies are evident, for instance, in Anthony Nixon's story of how Robert Sherley, frustrated in his attempt to trade thirty captured Turkish captains for his brother imprisoned in Constantinople, instead cut off their heads and '(according to the custome of Persia) caused them to bee carried in triumph about the Market place, on the top of his Souldiers Pikes'.[27] The echo of Abbas' earlier triumph is clear, a piece of narrative symmetry; and the implication is not that Robert has 'turned Turk' in a savage land but that he has legitimized Persian custom by making it a tool of Christian retribution, and at the same time asserts a moral authority that is inevitably absent from pagan triumphs.

A more subtle version of this argument emerges from the way Day, Rowley and Wilkins dramatize Abbas' entry into Qasvin in *The Travels of the Three English Brothers*. The Sophy (i.e. the Shah) makes his appearance simply *with drums and colours*; and he offers to make up for greeting the Sherleys 'in weatherbeaten steel' by staging for them 'the manner of our Persian wars, Our music and our conquests' (1.43–4).[28] His followers divide into two groups, representing Persians versus the Turks, and a battle is staged: *the one half drive out the other, then enter with heads on their swords*. After this demonstration of Islamic schism, the Sherleys reciprocate with *A Christian battle shown between the two brothers*, in which Anthony takes Robert and his followers prisoner, and the Sophy declares enthusiastically that

> Your wars are royal,
> So joined with music that even death itself
> Would seem a dream; your instruments dissolve
> A body into spirit but to hear
> Their cheerful clamours.
>
> (1.89–93)

Notice how the playwrights have avoided any suggestion that the heads on Persian swords are meant to be real: this is not a representation of an actual triumph, as it would have been if they had simply dramatized what they found in their sources, but a show of a show, a representation of courtly make-believe, a masque or pageant within a play. And it is clear that such a strategy is necessary to keep the Persian triumph within the same discursive arena as its Christian counterpart – as if the dramatists recognized that to *show* the procession of severed heads as part of the main action (and so early in the play) is a strong visual statement that might generate unwanted responses. As it is, the pageant of mock-battles establishes the context for a debate, initiated by the Sophy's puzzlement about one element in the Christian charade:

> SOPHY.   But what means those in bondage so?
> SIR ANTHONY.   These are our prisoners.
> SOPHY.   Why do they live?
>
> (1.100–1)

To which Anthony replies that it is Christian practice to show clemency to a yielding foe. A significant portion of the later action is shaped by this issue, as Robert Sherley, Hotspur-like, first refuses to yield up his Turkish prisoner to Halibeck, who relishes the prospect of putting him to death – a fate which his victim accepts as part of the 'Custom of tyranny' between the two nations (II. 105); and later (in a telling departure from Nixon's account cited above) successfully justifies to the enraged Sophy his decision to release the captured Turkish captains in exchange for his brother Thomas.

A similar manipulation of historical detail is evident also in the playwrights' handling of another piece of the Sherley myth, namely that the brothers were responsible for turning the Persian forces into a modern army. The definitive statement of this is in Purchas' 'briefe Memoriall':

The mightie Ottoman, terror of the Christian World, quaketh of a Sherly-Fever, & gives hopes of approching fates. The prevailing Persian hath learned Sherleian Arts of War, and he which before knew not the use of Ordnance, hath now 500. Peeces of Brasse, & 60000. Musketiers; so that they which at hand with the Sword were before dreadfull to the Turkes, now also in remoter blowes and sulfurian Arts are growne terrible.[29]

In fact the Persians had been using firearms, including cannon, for much of the sixteenth century, though it is likely that Robert Sherley did teach them new fighting methods. But the playwrights are quick to seize on this popular image of Persian military backwardness to create a scenario more redolent of New World encounters, as Anthony Sherley boasts of the power of his artillery and is more than ready to provide a demonstration:

> *Chambers go off.*
> HALIBECK. Mahomet! It thunders.
> SOPHY. Sure this is a god...
> [*To Sherley.*] First teach me how to call thee ere I speak.
> I more and more doubt thy mortality.
> Those tongues do imitate the voice of heaven
> When the gods speak in thunder; your honours
> And your qualities of war more than human.
> If thou hast godhead, and disguised art come
> To teach us unknown rudiments of war,
> Tell us thy precepts and we'll adore thee.
> (I.117–27)

This speech, so reminiscent of reported first encounters in the New World, is hardly appropriate to the present context, though it is certainly revealing of the potential for misunderstanding and self-betrayal in any dialogue between widely dissimilar cultures. Anthony's response is in effect a tactful corrective, and the means by which the play recovers its balance:

> SIR ANTHONY [...] No stranger are the deeds I show to you
> Than yours to me. My country's far remote,
> An island, but a handful to the world;
> Yet fruitful as the meads of paradise;
> Defenced with streams such as from Eden run;
> Each port and entrance kept with such a guard
> As those you last heard speak. There lives a princess
> Royal as yourself, whose subject I am
> As these are to you.
>
> (1.130–8)

This has the pristine idealism of Jacobean masque, conjuring an imaginative alliance between far-flung courts that transcends doctrinal differences and historical divisions. The encomium to Britain is the basis for a vision of reciprocity, for her isolation is perceived as a source of strength, leaving her free to reinvent the diplomatic map and turn the micro-empire of Great Britain into a global commonwealth of strong and benevolent monarchies. It was popularly believed that Abbas I had civilized Persia single-handed: as Nixon puts it, 'they have heretofore beene held a people fierce and uncivill, little better than the Turkes; But of late they are growne very courteous, and respective unto strangers, by whose conversation they have much bettred their manners & conditions.'[30] In popular writing's view of the matter, arguably, Persia is rescued by enlightened despotism from the miasma of a Turkish-dominated Middle East and restored to exotic respectability, one of a confederation of oriental courts with which a British monarch can do business.

Needless to say, this romantic view could be sustained only by ignoring some thorny diplomatic problems. When Robert Sherley travelled to Europe on his first embassy in 1609 he was wearing, in addition to his Persian robes, a turban with a jewelled crucifix attached to it (the latter a gift from the Pope). This provocative symbol of the *rapprochement* between East and West caused consternation and attracted scorn in diplomatic and court circles; and Robert's oriental dress led to further difficulties, such as whether he could and should remove his turban in the King's presence.[31] Each of the elements that contributed to the Sherley legend – the brothers' taste for adventure, Robert's military knowledge and skill, his glamorous marriage to a Circassian woman, his genuine commitment to the anti-Turkish alliance – became in time a source of controversy, and in one instance at least the popular accounts seem to have provoked a diplomatic incident, when a rival Persian ambassador sent to King James in 1625 assaulted Robert because, he said, he was furious that 'so meane a fellow and an Imposter should presume to say he had married the King his Masters Neece'.[32] That Robert's wife was a niece of Shah Abbas is the claim of the play we have been examining and of the title-page – though not the text – of Nixon's pamphlet; but it is hardly one that Sherley would have made; and there is something both poignant and amusing about the aggrieved ambassador doing battle with a popular fiction. It shows, on the one hand, how unamenable in reality the diplomatic issues were to Purchas' vision of royal co-operation, and, on the other, how the conventional resolutions of pamphlet and play exert a powerful influence on how people think about the foreign and accommodate it to their own priorities and assumptions. Popular culture will not always appeal to chauvinism and prejudice in addressing foreign subjects; it can also be inclusive and homogenizing, using its own conventions to incorporate the unfamiliar, as in the hint that Robert Sherley, by marrying the Sophy's niece, is father to an Anglo-Persian dynasty, a hint reinforced by the *show of the Christening* at the end of the play in which the Sophy stands godfather to their child.

Educated commentators at the time were pretty disparaging about *The Travels of the Three English Brothers*: Fuller called it 'but a friendly foe' to the memory of the Sherleys, one 'more accommodated to please the present spectators than inform posterity';[33] and the Reverend John Cartwright, who visited Persia a few years before it was written, complained of the liberties taken by the play.[34] But while the gap between historical actuality and commercial rehash is at times a wide one, so that Nixon's book and the play that flowed from it have little value either as biography or as chronicle, nonetheless we cannot assume, as seventeenth-century commentators like Fuller tended to, that such work has no cultural significance. It is clear that the British imperial idea, based on a notion of 'perfect conquest' that invites co-operation, is being canvassed in embryonic form in these texts; and in that sense they are laying the foundations of national attitudes. Samuel Purchas can afford to ignore them not just because they lack the authenticity of first-hand travel accounts – they are not the sort of thing he put in his *Pilgrimes* – but also because they have done some of his work for him. In terms of the home book market and the business of creating an audience for his political missionaries, plays and pamphlets like *The Three English Brothers* are in another, broadly cultural sense the primary texts upon which Purchas can erect the fantastical superstructure of *Purchas His Pilgrimes*.

NOTES

1 Samuel Purchas, *Purchas His Pilgrimes*, 20 vols. (London, 1625; rpt. Glasgow, 1905), I, p. 374.

2 Hakluyt documents the 'memorable exploytes' of Anthony Sherley in the West Indies (*Principall Navigations* (London, 1598, rpt. Glasgow 1903–5), 12 vols.), x, pp. 266–76. Thomas Sherley's earlier adventures were also written up in Hakluyt, and acidly noted in John Chamberlain's letter to Dudley Carleton on 27 June 1602 (*Letters*, ed. N. E. McClure (Philadelphia, 1939), I, p. 151).

3 Anthony Sherley, *His Relation of his Travels into Persia* (London, 1613), p. 12.

4 The fullest account of the Sherleys' adventures is D. W. Davies, *Elizabethans Errant* (Ithaca, NY, 1967). See also Samuel Chew's indispensable study of Islam and the West, *The Crescent and the Rose* (New York, 1963), and Niels Steensgaard, *The Asian Trade Revolution of the Seventeenth Century* (Chicago, 1973), on the wider contexts of the Persian mission.

5 Quoted by Chew, *ibid.*, p. 269.

6 George Manwaring, *A True Discourse of Sir A. Sherley's Travel into Persia* (Sloane MS 105), in Sir E. Denison Ross, *Sir Anthony Sherley and his Persian Adventure* (London, 1933), p. 176.

7 John Cartwright, *The Preachers Travels* (London, 1611), p. 69.

8 For more on this, see my edition of the play in *Three Renaissance Travel Plays* (Revels Companion Library (Manchester, 1995)).

9 Sir Robert Sherley...His Royall entertainement into Cracovia...with his pretended Comming into England (London, 1609). On the genesis of this pamphlet, see G. B. Shand, 'Source and Intent in Middleton's *Sir Robert Sherley*', *Renaissance and Reformation* 19 (1983), 257–64.

10 Michael Drayton, *Polyolbion* (London, 1622), part 2, p. 9.

11 Purchas, *Purchas His Pilgrimes*, x, p. 375.

12 Several first-hand accounts of the mission, including the previously unpublished narratives by Manwaring and Pinçon, are collected in Denison Ross, *Sir Anthony Sherley*.

13 Edward Said, *Orientalism* (New York, 1978), p. 70.

14 See Shand, 'Source and Intent'.

15 Sherley, *Relation*, p. 29.

16 *Ibid.*, p. 32.

17 Purchas, *Purchas His Pilgrimes*, VIII, p. 418.

18 See also my *Three Renaissance Travel Plays*, introduction, note 21.

19 James Boon, *Other Tribes, Other Scribes* (Cambridge, 1982), pp. 160, 157.

20 Purchas, *Purchas His Pilgrimes*, x, pp. 375–6.

21 Denison Ross, *Sir Anthony Sherley*, p. 116.

22 *Ibid.*, pp.154, 117, 204–5.

23 Sherley, *Relation*, p. 63.

24 G. le Strange, *Don Juan of Persia* (London, 1926), p. 226.

25 *Heart of Darkness* (Harmondworth, 1973), pp. 96–7.

26 Stephen Orgel, *The Illusion of Power: Political Theatre in the English Renaissance* (Berkeley, 1975), a searching study of the court masque.

27 Anthony Nixon, *The Three English Brothers* (London, 1607), K3.

28 All references are to the edition in *Three Renaissance Travel Plays*. I have borrowed here a few sentences from my introduction to that volume.

29 Purchas, *Purchas His Pilgrimes*, x p. 376.

30 Nixon, *The Three English Brothers*, H2 v.

31 Chew, *The Crescent and the Rose*, pp. 306–11, 325.

32 *Ibid.*, pp. 327–8.

33 Thomas Fuller, *The Worthies of England* (London, 1662), p. 108.

34 Cartwright, *The Preachers Travels*, pp. 70–1.

CHAPTER 3

'The naked and the dead': Elizabethan perceptions of Ireland

Andrew Hadfield

Just over a third of the way into Edmund Spenser's lengthy prose dialogue, *A View of the Present State of Ireland* (*c.* 1596), the dominant interlocutor, Irenius, substantiates a point about the cultural practices of the indigenous Irish with an anecdote based on his own observation of the people:

[T]he Gaules used to drinke their enemyes blood and to painte themselves therewith So allsoe they write that the owlde Irishe weare wonte And so have I sene some of the Irishe doe but not theire enemyes but friendes blodd as namelye at the execution of A notable Traitour at Limericke Called murrogh Obrien I sawe an olde woman which was his foster mother take up his heade whilste he was quartered and sucked up all the blodd runninge thereout Sayinge that the earthe was not worthie to drinke it and thearwith allso steped her face, and breste and torne heare Cryinge and shrikinge out most terrible.[1]

The incident has frequently been cited to argue that Spenser was in Ireland as early as 1577, when Murrogh O'Brien was executed.[2] Reading the episode in this way is by no means to be dismissed out of hand, but it does risk riding roughshod over the layers of rhetorical and cultural codes which the text places between us as readers and the putative eyewitness.[3] Firstly, it assumes that the character, Irenius, can be equated with the historical figure of Edmund Spenser, an identification between narrated and authorial self which can be problematic enough in 'travel literature' that purports to be directly autobiographical, as well as assuming that the dialogue form was not read as fiction in the sixteenth century.[4] Secondly, and more relevant to my argument here, such an equation assumes that Spenser would only have described the incident had he been an observer of the scene, which is clearly not the case. In the relevant section of the *View*, Irenius is attempting to establish a genealogy of the contemporary Irish, showing that they are primarily Scythian in origin, but also owe much to the Spanish, Gauls and ancient Britons. In order to prove these lines of descent, he relies upon a form of cultural anthropology whereby an instance of a shared custom argues not simply a homologous social formation, but a blood relationship.

Irenius employs (at least) three interrelated discourses in order to authorize his identification of the Irish. He invokes a classical paradigm, citing Caesar's *Conquest of Gaul* and Johannes Boemus in the same paragraph to establish their ancestral relationship and elsewhere refers to Tacitus, Herodotus and Diodorus Sicilius.[5] Secondly, in highlighting the detail of the ritualized blood-drinking, he is signalling a dichotomy of savage/civilized between the Irish subject and the observer of the scene, a distinction frequently used to denote both a classical and a New World reference. Sir Thomas Elyot's *Boke of the Governor* (1531) advised English aristocrats to read Caesar's *Conquest of Gaul* to instruct them 'concerning the wars against the Irishmen or Scots, who be of the same rudeness and wild disposition that the Swiss and Britons were in the time of Caesar'.[6] The comparison is repeated in the unpublished chapters of Fynes Moryson's *Itinerary* (1617), illustrating the prevalence of a notion of cultural advance: what the Britons once were the Irish are now; what the Romans once were, the Britons/English have become.[7] William Strachey claimed that if the Romans had not conquered and civilized Britain it would still be a savage nation, its inhabitants practising cannibalism.[8] The model of progress worked spatially too: Theodore De Bry, in his retouchings and additions to the New World drawings of John White, decided to place the figures of five 'Pictes which in the Old tyme dyd habite one part of the great Bretainne have bin in times past as savage as those of Virginnia'.[9] The patterns of the development of peoples have been flattened out into a simple model of necessary and inevitable progress from the savage to the civilized, one which can be imposed upon time and space.[10] In observing the contemporary Irish to be blood-drinkers, Irenius signifies their relationship to the savages of the ancient world, a British past and the New World.

A third discourse which is invoked is one already used to classify the Irish, that of Gerald of Wales, the ghost-in-the-machine of all Tudor descriptions of Ireland and the Irish.[11] In his *Expugnatio Hibernica* (1185), Gerald narrates the act of the Irish chieftain, Dairmait, who has the heads of two hundred enemies at his feet:

When he had turned each one over and recognised it, out of an excess of joy he jumped three times in the air with arms clasped over his head, and joyfully gave thanks to the Supreme Creator as he loudly revelled in his triumph. He lifted up to his mouth the head of one he particularly loathed, and taking it by the ears and hair, gnawed at the nose and cheeks – a cruel and inhuman act.[12]

Dairmait's anthropophagism defines him as a savage 'Other' (his behaviour resembles the Gaulish practice of drinking their enemies' blood) to be distinguished from the civility of the purported eyewitness. Like Spenser, Gerald writes as if he had observed the scene, but this does not mean that he was there. Medieval and Renaissance historians frequently reconstructed events or placed speeches in the mouths of historical actors which they could not possibly have witnessed to add authenticity to their accounts and afford the reader a psychological insight into events.[13]

Irenius' attempt to define the Irish involves elaborating a savage/barbarian character which is simultaneously natural and cultural, and, in both a crude and sophisticated sense of the term, his project is an intertextual one.[14] His use of an eyewitness account serves to justify a position of authority (a civilized observer of savage customs) and identify a people. Empirical perception – especially an example as obviously foregrounded as this – is always culturally mediated.

English observers (principally, colonists, administrators and the occasional traveller)[15] of the native Irish all work within this long-established model of a fundamental distinction between the savage and the civil. The essential details of a sketch of an Irish character had already been established in Gerald's *Topographia Hibernica* (1185) and no Elizabethan writer differed significantly from his 'observations':

[The Irish] are so barbarous that they cannot be said to have any culture...they go naked and unarmed into battle. They regard weapons as a burden, and think it brave and honourable to fight unarmed...They are a wild and inhospitable people. They live on beasts only, and live like beasts. They have not progressed at all from the primitive habits of pastoral living...They use the fields generally as pasture, but pasture in poor condition. Little is cultivated and even less sown...they do not devote their lives to the processing of flax or wool, or to any kind of merchandise or mechanical art. For given only to leisure, and devoted only to laziness, they think that the greatest pleasure is not to work, and the greatest wealth is to enjoy liberty...This people is, then, a barbarous people, literally barbarous. Judged according to modern ideas, they are uncultivated, not only in the external appearance of their dress, but also in their flowing hair and beards. All their habits are the habits of barbarians.[16]

The Irish are a naked people: they lack the accoutrements of the civilized. They do not use their land properly, they have defective systems of law and social organization, they lack even the most basic forms of technology because they refuse to work, their marriage customs lead only to libidinousness and the break up of stable inheritance, they have no rationality or religion, they are slaves to the unconscious desires of their naked bodies. In one of the most frequently cited descriptions of the native Irish, Fynes Moryson, who served as Mountjoy's secretary during his spectacularly successful victories in the Nine Years War (1594–1603) and then included his experiences and recollections in his massive account of his travels throughout Europe, has an Italian friar exclaim: 'Vain Armagh city, I did thee pity, / Thy meat's rawness and women's nakedness'.[17] Most obviously, the nakedness and the rawness connote clothing and cooking as the true order of things.[18] More importantly, the connection made between *women* and nakedness serves to feminize the savage Irish who are synecdochially represented as female. Yet again, an eyewitness account is produced which serves to verify this relationship. Moryson claims to have seen nude Cork girls grinding corn 'and striking off into the tub of meal such reliques thereof as stuck upon their belly, thighs, and more unseemly parts'.[19] The savage body is dangerous because uncontrollable; the description links an absence of civilized values with a repulsive libidinousness. What should be private, the pudenda of the girls, is made public and therefore perverse, so that the discrete ordering of society is thrown out of control. The desires of the body (female, Irish, savage, private) threaten to engulf the rational ordering of society (male, English, civilized, public).

Andrew Trollope, writing to Walsingham in 1581, makes a similar connection between nakedness and savagery:

The Irishe men, except [in] walled townes, are not Christians cyvell or humane creators, but heathen, or rather savage, and brute beasts. For many of them, as well women as men, goe commonly all naked saveing onely a lost mantle hangeing aboute them; if eny of them have a sherte and a payre of syngle sowled shoes, which they cal broges, they are especyally provyded for.

The absence of clothes/civility demonstrates both an excess and a lack, so that the Irish are dangerously violent and less than human in being so: 'Every chief rebel's pardon is a hundred men's deaths. Feagh M'Hugh's boast that he could murder and rob whom he listed...Practice lately at Dublin to cut the throats of all the English at one instant'.[20] The naked body signifies destruction and the overthrow of a civilized order.

However, a discourse of savagery/civility did not always use the signifier of nakedness to represent an evil and hostile creature. The aggressive naked savage is a form of post-lapsarian man; there is also a pre-lapsarian variant who, more often than not, inhabits the Garden of Eden.[21] Travel accounts of voyages to the Americas contain numerous instances of encounters with such peoples:

When he [Columbus] wente a lande and commaunded his chaplaine to say masse on the sea bankes, a great confluence of the naked inhabitants flocked thither symply and without feare bringynge with them plenty of meate and fresh water, mervelyynge at oure men as they had byn summe straunge miracle.[22]

Elsewhere, the same text describes groups of Indians as 'Civile and humane peoples' and 'Relygious and humane people'; they are well disposed towards the civilization they lack and wish to acquire it.[23] Columbus narrates his encounter with a group of Arawak Indians who imitate European religious practices by kneeling in prayer, and 'after what maner so ever they sawe them praye to the crosse, they followed them in all poyuntes as well as they could'; Walter Ralegh described an identical experience among the Trinidadians, when he explained the virtues of Elizabeth, then showed them a picture of her, 'as it had bene easie to have brought them idolatrous thereof'.[24] The icon of civilization leads to an excess of zeal, which is pleasurable rather than threatening according to Ralegh's witty trope. Such naked savages are to be contrasted to the most fearsome naked men of all, the cannibals: 'In all these places for the most part the Indians go naked, and are wilde people. Their common armour is bowes and arrowes: they use to eate up such Christians as they come by'.[25]

Whilst the Irish are most usually represented as the post-lapsarian branch of naked man – in some cases as cannibals – perceptions of them as docile *tabulae rasae* are extant. Edmund Campion, in his *History of Ireland* (*c.* 1571), emphasized their lack of clothes, notably for babies who are 'foulded up starke naked into a blankett tyll they can goe, and then yf they gett a peece of rugg to cover them they are well spedd'. 'Lynnen shirtes' are the only adult clothes he describes in his sketchy analysis of customs.[26] In the *History*, the Irish are a nation characterized by the absence of civility which, like the good Arawak Indians, they are keen to correct, being 'sharpe witted, lovers of learning, capable of any studie whereunto they bende themselves'. Campion has an implicit faith in the absolute power of education to produce human nature:

Hitherto the Irishe of boothe sortes, meere and English, are affected muche indiferently, save that in theis by good order and breaking the same vertues are far more pregnant, in those other by licencious and evil custome the same faculties are more extreame and odious. I saie by lycentiousnes and evill custome, for that there is daily traill of good natures amonge them; howe some they be reclaymed and to what rare giftes of grace and wisdome they doe have aspired, againe the veary Englishe of the birthe conversant with the brutish sorte of that people become degenerate in shoirt space, and are quite altered into the worst ranke of Irish rooges. Suche a force hathe education to make or marre.[27]

There is no sense here of a dialectical process, man being both determining and determined by a state of being: an individual is simply inserted into an environment which then produces his or her nature. The people need not be deracinated from the land because they are blank sheets waiting to be inscribed with the discourse of English civility. Both can easily be colonized, or, in Campion's phrase, 'reclaymed'.[28]

For Campion, the Irish are seen as a naked, innocent people, rather like the cannibals in Montaigne's famous essay, who are also without clothes: 'they weare no kinde of breeches nor hosen'.[29] His hastily assembled *History* has been described as little more than a plea for education: it ends with an oration by James Stanihurst, speaker of the Irish House of Commons, and the reply by Sir Henry Sidney, the outgoing Lord Deputy, both of whom stress this need.[30] Sidney passes over control to Fitzwilliam and Perrot and the text concludes with the assumption that although the realm is not yet fully secure and reformed, it soon will be.[31]

Stephen Greenblatt has pointed out that the metaphor of natural man functioned either to represent a people designated as savage as opaque (beyond reason, an alien Other), or transparent (innocent, ready to be completely assimilated).[32] The Irish are represented as either of these two poles of meaning: Campion sees through them, recognizing only traits which can be defined as civilized or English, whereas writers like Trollope or Moryson can see only inherent evil and a bestiality beyond reform. The difference is easily accounted for: Campion was writing in 1571, at a time of relative peace and stability, after the defeat of Shane O'Neill and before the disastrous attempts of Essex and Sir Thomas Smith to colonize Ulster. Peace seemed a genuine possibility.[33] Trollope's letter was written ten years later during the Desmond rebellion and soon after Spanish and Papal forces had landed in Munster, when a pan-Catholic-inspired invasion seemed likely to many English officials and observers.[34] Moryson was writing about the height of the Nine Years War when the same threat loomed even larger.[35] Such writers were more than likely to make very different assesssments of Ireland's malleability and consequently employ directly opposed representations from within the same paradigms of a colonial discourse. Only after the defeat of the Irish forces at Kinsale (1601) do metaphors like Campion's abound once more: Mountjoy, the architect of the English victory, submitted a 'Discourse concerning Ireland' (March 1601) to the Privy Council, in which he confidently (and accurately) predicted that the war would be over by the end of the next winter and stated that Elizabeth would be able to 'work this kingdom into what fashion she will, either to make a long and lasting peaceable government between some mere Irish and her English subjects, or else to make it as a *tabula*, and to write in it what laws shall best please herself' (Mountjoy's emphasis).[36]

The influence of this particular system of discourse upon Elizabethan perceptions of Ireland can perhaps be illustrated via a comment made by Mountjoy slightly earlier in the campaign. It was believed that the Irish were incapable of the civilized practice of crop cultivation because they were essentially a nomadic people who followed their wandering herds of cattle.[37] For example, on his deathbed, Con O'Neill was supposed to have confessed that he hated husbandry and preferred a wild life.[38] During his northern campaign in the summer of 1600, Mountjoy wrote to Robert Cecil and expressed his surprise at seeing cornfields in Ulster, the least anglicized province of Ireland before the Londonderry Plantation: 'It is incredible in so barbarous a country how well the ground was manured, how orderly the fields were fenced, their towns inhabited, and every highway and path so well beaten.'[39] Again, this empirical observation has be to read as part of – or against – a series of representations which served to define an Irishness for the English.

Irish property inheritance was believed to be the cause of the lack of agricultural production because the Irish did not practise primogeniture but the 'corrupt custome of tanistry…[which] was the roote of all the barbarisme and Disorder in Ireland'.[40] This meant that succession went to 'the strongest personality in the group' (tuatha), who was often nominated by the current chieftain: if no heir was apparent, one emerged from either election or force of arms. The defect which the English perceived was the rarity of stable land inheritance under this system, which often resulted in 'a certain amount of repartitioning at a succession'.[41] Sir John Davies, in his legal treatise, *A Discovery of the True Causes why Ireland was never entirely subdued* (1612), links the practice of tanistry – and gavelkind, which decreed that 'the inferior territories were partible amongst all the males of the sept, both bastards and legitimate' – with the 'desolation and barbarism' he perceived in early Jacobean Ireland, 'the like was never seen in any country that professed the name of Christ'.[42] Ireland had no cities, castles or permanent property, save what was copied from the English

Neither did any of them in all this time plant any gardens or orchards, enclose or improve any lands, live together in any settled villages or towns, nor make provision for posterity, which, being against all common-sense and reason, must needs to be imputed to those unreasonable customs which made their estates so uncertain and transitory in their possessions.[43]

The savage lives only for the present, being ruled by the dictates of the body's desires, and is unable to accumulate like civilized man. He underuses his land and so this can be claimed by those who will use it more efficiently. Sir Thomas Smith's plans for the establishment of a colony of English in the Ards Peninsula in the early 1570s concentrated on the problem of overpopulation in England, especially for younger sons, who were unable to inherit under a system of primogeniture and so often became impoverished, rootless and dangerous.[44] Smith argued that their needs would best be fulfilled through colonizing the wastelands of other countries and that his Irish venture was a noble examplar.[45] The younger English sons would be replacing the Irish first-born who had forfeited their rights to the land through their refusal to follow a natural law of inheritance, designed to increase wealth for all.

Exactly the same logic was applied to Indian land in the Americas. The natives were seen to be unable to use their land efficiently despite the 'great abundance' of it they possessed:

God created land 'to the end that it should by culture and husbandry yield things necessary for man's life'. The Indians make 'small account' of their land, 'taking no other fruits thereby than such as the ground itself doth naturally yield'...When the Indians have assimilated the knowledge to put their land to some use, they will be on their way from brutish ignorance to civility and knowledge.[46]

Until then, the laws of international trade decree that those who can use the land should be free to do so.[47]

Both Irish and Indians are seen as barbarous, naked people who do not possess the benefits of civilization and it would be possible to enumerate far more instances of similar descriptions of their cultural practices by English observers, illustrating that both peoples were represented in analogous ways.[48] However, to suggest that the Irish were regarded solely as Amerindians and that Ireland was no more than a stepping stone *en route* to the colonization of the Americas would be highly misleading.[49] The Irish were also supposedly subjects of the English crown and were thus represented within a whole series of discourses of state many of which had been formulated during the reign of Henry VIII after the break with Rome and, importantly, during the suppression of the Pilgrimage of Grace (1536–7).[50] It is erroneous to see an expanding frontier, a progressive loosening of morality, and to claim that English governors 'were absolved of all ethical restraints' in Ireland, serving an apprenticeship before they went off to the New World.[51] Sir Walter Ralegh, for example, in his account of his voyage to Guiana (1596), advocated humane treatment of the natives to win them over from Spanish control: the Spanish, according to Ralegh, treated the Indians with the utmost cruelty.[52] In Ireland, Ralegh was as ruthless as such notorious 'hard men' as Sir Humphrey Gilbert and Sir Peter Carew, being prepared to enforce law and order pitilessly, most notoriously at the massacre at Smerwick, rumours of which appear to have disturbed court officials in England and led to the recall of the Lord Deputy responsible, Arthur, Lord Grey De Wilton.[53] Gilbert himself, although he considered forcing 'a violent entry' into the lands of the northern American Indians, concluded that this would be too difficult and that his crew should 'winne the Barbarians favour by some good meanes'; in Ireland, Gilbert made no such distinctions.[54] Richard Hakluyt also advocated humane treatment of New World Indians and hoped for mutual toleration, surmising that there was land enough for all to use.[55] It was clearly possible – in theory, at least – to live in harmony with American natives, something which could not be countenanced on the same terms with Irish within the boundaries of state.

A comparison of the ways in which rebellions in England and Ireland were regarded and dealt with in the sixteenth century illustrates that a complex grid of intersecting discourses was in operation over the territories ruled by the English monarch.[56] Tudor theories of absolute loyalty to the monarch had been formulated after Henry VIII's break with Rome and, specifically, in response to the serious rebellion which that act provoked in the north, the Pilgrimage of Grace. Richard Morison, one of the most important Henrician theorists and propagandists, whose tracts were widely circulated in response to the revolt, argued that subjects must serve with unquestioning obedience: 'He is none of mine sayth Christ, nor worthy to be my servant that can not, if just cause require hym so to do, forsake his father and mother to doo mke servyce. He is none of myne saythe Englande, that canne not hate his father and his mother, that canne not kyll them bothe, sooner than ones consente to my destruction.'[57]

For Morison, state and rule are synonymous as *loci* of authority: 'Take awaye the commandments of God, destroye all the lawes of nature and of man, may not eyther the hygh commodyties, that come of mutuale concorde betwene all the kyngs subjectes, and the kyngs grace, or the excedynge damagers, that ensue open sedition, kepe any honest harte, in maynteynynge the one, and fleinge the other?'[58] The king represents the land in a metonymic relationship, rather as the Ditchley portrait has Elizabeth standing on her country ready to face and repel the invading force of the Armada.[59] Elsewhere, Morison compares the bond between ruler and subject as that between father and children, a patriarchal power relation openly declared and writ large.[60]

Other writers like Thomas Starkey and John Cheke, the noted humanist and Greek scholar, also inveighed against any form of civil or military disobedience. Cheke argued that rebellions were often pedagogically useful events – provided they were unsuccessful – as they would show loyal subjects the futility and destructiveness of opposition to the monarch. Rebels, he pointed out, claim that they desire to help the commonwealth by drawing attention to its vices in the hope of curing them; but the manifest result of rebellion is poverty for the majority of subjects because husbandry is halted and its products destroyed.[61] William Camden stated that 'all rebellions do *touch* the body of the prince' and criticized Sir John Perrot for even thinking of words against the monarch: 'he had bolted out some words against his sovereign who is not to be *violated* by word or thought' (my emphases).[62] This was no more than the 1534 Treason Act had stated.[63]

Similar juridico-political statements have been analysed by Michel Foucault who argued that the most spectacular manifestation of these power relations took place in the public execution:

Its aim is not so much to re-establish a balance as to bring into play, as its extreme point, the dissymmetry between the subject who has dared to violate the law and the all-powerful sovereign who displays his strength...And this superiority is not simply that of right, but beating down upon the body of his adversary and mastering it; by breaking the law, the offender has touched the very person of the prince; and it is the prince – or at least those to whom he has delegated his force – who seizes upon the body of the condemned man and displays it marked, beaten, broken.[64]

In *The Image of Ireland* (1581), John Derricke places a long narrative in the mouth of the rebel, Rory Oge O'More.[65] Even when dead, justly executed by the Queen – or rather, her representative in Ireland, the Viceroy[66] – the corpse is able to speak, to signify and take its place within the pageant of state power. As his severed head looks down from the battlements of Dublin Castle it warns subjects:'Against the Crowne royall doe nothyng attempt, / For if against it, ye, falyng at odde, / Doe feele as I felt, the Strength of the Rodde.'[67] The sixth woodcut which accompanies the text shows Sir Henry Sidney setting out from Dublin Castle with rebels' heads on poles. A verse attached to it states: 'These trunkles heddes do playnly showe each rebelles fatal end, / And what a haynous crime it is the Queene for to offend.'[68]

Clearly, the same logic of obedience to the crown which applied in England was capable of warranting the theatrical public violence which took place in Ireland, rather than it bring the product of a perception of the Irish as semi-human savages. In *The Faerie Queene*, v.ix, Arthur and Artegall, the Knight of Justice, have to defeat a shadowy figure named Malengin, whose name is glossed in the head-verse to the canto as 'Guyle'. A description of him strongly resembles a sketch of Irish kerns in the *View* and his garment ('And on his back an uncouth vestiment / Made of strange stuff, but all to-worn and ragged' (v.ix.10)) recalls Irenius' comments on the Irish mantle.[69] Malengin escapes the knights through a bewildering range of metamorphoses; eventually, however, he is captured and killed by Artegall's servant, the iron man, Talus:

> But when as he [Malengin] would to a snake again,
> Have turn'd himselfe, he [Talus] with his yron flaile
> Gan drive at him, with so huge might and maine,
> That all his bones, as small as sandy grayle
> He broke, and did his bowels disentrayle;
> Crying in vaine for helpe, when helpe was past.
> So did the selfe deceiver fayle,
> There they him left a carrion outcast;
> For beasts and foules to fede upon for their repast.
>
> (v.ix.19)

Like Rory Oge O'More, Malengin is said to destroy himself ('selfe deceiver') by threatening the power of the prince and so suffers a vividly brutal and theatrical death. His body is reduced to its constituent parts and so anatomized for all to see, serving as a lesson for good subjects as Cheke recommended, before it is dissipated and removed entirely from the body politic by the obliging 'beasts and foules'. The stanza describes a political myth, the extension of a discursive practice to its logical extreme: the body of the alien subject, the rebel, is removed by natural forces so that it disappears.[70] Just as the representation of the savage permits difference only when it can be assimilated, so does a discourse of state demand that subjects be either transparent or destroyed by the spectacular power of the state's judicial machinery. Both modes of discourse have the same vanishing point: an anonymous treatise written in 1599 concludes with the desire that Ireland become 'merely a West England' and will do so if the author's brutal proposals are followed; some years earlier, Sir Henry Sidney had enthused about the citizens of Cork: 'I found such humbleness in them and willingness to become English, and accordingly to lyve under English law, and by the same to be defended, each weaker from his stronger neighbour, as I did ask nothing but it was granted.'[71] Malengin is clearly a problematic construct within a fiction: he serves as a lesson to good subjects, then conveniently dematerializes, providing no resistance to the forces of law and order or colonial authority. The land is removed of its stubborn people, becomes blank and empty, ready to be inscribed with a whole series of new languages.[72] Spenser's depiction of the court of Mercilla in the same canto, a place where poets who oppose the Queen have their tongues nailed to posts and the monarch has to be forced by her council to execute her most dangerous rival, illustrates that Spenser himself realized that his representation of Malengin's death was a fantasy, as does the bitingly savage allegory of Elizabeth's failure in Ireland which concludes book v of *The Faerie Queene*.[73]

Dissent in sixteenth-century England was also represented as vagabondage as well as rebellion and it was frequently assumed that the two malpractices were intimately linked. John Cheke contended that wherever there were rebels there would also be vagabonds:

But what talke I of disobedience so quietlie? Have not such mad rages run in your heads, that forsaking and bursting the quitnesse of the common peace, ye have heinouslie and traitorouslie incamped your selves in field, and there like a bile in a body, naie a sinke in a town, have gathered togither all the nastie vagabonds and idle loiterers to beare armour against him [the King], whom all godlie and good subjects will live and die withall.[74]

Cheke implies that vagabondage, like rebellion, is caused by an evil state of mind which infects people. His treatise is introduced as 'a necessarie discourse for everie good English subject' and the act of reading the work is envisaged as beneficial to the creation of loyal obedience: 'the verie reading of this treatise is able to turne a rebellious mind to meeknesse: if reason be not altogether led awaie by lust'.[75]

I have already referred to representations of the Irish as lazy, nomadic savages incapable of using their land correctly like many Amerindians and other exotic peoples scattered throughout the pages of Hakluyt's *Principal Navigations*: an English perception of Irish character from Gerald's works onwards.[76] What needs to be challenged is a confidence that such a link between idleness, nomadic behaviour and rebellion necessarily belongs to a discourse which hinges on the axis of savagery versus civility. As the quotation from Cheke illustrates, the duty of a subject was to be useful and hence to be idle was to be useless and therefore constituted a form of rebellion against the monarch.[77] Failure to cultivate land could be interpreted within the paradigm of state loyalty. Edward Phyton wrote to Burghley in 1587 that Munster was wasted and full of the poorest people he had ever seen: he attributed their lamentable state to their idleness and, therefore, believed it to be richly deserved.[78] Another commentator noted that idle kerns and gallowglasses lived off the spoils of ordinary herdsmen: the Irish socio-economic system was seen to cause division and strife through an inherent disorder which opposed English order.[79] This was reinforced through a practice of holding only tenants-at-will rather than freeholders, which also discouraged efficient land usage.[80] A general reason for the decay of Ireland was felt to be the Irish vice of idleness which infected English settlers with a vengeance.[81] In an Irish context, Englishness is seen as a mark of industry, productivity and obedience; Irishness leads only to anarchy and rebellion.

It would be inaccurate to argue that there was no difference at all between the reactions of English authorities to rebellion and disorder in England and Ireland. Judicial execution rather than widespread slaughter was the norm in England whereas the reverse was the case in Ireland.[82] Nevertheless, in addition to the discursive links made between the representation of rebels in the two countries, mention should also be made of the fact that many government officials who were responsible for the suppression of rebellion in Ireland were also instrumental in performing the same task in England, a relationship which has received far less attention than the overlap between those who sought their fortunes in both Ireland and the New World.[83] To cite two examples: Thomas Ratcliffe, Earl of Sussex and Lord Deputy of Ireland under both Mary and Elizabeth, supervised the planting of English colonies at Leix and Offaly and was also President of the Council of the North during the rebellion of 1569–70, and thus responsible for its suppression; Sir Peter Carew, who procured a huge fortune in Irish land through the actions of his solicitor and biographer, Sir John Hooker, had been particularly severe in his treatment of rebels during the Western Rising of 1549.[84] At times English rebels were described as 'ignorant, superstitious and altogether blinded with the old papish doctrine'; at others, it was stated that they should rather be 'rebuke[d] for their stubbornesse than despise[d] for their ignorance'.[85] Exactly the same judgements are applied as were to the Irish when seen as New World savages, illustrating how easily seemingly separate discursive areas employ the same logic and are inextricably linked.

English descriptions of the Irish cut across any boundaries of ethnic identity and throw a belief in such putatively stable categories into crisis; again, attempts to order the material into discrete categories are thwarted by the problematic and transgressional nature of the evidence. Ireland contained two competing colonial communities, the Old English, those who had come over in the wake of the Norman English invasion, and the New English who had come to Ireland with the Tudors' renewed interest in the country.[86] The existence of these two communities, each trying to claim that they alone represented an English identity in Ireland and had the right to speak directly to the central authorities in London, demonstrates that problems of defining Self/Other cannot be confined to English perceptions of the Irish. English identity itself was redefined in Ireland. This subject has been extensively analysed elsewhere and lengthy treatment here would only involve duplication of other conclusions.[87] Old and New English both tended to employ the whole gamut of representations of the indigenous Irish established by Gerald; they differed in their perceptions of what was to be done in order to reform the country. The Old English, more often than not, argued that the administrative structure in place in Ireland was workable and that greater education and the spread of the law would make the country peaceful and profitable to the crown.[88] The New English countered that a radical overhaul of the edifice of government was necessary as the Irish were too hostile to English attempts to govern them and enable the current apparatus to work. They demanded that their representatives replace the existing Old English officials in Dublin, greater military intervention and the use of martial law to quell rebellion and a further influx of settlers to establish a more dominantly English presence in Ireland.[89] The crucial point which needs to be made is that what divided these two groups was the matter of religion: the Old English were predominantly catholic and hence their perception of their difference from the native Irish was based on a dichotomy of civilized/barbarian; the New English were Protestant and reinforced this division with a religious one so that Englishness was seen to depend upon the possession of the reformed faith. Writers like Spenser and Barnaby Rich argued that the Old English had really 'degenerated' and become Irish, but whereas they claimed that the Irish were ignorant and naive in their adherence to a false form of Christianity, the Old English were far worse because they had chosen to oppose civilized values.[90] The Old English became caught between assuming an identity based upon their genealogical lineage and one which foregrounded their religion.[91] By the end of the

seventeenth century, the range of identities in Ireland became
dependent upon religious affiliation, a split which still operates
today.[92]

What can be learnt from this brief survey of English representations
of Ireland and Irishness? Perhaps the most important lesson is how
difficult it is to separate categories which are all too often taken for
granted as distinct and self-sufficient entities. Evidence cannot exist
as pure empirical data ready to be placed into a theoretical
framework because it already exists within one possessed by the
observer or recorder.[93] Similarly, analyses of sixteenth-century
British history which accept a division of events and territories into
the domestic and the exotic are seriously flawed. All too often a
narrative of 'early modern' history fails to make any connection
between the process of colonialism and the assertion of a national
unity; too much colonial and post-colonial theory assumes that
certain conflicts and contradictions inherent in the formation of
identity are products of the colonial scene alone.[94]

Hayden White has argued that when sixteenth-century Europeans
wrote about the 'noble savage', the dominant referent in the
comparison was not savageness but nobility. The period in
question can be seen as 'the ironic stage in the evolution of the Wild
Man motif in European thought' when the image was used to
attack class systems in Europe, not exalt the natives of the New
World and protect their rights. In the New World, according to
White, the term 'humanity' was being tested: the natives appear as
either continuous (human), or contiguous (different, whether
superior or inferior). The American Indians became a European
'fetish', just as the 'dangerous classes' of a later period were viewed
as malevolent wild animals, 'grotesque objects of fear and anxiety',
or God-like guardians of the future of humanity.[95] Such an analysis
points out the difficulty of prising apart discourses of race and class
and provides us with a useful framework with which to approach
the contemporary relationship between English authorities and
Irish subjects, the Irish forming the explicit link between the two
poles of English lower orders and alien savages.

English perceptions of Elizabethan Ireland would seem to
suggest that the formation of a colonial identity cannot be
separated from the concomitant development of a specific national

identity, a notional Britishness which is subordinate to a hegemonic Englishness: the representation of Ireland as simultaneously a domestic state and an exotic conquered territory would appear to elide both the difference between Britain and England, as well as throw any reliance upon a stable identity into crisis.

NOTES

1 *The Works of Edmund Spenser: a Variorum Edition*, 10 vols., ed. Edwin Greenlaw *et al.* (Baltimore, 1932–49), x, *The Prose Works* (1949), ed. Rudolph Gottfried, p. 112. All subsequent references to this edition. u/v and i/j have been modernized.

2 For a recent comment on this assumption see Donald Bruce, 'Spenser's Irenius and the Nature of Dialogue', *Notes and Queries* 237 (1992), 355–7. On Murrogh O'Brien, see Richard Bagwell, *Ireland Under the Tudors*, 3 vols. (London, 1885–90), II, p. 338.

3 See Joan W. Scott, 'The Evidence of Experience', *Critical Inquiry* 17 (1991), 773–9.

4 See Bruce, 'Spenser's Irenius'; Mary Louise Pratt, 'Scratches on the Face of the Country: or, what Mr Barrow Saw in the Land of the Bushmen', in *'Race', Writing and Difference*, ed. Henry L. Gates, Jr (Chicago, 1986), pp. 138–62; Virginia Cox, *The Renaissance Dialogue: Literary Dialogue in its Social and Political Contexts, Castiglione to Galileo* (Cambridge, 1992).

5 *Variorum*, x, pp. 342–3, for details. Herodotus is mentioned on pp. 99, 103 and 107; Tacitus on pp. 86 and 89; Diodorus Sicilius on pp. 95, 99, 103, 105 and 131. See *Variorum*, x, commentary, for analysis.

6 Sir Thomas Elyot, *The Book Named the Governor*, ed. S. Lehmbert (London, 1966), p. 38.

7 Fynes Moryson, *Shakespeare's Europe: Unpublished Chapters of Fynes Moryson's Itinerary*, ed. Charles Hughes (London, 1903), pp. 193, 473.

8 Cited in D. B. Quinn, 'Renaissance Influences in English Colonisation', *Transactions of the Royal Historical Society*, 5th series, 26 (1976), 73–93, especially p. 89.

9 Paul Hulton, 'Images of the New World: Jacques Le Moyne de Morges and John White', in K. R. Andrews *et al.*, eds. *The Westward Enterprise: English Activities in Ireland, the Atlantic and America, 1480–1650* (Liverpool, 1978) pp. 195–214, quote p.211.

10 See Arthur B. Ferguson, 'Circumstances and the Sense of History in Tudor England: the Coming of the Historical Revolultion', *Medieval and Renaissance Studies* 3 (1967), 170–205, especially pp. 194–5.

11 See John Gillingham, 'Images of Ireland, 1170–1600: the Origins of

English Imperialism', *History Today* 37 (February 1987), 16–22.

12 Gerald of Wales, *Expugnatio Hibernica*, eds. F. X. Martin and A. B. Scott (Dublin, 1978), p. 37.

13 Peter Burke, *The Renaissance Sense of the Past* (London, 1969), ch. 5.

14 See Richard Hillman, *Intertextuality and Romance in Renaissance Drama: the Staging of Nostalgia* (London, 1992), introduction.

15 On English travellers to Ireland, see Andrew Hadfield and John McVeagh, eds., *'Strangers to that Land': British Perceptions of Ireland from the Reformation to the Famine* (Gerrard's Cross, 1994), ch. 4.

16 Gerald of Wales, *The History and Topography of Ireland*, trans. J. J. O'Meara (Harmondsworth, 1982, rpt. of 1951), pp. 101–2.

17 Fynes Moryson, 'A Description of Ireland', in *Ireland under Elizabeth and James I*, ed. Henry Morley (London, 1890), 411–30, p. 430.

18 See Claude Lévi-Strauss, *The Raw and the Cooked: Introduction to a Science of Mythology*, trans. Doreen and John Weightman (London, 1970), I; 'The Culinary Triangle', *New Society* 221, (22 December 1966), 937–40.

19 Moryson, 'Description of Ireland', pp. 424–6.

20 Andrew Trollope to Walsingham, 12 September 1581, in *Calendar of State Papers, Ireland (CSPI)* (1574–85), p. 318.

21 See Bernard W. Sheehan, *Savagism and Civility: Indians and Englishmen in Colonial Virginia* (Cambridge, 1980), ch. 1.

22 Edward Arber, ed., *The First Three English Books on America* (Birmingham, 1885), p. 150. See also pp. 152, 343–4 for similar descriptions.

23 *Ibid.*, pp. 66, 151.

24 *Ibid.*, p. 66; Richard Hakluyt, *The Principal Navigations, Voyages, Traffiques and Discoveries of the English Nation*, 8 vols. (London, 1907), VII, p. 285.

25 Hakluyt, *Principal Navigations*, VI, pp. 267–8.

26 Edmund Campion, *Two Bokes of the Histories of Ireland*, ed. A. F. Vossen (Assen, 1963), p. 23.

27 *Ibid.*, pp. 19–20.

28 See also the three treatises by Sir William Herbert deposited in the State Papers: *CSPI* (1586–8), pp. 527–47; *Croftus Sive De Hibernica Liber*, eds. Arthur Keaveney and John A. Madden (Dublin, 1992).

29 *The Essays of Michael Lord of Montaigne*, trans. John Florio (1613), 3 vols. (London, 1910), I, p. 229.

30 Campion, *Two Bokes of the Histories of Ireland*, pp. 144–6. For details of Campion's life and his relationship to the Sidney circle see *Dictionary of National Biography* entry and Vossen's introduction.

31 Campion, *Two Bokes of the Histories of Ireland*, p. 151.

32 Stephen J. Greenblatt, 'Learning to Curse: Aspects of Linguistic Colonialism in the Sixteenth Century', in *First Images of America: the*

Impact of the New World on the Old, ed. Fredi Chiapelli (Berkeley, 1976), pp. 561–80.

33 For an overview, see Steven G. Ellis, *Tudor Ireland: Crown, Community and the Conflict of Cultures, 1470–1608* (Harlow, 1985), ch. 8.

34 See Ciaran Brady, 'Faction and the Origins of the Desmond Rebellion of 1579', *Irish Historical Studies* 22 (1981), 289–312; Ellis, *Tudor Ireland*, pp. 278–85.

35 For a recent overview, see Hiram Morgan, 'The End of Gaelic Ulster: a Thematic Interpretation of Events Between 1534 and 1610', *Irish Historical Studies* 26 (1990), 8–32.

36 'My Lord Mountjoy's Discourse concerning Ireland, sent in March, 1601', *CSPI* (1600–1), p. 254.

37 See, for example, Spenser, *View*, pp. 97–9, 217–8; D. B. Quinn, *The Elizabethans and the Irish* (Ithaca, NY, 1966) pp. 76–9.

38 'A Discourse to Show that Planting of Colonies, and that to be Begun Only by the Dutch, Will Give Best Entrance to the Reformation of Ulster', *CSPI* (1598–99), pp. 438–42, especially p. 440.

39 Mountjoy to Robert Cecil, 7 August 1600, *CSPI* (1600), p. 338.

40 R. Rawlindson, ed., *A History of that most Eminent Statesman, Sir John Perrot* (London, 1727), p. 177.

41 Quinn, *Elizabethans and the Irish*, p. 16.

42 Sir John Davies, *A Discovery of the True Causes why Ireland was never entirely subdued*, reprinted in *Ireland Under Elizabeth and James I*, ed. Morley, p. 291.

43 *Ibid.*, pp. 291–2.

44 D. B. Quinn, 'Thomas Smith and the Beginnings of English Colonial Theory', *Proceedings of the American Philological Society* 89 (1945), 543–60, especially p. 552.

45 Hiram Morgan, 'The Colonial Venture of Sir Thomas Smith in Ulster, 1571–5', *History Journal* 28 (1985), 261–78, pp. especially 269–70.

46 Sir George Peckham cited in H. C. Porter, *The Inconstant Savage: England and the North American Indian, 1500–1660* (London, 1979), pp. 217–18.

47 Hakluyt, *Principal Navigations*, VI, pp. 18, 49.

48 Anne Laurence, 'The Cradle to the Grave: English Observations of Irish Social Customs in the Seventeenth Century', *The Seventeenth Century* 3 (1988), 63–84.

49 Nicholas P. Canny, 'The Ideology of English Colonisation from Ireland to America', *William and Mary Quarterly* 30 (1973), 575–98.

50 Franklin Le Van Baumer, *The Early Tudor Theory of Kingship* (New Haven, 1940); Walter Ullmann, '"This Realm of England is an Empire"', *Journal of Ecclesiastical History* 30 (1979), 175–203.

51 Nicholas P. Canny, *The Elizabethan Conquest of Ireland: a Pattern Established, 1565–76* (Hassocks, 1976), pp. 122, 159.

52 Walter Ralegh, *A Voyage for the Discovery of Guiana*, in *Works*, 8 vols. ed.

W. Oldys and T. Birch (Oxford, 1829), VIII, pp. 377–476, especially pp. 421, 430.

53 Philip Edwards, *Sir Walter Ralegh* (London, 1953), pp. 3–5; Alfred O'Rahilly, *The Massacre at Smerwick (1580)* (Cork, 1938).

54 Hakluyt, *Principal Navigations*, V, pp. 128–9.

55 *Ibid.*, VI, pp. 51–2.

56 On Britain as a 'multiple kingdom', see Hiram Morgan, 'Mid-Atlantic Blues', *The Irish Review* 11 (Winter 1991–2), 50–5.

57 Richard Morison, *A Remedy for Sedition* (London, 1536).

58 Richard Morison, *A Lamentation in which is shewed what ruyne and destruction cometh of seditious rebellion* (London, 1536).

59 Richard Helgerson, 'The Land Speaks', in *Forms of Nationhood: the Elizabethan Writing of England* (Chicago, 1992), pp. 105–47, especially p. 114.

60 Morison, *Lamentation*; see also John Cheke, in Raphael Holinshed, *Chronicles of England, Scotland and Ireland*, 6 vols. (Dublin, 1807), III, pp. 991, 1006.

61 Holinshed, *Chronicles*, III, p. 988; Thomas Starkey, *An Exhortation to the People, instructynge theym to unitie and Obedience* (London, 1540).

62 William Camden, *Britannia*, ed. Edmund Gibson (London, 1695), p. 1032.

63 See Penry Williams, *The Tudor Regime* (Oxford, 1986, rpt. of 1967), p. 376 for details.

64 Michel Foucault, *Discipline and Punish: the Birth of the Prison*, trans. Alan Sheridan (Harmondsworth, 1977), pp. 48–9.

65 On Rory Oge O'More see Bagwell, *Ireland Under the Tudors*, II, pp. 340–5.

66 On the viceroyalty see Ciaran Brady, 'Court, Castle and Country: the Framework of Government in Tudor Ireland', in *Natives and Newcomers: the Making of Irish Colonial Society, 1534–1641*, eds. Ciaran Brady and Raymond Gillespie (Dublin, 1986), pp. 22–49.

67 John Derricke, *The Image of Ireland* (1581), ed. T. Small (Edinburgh, 1883), p. 97.

68 *Ibid.*, woodcut 6.

69 Spenser, *View*, p. 82. Malengin has been identified as an Irish rebel by many literary critics: see, for example, Graham Hough, *A Preface to the Faerie Queene* (London, 1963), p. 200; T. K. Dunseath, *Spenser's Allegory of Justice in Book V of The Faerie Queene* (Princeton, 1968), p. 203.

70 On 'discursive practice', see Michel Foucault, *The Archaeology of Knowledge*, trans. A. M. Sheridan Smith (London, 1972), part 2.

71 D. B. Quinn, ed., '"A Discourse on Ireland (circa 1599)": a Sidelight on English Colonial Policy', *Proceedings of the Royal Irish Academy* 47, Section C, 3 (1942), 151–66, especially p. 166; Sir Henry Sidney, 'Memoir, Addresses to Sir Francis Walsingham, 1583', ed. H. J. Hore, *Ulster Journal of Archaeology*, 1st series, 3 (1855), 37–52, 91–109, 336–53; 5 (1857), 299–323; 8 (1860), 179–95; quote at pp. 5, 311.

72 Pratt, 'Scratches on the Face of the Country', pp. 138–45.

73 See, for example, J. W. Bennett, 'The Allegory of Sir Artegall in *The Faerie Queene*, v, xi–xii', *Studies in Philology* 37 (1940), 177–200; 'Malengin' in *The Spenser Encyclopedia*, ed. A. C. Hamilton (London and Toronto, 1990), p. 450.

74 Holinshed, *Chronicles*, III, p. 992.

75 *Ibid.*, III, p. 987.

76 Gerald, *Topographia*, p. 102; Quinn, *Elizabethans and the Irish*, pp. 76–9; Sir George Peckham, 'A True Report of the Late Discoveries...of the Newfound Lands', in Hakluyt, *Principal Navigations*, VI, pp. 42–78.

77 See, for example, Holinshed, *Chronicles*, III, pp. 1061–62; John Pound, *Poverty and Vagrancy in Tudor England* (Harlow, 1971), p. 40.

78 Edward Phyton to Burghley, 30 July 1587, *CSPI* (1586–8), p. 392.

79 'Reasons collected to maintain the action of the undertakers for the peopling of Munster', 22 December 1587, *CSPI* (1598–9), pp. 141–2.

80 Quinn, *Elizabethans and the Irish*, pp. 37–8.

81 W. Weston to Burghley, 28 August 1593, *CSPI* (1592–6), pp. 141–2; 'Book on the State of Ireland, addressed to Robert, Earl of Essex by H. C.', March 1599, *CSPI* (1598–9), pp. 505–7.

82 See A. D. Hadfield, 'The English Conception of Ireland, *c.* 1540–1600, with Special Reference to the Works of Edmund Spenser' unpublished D.Phil. thesis, University of Ulster, 1988, pp. 165–7.

83 See the work of Nicholas Canny, especially, *The Elizabethan Conquest*, ch. 6.

84 Susan Doran, 'The Political Career of Thomas Ratcliffe, Third Earl of Sussex (1526?–83)', unpublished Ph.D. thesis, University College London, 1977, chs. 3, 6; John Hooker (alias Vowell), *The Lyffe and Times of Sir Peter Carew*, ed. John McLean (London, 1857), pp. 48–50 *passim*.

85 Ralph Sadler to William Cecil, 6 December 1569, *CSPD* (1566–79), addenda), pp. 139–40; Holinshed, *Chronicles*, III, pp. 926, 1008.

86 James Lydon, ed., *The English in Medieval Ireland* (Dublin, 1981); Nicholas P. Canny, 'Identity Formation in Ireland: the Emergence of the Anglo-Irish', in *Colonial Identity in the Atlantic World, 1500–1800*, eds. Nicholas P. Canny and Anthony Pagden (Princeton, 1987), pp. 159–212.

87 For an overview see A. D. Hadfield, 'Colonialism and National Identity in Early Modern Ireland', *Eire/Ireland* 28, 1 (Spring 1993), 82–100.

88 For an overall view see Brendan Bradshaw, *The Irish Constitutional Revolution of the Sixteenth Century* (Cambridge, 1979).

89 Ellis, *Tudor Ireland*, pp. 169–70, 179–80 *passim*.

90 Spenser, *View*, pp. 113–20; Barnaby Rich, *A New Description of Ireland* (London, 1610), ch. 21.

91 See Colm Lennon, 'Recusancy and the Dublin Stanihursts', *Archivium Hibernicum* 33 (1975), 101–10.

92 R. F. Foster, *Modern Ireland, 1600–1972* (London, 1988), 'Prologue: Varieties of Irishness'. But see also Brian Walker, '1641, 1689, 1690 and All That: the Unionist Sense of History', *The Irish Review* 12 (Spring/Summer 1992), 56–64.

93 Natalie Zemon Davies, *Fiction in the Archives: Pardon Tales and their Tellers in Sixteenth-Century France* (Stanford, 1987), introduction.

94 See, for example, Homi K. Bhabha, 'The Other Question: the Stereotype and Colonial Discourse', *Screen* 24 (1983), 18–36. The problem is partly dealt with in Michael Hechter, *Internal Colonialism: the Celtic Fringe in British National Development 1536–1966* (London and Berkeley, 1975).

95 Hayden White, 'The Noble Savage: Theme as Fetish', in *First Images of America*, ed. Chiapelli, pp. 121–35.

CHAPTER 4

The Elizabethans in Italy

Jonathan Bate

Italy, the Paradice of the earth and the Epicures heaven, how doth it forme our yong master? It makes him to kis his hand like an ape, cringe his necke like a starveling, and play at hey passe repasse come aloft, when he salutes a man. From thence he brings the art of atheisme, the art of epicurising, the art of whoring, the art of poysoning, the art of Sodomitrie. The onely probable good thing they have to keepe us from utterly condemning it is that it maketh a man an excellent Courtier, a curious carpet knight: which is, by interpretation, a fine close leacher, a glorious hipocrite. It is nowe a privie note amongst the better sort of men, when they would set a singular marke or brand on a notorious villaine, to say, he hath beene in *Italy*.[1]

This expatiation on Italy as perceived by an Elizabethan Englishman is characterized by, shall we say, a certain extremity. It begins with an image of the place as an earthly paradise, but quickly modifies it into a decadent one – for epicures only. It then descends into making Italy a kind of hell, associated with false religion or no religion, with villainy and sexual transgression. Is it a place where you educate yourself in the qualities of a courtier or the characteristics of a flatterer, insinuator and hypocrite? Or is it where you learn that to be a courtier and an insinuator are one and the same thing?

The passage is from one of the richest productions of the Elizabethan imagination, Thomas Nashe's *The Unfortunate Traveller*, published in 1594. My argument will move towards a reading of the Italian part of this narrative – the location of its most spectacular adventures – which, I will suggest, holds together the Elizabethans' widely divergent views of Italy.[2] *The Unfortunate Traveller* has the universalizing truth of a fiction. Before reaching it, I shall give brief consideration to three other English accounts of Italy, which become progressively more fictive. The first is factual: it will concern something of the experience of an English gentleman and ambassador in Italy. The second is based on fact: it will draw on an Englishman's reminiscences of his journey to Italy, apparently thrown casually into a book and thus suggesting the chaos of experience but tending towards the ordering of artistic narrative. And the third is fictional: a dramatic representation of an English gentleman abroad. To give some unity to my account, I shall be focusing principally on Venice, where my ambassador had his residence and which, to Elizabethan eyes, offered the best of Italy. The progression from fact to fiction cannot, however, be a strict one: we only know about the 'real' gentleman from letters and biography, which have fictive arts of their own, while the fictional gentleman may in some part be based on a real one.

To begin, then, with Sir Henry Wotton, the most famous of the Elizabethan Englishmen in Italy. He underwent the typical education of a gentleman – a couple of years at Oxford and then, in the words of his biographer, Sir Izaak Walton, he 'laid aside his Books, and betook himself to the useful Library of Travel, and a more general Conversation with Mankind; employing the remaining part of his Youth, his industry and fortune, to adorn his mind, and to purchase the rich Treasure of Foreign knowledge'.[3] Here travel is seen as a text, an extension of book learning, which according to classical humanist principles stores the mind with experience and prepares the gentleman for a life of civic virtue. Wotton's grand tour took him to Florence, which he described in a letter of June 1592 to Lord Zouche as 'a paradise inhabited with devils'.[4] But he appreciated the pure Tuscan dialect. He consequently considered the city to be a place where one could learn to speak well and to do ill.[5] This initial impression of Italy as a place of paradox was typical of the Elizabethan response; the Italians are characterized by a combination of politeness and perfidy. One of John Donne's verse-epistles to Wotton describes how Sir Henry 'sucked' all there was of worth from 'faire Italie' while remaining immune to its 'faithlessnesse'.[6] The juxtaposition of opposed alliterative epithets emphasizes the ambivalence of the perception.

It was Italy, home of Machiavelli, that seemed to teach Wotton the politic arts which led to his advancement.[7] He was rewarded as a result of an action achieved through a combination of disguise and linguistic skill. Ferdinand Duke of Florence had intercepted letters concerning a plot on the life of James VI, King of Scotland. The plot was interpreted as a Spanish-inspired attempt to secure the English succession for the Infanta by getting rid of James. The position of Florence in terms of the delicate balance of European powers was such that it was imperative for Ferdinand to prevent this. Wotton served as his messenger, taking a warning to James. Walton's *Life* describes the incident vividly: 'Having parted from the *Duke*, he took up the Name and Language of an *Italian*; and thinking it best to avoid the line of *English* intelligence and danger, he posted into *Norway*, and through that country towards *Scotland*, where he found the King at *Sterling*' (p. 111). The name he travelled under was Octavio Baldi. Walton then dramatizes the denouement, placing a strong emphasis on Wotton's sheer style, his poise. An Italianate coolness and elegance are manifest in his costume, his sense of timing, his controlled exit:

When *Octavio Baldi* came to the Presence-Chamber-door, he was requested to lay aside his long *Rapier* (which *Italian*-like he then wore) and being entred the Chamber, he found there with the King three or four *Scotch* Lords standing distant in several corners of the Chamber: at the sight of whom he made a stand; which the King observing, *bade him be bold, and deliver his Message; for he would undertake for the secresie of all that were present.* Then did *Octavio Baldi* deliver his Letters and his Message to the King in *Italian*; which, when the King had graciously received, after a little pause, *Octavio Baldi* steps to the Table,

– note the dramatic shift into the present tense –

and whispers to the King in his own Language, that he was an *English* man, beseeching Him for a more private conference with His Majesty, and that he might be concealed during his stay in that Nation; which was promised, and really performed by the King during all his abode there (which was about three Months) all which time was spent with much pleasantness to the King, and with as much to *Octavio Baldi* himself, as that Countrey could afford; from which he departed as true an *Italian* as he came thither. (pp. 111–12)

To be a 'true' Italian is to put on a feigned appearance, to inhabit a role with ease and apparent naturalness. This is the *sprezzatura* recommended in courtiers' manuals descending from Castiglione, such as Puttenham's *The Art of English Poesie*.

According to Walton, Wotton was rewarded once James became King of England with a choice of three embassies – France, Spain and Venice. This is probably biographer's licence; it is more likely that he was simply offered Venice. But Walton's account of Wotton's reasons for his choice between the three posts gives a valuable sense of both the image of the cultivated, gentlemanly and modest knight and of the lure of Venice to an Elizabethan Englishman: Wotton,

considering the smallness of his own Estate (which he never took care to augment) and knowing the Courts of great Princes to be sumptuous, and necessarily expensive, inclined most to that of *Venice*, as being a place of more retirement, and best suiting with his *Genius*, who did ever love to join with Business, Study, and a tryal of natural Experiments; for both which fruitful *Italy*, that *Darling of Nature, and Cherisher of all Arts, is so justly fam'd in all parts of the Christian World.* (p. 113)

Here, instead of a positive and negative pair of epithets, there is a double positive implying a harmonious relationship between art and nature. Venice becomes a natural retreat, a kind of aquatic *hortus conclusus*, in which Wotton can simultaneously live the *vita activa* in service of his nation and the *vita contemplativa* of study and reflection. The image provides a sharp contrast to those far-from-idealizing accounts which treat the art and artifice of Italy as being against nature. But within the structure of Walton's *Life*, once Wotton is established in Venice, there is a reversion to the ambivalent view of Italy. According to the biographer, the ambassador's experience soon showed him that '*Italy* is observed to breed the most vertuous, and most vicious men of any Nation' (p. 117). And Venice was soon discovered to be anything but a retreat from the world as Wotton became actively involved in the perpetual hostilities between the Serenissima and the Papal empire.[8]

Wotton lost his post when his past came back to haunt him. On his way to take up the post, he had inscribed a witty text in a visitors' book in Germany to the effect that 'An Embassadour is an honest man, sent to *lie* abroad for the good of his Country.' This is a good pun, with the virtue that the text remains open to an innocent construction. Unfortunately, Wotton wrote the inscription in the universal language of the period, Latin. And there it is not a pun:

'Legatus est vir bonus peregrè missus ad mentiendum Reipublicae causâ.'[9] 'Mentiendum' suggests only the mendacious sense of 'lie'. Eight years later, the inscription fell into the hands of a papist who printed it in a book directed against King James – the citation served to indicate how deceitful the King's diplomatic practices were. Wotton was promptly called home.

There is, however, a kind of appropriateness about the Latin inscription, for its two key words suggest much about the function of Italy for an Elizabethan. 'Mentiendum' brings to mind the Elizabethan perception of the deceits of Italy and its associations with Machiavellian policy. And 'peregrè', peregrination, implies a place to journey to and to wander around in, as if in quest of its identity. Since Italy was not a unified country, different impressions were gained from different cities and principalities; its truth was to be found not in one place but in the peregrinations, the links (and differences) between places. 'Peregrè' also carries a sense of pilgrimage, reminding us of the deeply problematic status of Rome for a post-Reformation gentleman. Rome was, of course, a base for English Catholics, as described in detail in Anthony Munday's *English Romayne Life*. Part of the attraction of Venice was its independence from the Pope; it could be imagined as an anti-Romish island like England itself.[10] Wotton in fact became associated with rumours that the city had actually turned Protestant.

Peregrination is the leitmotif of my next traveller, whose Italian journey was described in the book with the appetizing title of *Coryats Crudities Hastily gobled up in five Moneths travells in France, Savoy, Italy, Rhetia commonly called the Grisons country, Helvetia alias Switzerland, some parts of high Germany, and the Netherlands; Newly digested in the hungry aire of Odcombe in the County of Somerset, & now dispersed to the nourishment of the travelling Members of this Kingdome*. The *Crudities* carried a dedication to Henry Prince of Wales, signed Thomas Coryate, Peregrine of Odcombe. They came with one hundred pages of commendatory verses to the author, stressing his oddity and his arduous travels on foot. Among these are a poem by Hugo Holland addressed 'To Topographicall Typographicall Thomas' – the word-play cleverly links the acts of visiting new topographies and going into print on the subject of them. The poem begins with a mock-epic invocation to the attributes of the travelling man:

> I sing the man, I sing the wofull case,
> The shirt, the shoes, the shanks that serv'd to trace
> Seven Countries wide...

Henry Peacham's dedicatory contribution was actually an emblem of these shoes, in which Coryate walked from Somerset to Venice and which he eventually left as a votive-offering in his church before setting off again, this time to walk to India, where he died.[11] The shoes were also remembered by Ben Jonson:

> How well and how often his shoes too were mended,
> That sacred to Odcombe are now there suspended,
> I mean that one pair, wherewith he so hobbled
> From Venice to Flushing, were not they well cobbled?[12]

Jonson's dedicatory poem refers to the content of the *Crudities* but was in fact published with its sequel, *Coryats Crambe* ('crambe' means 'cabbage': the vegetable succeeds the crudités). The poem is called 'To the London Reader, on the Odcombian Writer, Polytopian Thomas the Traveller', a title which suggests how Coryate provided a doubly fresh perspective for the London reader, that not only of poly-topia, of everywhere abroad, but also of the country, of a small parish in the distant west of England. Coryate relished being Rector of Odcombe because he was an odd fellow and a kind of living coxcomb. He was fascinated by the sheer oddity of other countries to his provincial English eyes, by the strangeness to which travel gave access.

To travel was to observe novelties, such as the Italian habits of using forks at table and fans in the hand, or sprinkling cheese on all manner of dishes. Unlike some more elevated travellers, Coryate is always acutely aware of his body – which can sometimes get in the way of the observation that is expected of the man abroad. As in Turin:

I am sory I can speake so little of so flourishing and beautifull a citie, for during that little time that I was in the citie, I found so great a distemperature in my body, by drinking the sweete wines of Piemont, that caused a grievous inflammation in my face and handes; so that I had but a smal desire to walke much abroad in the streets. Therefore I would advise all English-men that intend to travell into Italy, to mingle their wine with water as soone as they come into the countrey, for feare of ensuing inconvenience.[13]

The mark of the writing here is its personal immediacy and its practicality; this is what renders it a form of 'crudité', an art that is not fully cooked.

Coryate offers perspectives on most of the major Italian cities. Mantua, for example, is seen as a paradise, remarkable for the sweetness of its flowers and its reputation as the birthplace of Virgil. The only things, says the traveller, that prevent him from wanting to live there are his love of his native parish in Somersetshire and the superstitious, idolatrous religion. Mantua, however, is but a prelude to Venice. When he arrives there, Coryate looks back on his journey, computing that he has travelled 952 miles from Odcombe to London to Dover to Calais to Paris to Lyons to Turin to Milan to Padua to Venice.

Venice is described as a glorious sight and also a 'mayden' city because it has never been conquered. There is a thoroughgoing gendering of the place: she is 'The fairest Lady, yea the richest Paragon and Queene of Christendome' (p. 160). Her virtues and her virginity are also, remarks Coryate, apparent from the presence of two hundred churches, fifty-four monasteries and twenty-six nunneries. The city is variously described as an 'untainted virgine', as 'Paradise' and 'Tempe'; it is simultaneously Eden or Arcadia and Eve before the Fall or a classical nymph. But on the other hand, it is a place where a notorious friar has had children by no less than ninety-nine nuns (if he had made it to a hundred they would have let him off his punishment, says Coryate – p. 290). Once again, the writing is animated by the paradoxical attraction and repulsion of Italy.

Venice is also a place of performances: 'I saw women acte, a thing that I never saw before, though I have heard that it hath beene some times used in London' – (is this a country myth or an unknown fact about the London stage?) – 'and they performed it with as good a grace, action, gesture, and whatsoever convenient for a Player, as ever I saw any masculine Actor' (p. 247). Public performances are not confined to the theatre. They are also played out in the thoroughfares: Coryate is amazed by the dramatic gestures of Venetian street life, as the Clarissimoes kiss each other on both cheeks upon leave-taking and women walk abroad with visible breasts. In discussing women thus, Coryate switches from a language of purity to one of courtesanship. As Wotton found Florence a paradise inhabited by devils, so Coryate finds Venice a virgin inhabited by whores. (His image of the moral dubiety of Venetian woman is of a piece with the false preconceptions about Desdemona's kind on which Iago plays so cunningly.) Coryate gives a highly coloured account of the famous Venetian courtesans. He places a strong emphasis on their arts; where Walton's image in the *Life of Wotton* was of the harmonious coexistence of nature and art in Venice, Coryate treats the courtesans' artful dressing of themselves as something against nature: 'many of them which have an elegant naturall beauty, doe varnish their faces' with 'sordid trumperies' (p. 266). These arts are dangerously alluring, like those of the Sirens who endeavoured to turn Ulysses, western literature's archetypal traveller, from his course: 'the ornaments of her body are so rich, that except thou dost even geld thy affections (a thing hardly to be done) or carry with thee *Ulysses* hearbe called Moly which is mentioned by *Homer*, that is, some antidote against those Venereous titillations, shee wil very neare benumme and captivate thy senses, and make reason vale bonnet to affection' (p. 266). By fleshing out the middle of the word, Coryate transforms Ven-ice into a Ven-er-eous place. From the physical ornamentation of fine clothing, he then proceeds through a progression of less tangible arts of seduction:

shee will endevour to enchaunt thee partly with her melodious notes that shee warbles out upon her lute, which shee fingers with as laudable a stroake as many men that are excellent professors in the noble science of Musicke; and partly with that heart-tempting harmony of her voice. Also thou wilt finde the Venetian Courtezan (if she be a selected woman indeede) a good Rhetorician, and a most elegant discourser, so that if shee cannot move thee with all these foresaid delights, shee will assay thy constancy with her Rhetoricall tongue. And to the end shee may minister unto thee the stronger temptations to come to her lure, she will shew thee her chamber of recreation... (p. 267)

and thence to 'all her bedding sweetly perfumed', which is just what the traveller needs after long nights in dirty inns on the road, or even worse conditions (Jonson's dedicatory poem recalls the night in the *Crudities* when Coryate 'lay in straw with the horses at Bergamo').

Reading a passage such as this, one begins to see that part of the attraction of the courtesans for Coryate is the way in which their wiles match his own arts, his own skilful language. He is trying the reader's constancy with his rhetorical tongue, just as the courtesans try him with theirs. 'The truest poetry,' said Touchstone, 'is the most feigning': the writer is drawn to Venice because he is complicit in its play of art and nature. As he is played upon by the experience of travel, so he plays upon the reader, making their experience of reading a re-enactment of his own of travelling.[14]

As striking a performance as that of the courtesan is that provided in the streets by the mountebanks. Coryate realizes that the latter are hucksters, adept in the arts of counterfeit, but he is nevertheless – or, indeed, for this very reason – fascinated by their skill and in particular their linguistic art:

Truely I often wondred at many of these naturall Orators. For they would tell their tales with such admirable volubility and plausible grace, even *extempore*, and seasoned with that singular variety of elegant jests and witty conceits, that they did often strike great admiration into strangers that never heard them before: and by how much the more eloquent these Naturalists are, by so much the greater audience they draw unto them, and the more ware they sell. (p. 273)

As with the courtesans, the attraction here is the sense that the mountebanks are the writer's double. Coryate, too, has his oratorical arts and spice; the more eloquent he is, the more copies of the book he sells. When Ben Jonson's Volpone impersonates the mountebank Scoto of Mantua, there is an identification with the role on the dramatist's own part.

Volpone is characterized by an exceptionally detailed interest in the topography and *mores* of Venice.[15] The English eyes through which the city is seen are those of the travellers, Peregrine, who like the theatre audience is newly arrived in the geographical world of the play, and Sir Politic Would-be, the naive traveller who supposes himself experienced. On the first encounter of the two Englishmen, Sir Pol asks Peregrine if he has visited the ambassador – a sense of contemporaneity and realism is provided by this invocation of the central English figure living in Venice. The reference makes it highly unlikely that, as some critics have argued, Sir Pol is a satire on Wotton; there may, however, be elements of satire upon another celebrated traveller, Sir Anthony Sherley, who, like Sir Pol, was actually forced to leave the city (in his case because of a trading dispute).

Sir Pol is a master of misunderstanding. When Peregrine reports some gossip from England about a famous fool being dead, Sir Pol takes him to be referring to a famous spy; by a nice irony, in the course of the play's action Sir Pol himself becomes a fool taken for a spy, when as a result of his habit of noting Venetian customs down in his commonplace book he renders himself liable to the accusation of being engaged in espionage. He is also the quintessence of gullibility. When Volpone impersonates Scoto, Sir Pol is completely taken in. He especially admires the inventive, feigned language which makes up the performance; this, he thinks, is the *sprezzatura* of the Italian – the audience, of course, knows that it is an easy art adapted to the purposes of cunning and deceit. Peregrine, again serving as the audience's representative, sees through the language. By identifying with him, audience members can imagine themselves as worldly-wise as opposed to innocent travellers. At the centre of the play we see the Englishmen as spectators of the mountebank performance; more generally, they are spectators in Venice, thus replicating on stage the position of the theatre audience as English spectators of a Venice that is realized by means of performance.

Sir Pol is also a satire on a figure related to the traveller, that of the projector (where one goes to new places, the other introduces new schemes). He has various doomed projects, such as selling red herrings to the inhabitants of the city. Dramatically, the effect of his projects is to feed the audience with information about Venice, some of which is informative with regard to the main plot, some of which constitutes what we would now call red herrings in the proverbial sense. Sir Pol observes everything, but he only attends to the surface of things:

> And then, for your religion, profess none;
> But wonder, at the diversity of all;
> And, for your part, protest, were there no other
> But simply the laws o'the land, you could content you:
> Nick Machiavel, and Monsieur Bodin, both,

Were of this mind. Then, must you learn the use,
And handling of your silver fork, at meals;
The metal of your glass – these are main matters
With your Italian – and to know the hour,
When you must eat your melons, and your figs.[16]

He does not understand what are really the 'main matters' – in mockery of his own name, he misreads the politic Machiavelli and Bodin (though French, the latter, because 'politic', is associated with Italy); he attaches importance to a trivial custom like the use of forks at table (something also noticed by Coryate, though he views the habit merely as the kind of interesting oddity which makes travelling worth undertaking and writing home about). He fails to learn from his observations, just as his wife, Fine Madame Would-be, reads all the classic humanist texts, but fails to read as a proper humanist who lives well on the basis of reading.

'I know the forms so well', says Sir Pol (IV.i.139). 'And nothing else', interjects Peregrine as an aside: only the exterior forms of Italy are understood by the knight, not its internal essence. As a well-born innocent abroad, Sir Pol is the diametric opposite of Thomas Nashe's low-born traveller, Jack Wilton, who through all his misfortunes is a survivor who lives off his wits.

The first half of *The Unfortunate Traveller* narrates a series of adventures in a northern Europe which is riven by war and Protestantism. The second half moves south to Italy, where the civil as opposed to the military virtues – and vices – are explored. Nashe's pages tell of how Jack Wilton becomes a page in the service of Lord Henry Howard, Earl of Surrey. The fictional page is realized but also moved into the past by means of this reinvention of a historical figure from the reign of Henry VIII. Surrey serves as an idealized image of the poet: 'if there bee anie sparke of Adams Paradized perfection yet emberd up in the breastes of mortall men, certainelie God hath bestowed that his perfectest image on Poets' (II, p. 242). Surrey's narrative to Wilton concerning his service to his beloved Geraldine serves the reader as an introduction to the poetic image of Italy: 'Uppon a time I was determined to travell; the fame of Italy, and an especiall affection I had unto Poetrie, my second Mistris, for which Italy was so famous, had wholy ravisht me unto it' (II, p. 244). Poetic Italy brings with it positive images of a mistress and of ravishment; the Italy subsequently discovered by Wilton wholly darkens these images, as spiritual ravishment is replaced by physical rape. Surrey tells of how when he sought permission from his mistress to leave her in order to travel, she made a request: 'When thou commest to Florence (the faire Cittie from whence I fetcht the pride of my birth) by an open challenge defende my beautie against all commers' (ii, p. 244). Historically, only one of Surrey's love-sonnets calls his mistress Geraldine and gives 'biographical' details, but in that one she is said to come from Florence.[17] This may not be true of the real origins of Surrey's mistress – always supposing that the sonnets are inspired by a single woman, or even a real woman at all[18] – but it is intended to establish an echo of Dante seeing Beatrice in Florence, writing the *Vita Nuova* and initiating the love-sonnet tradition. In Nashe's recension of Surrey, Italy is associated with the idea of the noble poet's need to defend his mistress' honour and beauty, with a sense of love as a competitive display (as it is in the Italian encounter in *Cymbeline*).

It is, then, the poet, and the Petrarchan poet in particular, who leads the narrator of *The Unfortunate Traveller* to Italy: 'Italy still stuck as a great moate in my masters eie; he thought he had travelled no farther than Wales till he had tooke survey of that countrie which was such a curious molder of wits' (ii, p. 255). But it is important that Surrey is a famously dead poet – he was executed in 1547 on a treason charge. The Golden Age, 'Adams Paradized perfection', the high Renaissance poetic, Petrarchan Italy, are firmly located in the past. When the travellers arrive in Italy it is as if Surrey is wrenched out of that past into a darker present, for the first Italian encounter is with a figure who comes from no Golden Age. His linguistic facility serves a 'courtesy' very different from that of the court poet:

we made a long stride and got to Venice in short time; where having scarce lookt about us, a precious supernaturall pandor, apparelled in all points like a gentleman & having halfe a dosen several languages in his purse, entertained us in our owne tongue very paraphrastically and eloquently, & maugre all other pretended acquaintance, would have us in a violent kinde of curtesie to be the guestes of his appointment. His name was *Petro de campo Frego*, a notable practitioner in the pollicie of baudrie.

The place whether he brought us was a pernicious curtizans house named *Tabitha* the Temptresses, a wench that could set as civill a face on it as chastities first martyr *Lucrecia*.   (II, p. 255)

Lucrece, the image of chastity associated with the foundation of Rome, is replaced with a whore; the civil arts become a false face. Tabitha's room is full of false appearances in its resemblance to a saint's cell. Surrey's narrative has set up an expectation that the arrival in Italy will be graced by an encounter with a courtly Florentine lady like Geraldine, but instead we meet a cunning whore of Venice.

There is a further twist against Petrarchanism when Jack and his master find themselves in prison in the company of Diamante, who has been thrown there by her husband on an ungrounded jealous suspicion of her chastity. Surrey attempts to woo her in a courtly style, projecting the image of Geraldine on to her. Jack is more direct: 'My master beate the bush and kepte a coyle and a pratling, but I caught the birde' (II, p. 263). Elaborate Petrarchan courtship is reduced to ineffective prattle, while a frontal approach wins the woman. At this point in the text there is a long digression in the form of an encomium on Aretino. He is praised for his freedom of speech: 'His tongue & his invention were foreborne; what they thought, they would confidently utter. Princes hee spard not, that in the least point transgrest. His lyfe he contemned in comparison of the libertie of speech' (II, p. 265). That Aretino should care more for freedom of speech than saving his own skin contrasts sharply with the flattering uses of language that are employed by Petrarchans and, with more sinister motives, by the likes of de campo Frego. As a poet, sharing some of the licence of the court fool, Aretino could get away with what Wotton, as a diplomat, could not: Francis I bequeathed him a golden chain bearing the motto 'Lingua eius loquetur mendacium' ('His tongue speaks a lie'), to which Aretino retorted that if the motto were true he would be lying every time he praised Francis.[19]

Freedom of speech means not only political licence but also sexual licentiousness. Aretino is praised by Nashe's Wilton for his wanton verses: 'Tell mee, who is travelled in histories, what good poet is, or ever was there, who hath not hadde a lyttle spice of wantonnesse in his dayes?' (II, p. 266 – 'travelled in histories' plays on the perceived link between reading and journeying). In the context of the tale, this defence of wantonness is also a defence of Wilton, who has got Diamante with child. Petrarchan ladies, on the other hand, never become pregnant. Aretino was notable for his anti-Petrarchan verses; with this in mind, Nashe establishes an implicit opposition between Petrarch/Surrey and Aretino/Wilton. Where Surrey is being a failed Petrarchan, Wilton imitates the more 'modern' Italianism of Aretino and gets on with it. The narrative actually has Wilton going to visit Aretino, who promptly releases Diamante from her marriage, enabling her to travel round Italy as Wilton's courtesan (it might be worth remembering here that a strong precedent for the voyeuristic aspect of the *The Unfortunate Traveller* is to be found in Aretino's *Ragionamenti* and, furthermore, that his best-known play was *La cortigiana*, a title which probably means 'The Courtier's Play', but which was widely interpreted as 'The Courtesan').[20]

In Florence, Wilton briefly meets up again with Surrey, who is finally carrying out his mistress' wishes by defending her honour in a chivalric tournament. In contrast to Venice, whence the travellers have come, and Rome, whither Wilton goes, Florence is still associated with the courtly and the chivalric – although even there Nashe cannot resist his debunking mode, as he tilts at the art of tilting by having all the knights save Surrey miss the target. As for Rome, it offers an initial paradisal appearance, but that paradise is swiftly revealed to be an artificial one. The reality of the city turns out to be plague and rape.

The paradisal image is crystallized in a beautiful description of a building:

I sawe a summer banketting house belonging to a merchaunt, that was the mervaile of the world, & could not be matcht except God should make another paradise. It was builte round of greene marble like a Theatre with-out: within there was a heaven and earth comprehended both under one roofe; the heaven was a cleere overhanging vault of christall, wherein the Sunne and Moone and each visible Starre had his true similitude, shine, scituation, and motion, and, by what enwrapped arte I cannot conceive, these spheares in their proper orbes observed their circular wheelinges and turnings, making a certain kinde of soft angelical murmering musicke in their often windings & going about; which musick the philosophers say in the true heaven, by reason of the grosenes of our senses, we are not capable of. For the earth, it was counterfeited in that liknes that Adam lorded out it before his fall. (II, pp. 282–3)

Flowers are painted on the floor, 'which so lively were delineated that he that had viewd them a farre off, and had not directly stood poaringly over them, would have sworne they had lived in deede'. And in the trees there are artificial birds akin to those in Yeats' Byzantium, 'Who though there were bodies without soules, and sweete resembled substances without sense, yet by the mathematicall experimentes of long silver pipes secretlye inrinded in the intrailes of the boughs whereon they sate, and undiscerneablie convaid under their bellies into their small throats sloaping, they whistled and freely carold theyr naturall field note.' It is perpetual spring: 'No frosts to make...the mulberie tree a strange polititian, in blooming late and ripening early' – this is the opposite of the 'politic', Machiavellian perception of Italy. The description concludes: 'Such a golden age, such a good age, such an honest age was set forth in this banketting house' (II, pp. 283–5).[21]

But it is only in the enclosed, fictive space of this theatre-like structure that Rome is a paradise. Outside, people are dying of plague, while Diamante is raped; also raped, before Wilton's eyes, is a noble and chaste matron called Heraclide. These are the kinds of horror which lead a banished English earl – Italy was 'paradise of exiles' even then, as it was later for Byron and Shelley[22] – to voice an oration against travel: 'Countriman, tell me, what is the occasion of thy straying so farre out of *England* to visit this strange Nation? If it bee languages, thou maist learne them at home; nought but lasciviousnesse is to bee learned here' (II, p. 297). He does not believe, with Wotton, that travel is an extended means of reading the book of nature. Read books about the accidents, treasonings and poisons of Italy, says the banished earl, but don't actually go there. There is a nice self-referentiality about this, for it seems to have been Nashe's own case, and it would have been that of many of his middle-ranking readers. Neither he nor they had the means to follow the aristocracy and gentry on their Italian journeys; for them the book was a substitute for travel.

The earl's oration climaxes with the passage I quoted at the beginning of this essay: '*Italy*, the Paradice of the earth...' The oration's modulation from paradise to policy reveals the hollowness of the idealization, the flimsiness of the banqueting-house. *The Unfortunate Traveller* proceeds from this point towards another oration, this one an elaborate speech in praise of revenge, delivered by a murderer on the scaffold. But because the murderer, Cutwolfe, has killed Esdras, the man who raped Heraclide so brutally, the reader cannot avoid having some sympathy with his views. We thus find ourselves admiring a 'notable newe Italionisme' (II, p. 325) which consists of a contrivance to damn an enemy to eternal perdition, and appreciating the inversion of moral and judicial norms which proposes that 'Revenge is the glorie of armes, & the highest performance of valure: revenge is whatsoever we call law or justice.' Where in Protestant England under the Tudor polity revenge was supposed to be left to God or the courts, at the end of *The Unfortunate Traveller* it is something that will be honoured by all true Italians. Jack Wilton is led by this claim to flee from 'the *Sodom* of *Italy*' (II, p. 327) – the image of sexual abomination serving as shorthand for other kinds of violation of the moral law – but the structure of the story leaves the reader with more than a sneaking sympathy for what has been said on the scaffold, especially as the act of execution has a clinical cruelty which makes it in effect no different from the act for which it is a punishment. The narrative has made us discover the Italian within all of us.

The Italy of Nashe's tale begins with the Petrarchanism of Surrey and ends with the code of revenge that was being explored in the most popular dramas on the London stage at the time when it was written, Kyd's *Spanish Tragedy* (an Italianate play displaced to Spain and Portugal) and *Titus Andronicus* (which I suspect Shakespeare wrote or revised immediately after reading *The Unfortunate Traveller* and in which ancient Rome is seen to have declined from republican virtue into imperial decadence). The perception of Italy as both poet's paradise and revenger's inferno is both a cause and a symptom of the late Elizabethan literary tendency to move between elegance and violence, the erotic and the politic, the love-sonnet and the tragedy of blood.

For the Renaissance, travel, like reading, was a means of self-discovery (and conversely, humanist reading was a form of travel, a voyage into the classical past). The peregrine holds up a mirror to his own culture. Just as voyages to the New World of the Americas cast new light on the customs of the voyagers, so journeys to Italy, with its mix of literary and political traditions, its Popish religion, its codes of courtly style on the one hand and blood-revenge on the other, provided all sorts of illuminations for the English. The Italian mirror was a strong, sometimes a distorting one, but what it reflected back to the Elizabethans were some of the supremely influential images of their age.[23] It is appropriate that a copy of one of the great representations of the Virgin Queen, fan in hand, hangs in the Pitti Palace in Florence – appropriate not merely because the Elizabethan fashion for fans was Italian-influenced, but because the whole cult of the Queen was a political displacement of the poetic cult of Petrarchanism. The English Renaissance began when Sir Thomas Wyatt and the Earl of Surrey discovered, translated and imitated the poetry of Petrarch. Two generations later, the predominant image of Italy had darkened: in contrast to the frequently idealizing sixteenth-century travellers' accounts, several much more critical books concerning Italian institutions and the Italian character were published between 1605 and 1617.[24] The Elizabethan Englishman begins his Italian journey with Petrarch, but once he immerses himself in Italian culture, he will sooner or later fall under the spell of the Machiavelli who became both a demonic figure on the Elizabethan stage and a serious influence on politic historiography and practical politics in early modern England.[25] If Petrarch led to the cult of the Queen, Machiavelli led to an understanding of how power works and a demystification of divine right theory. We may remember the words with which Andrew Marvell began the great English Renaissance political poem, a poem steeped in the wisdom of Machiavelli and concerning the rise of a truly political man, not a Politic Would-be like Jonson's, his ode on the Englishman who did more than any other to change the course of the seventeenth century, Oliver Cromwell: 'The Forward Youth that Would Appear' – would make an impression on the political stage, that is – 'Must now forsake his Muses dear'. He must put down his *canzoniere* and pick up his *discorsi* and his *principe*.

NOTES

1 *The Unfortunate Traveller*, in *The Works of Thomas Nashe*, ed. Ronald B. McKerrow, rpt. with corrections by F. P. Wilson, 5 vols. (Oxford, 1966), II, p. 301. Subsequent references to this edition followed in text by volume and page number (u/v modernized in these and other quotations).

2 The bibliography on the subject of Renaissance Englishmen and Italy is substantial: see the references in Sergio Rossi's valuable survey, 'Italy and the English Renaissance: an Introduction', in *Italy and the English Renaissance*, eds. Sergio Rossi and Dianella Savoia (Milan, 1989), pp. 9–24. Another useful introduction is John L. Lievsay's brief *The Elizabethan Image of Italy* (New York, 1964). An engaging survey of the impressions of travellers, including Wotton and Coryate, is provided by A. Lytton Sells in his *The Paradise of Travellers: the Italian Influence on Englishmen in the Seventeenth Century* (London, 1964).

3 *The Life of Sir Henry Wotton, Late Provost of Eaton College* (1651), rpt. in *Lives* by Izaak Walton (World's Classics edition, London, 1927), p. 106. Subsequent references to Walton followed in text by page number to this edition.

4 Logan Pearsall Smith, *The Life and Letters of Sir Henry Wotton*, 2 vols. (Oxford, 1907, rpt. 1966), I, p. 281. Fittingly enough, the same phrase was used of England by an Italian traveller of the same period: see L. Einstein, *The Italian Renaissance in England* (London, 1902), p. 226.

5 See the same letter to Zouche.

6 'To Sir *Henry Wotton*' ('Sir, more then kisses'), in *The Poems of John Donne*, ed. Herbert J. C. Grierson, 2 vols. (Oxford, 1912), I, p. 182.

7 On the Elizabethan association between Machiavelli and the word 'politic', see Mario Praz, *The Flaming Heart* (New York, 1958), pp. 103–9 (part of his lecture 'The Politic Brain: Machiavelli and the Elizabethans').

8 On this, see in particular J. L. Lievsay, *Venetian Phoenix: Paolo Sarpi and Some of His English Friends* (Lawrence, KS, 1973), pp. 19–25. Day-to-day details of many of Sir Henry's meetings and dispatches may be found in *Calendar of State Papers and Manuscripts, Relating to English Affairs, Existing in the Archives and Collections of Venice*, especially vol. XI, 1607–1610 (London, 1904). A useful brief introduction to diplomatic relations between England and Venice, and to the role of ambassadors in political intrigue more generally, is provided by David Loades in *The Tudor Court* (London, 1986, revised Bangor, 1992), pp. 166–72.

9 Latin and English both cited in Walton, *Lives*, p. 121.

10 On the Elizabethan idealization of Venice's political structure, see J. G. A. Pocock, *The Machiavellian Moment: Florentine Political Thought and*

the Atlantic Republican Tradition (Princeton, 1975), pp. 272–330, where it is shown that Lewis Lewkenor's 1599 translation of Gasparo Contarini's *The Commonwealth and Government of Venice* (1543) in many places expanded on the original to favourable effect.

11 See further, Michael Strachan, *The Life and Adventures of Thomas Coryate* (London, 1962).

12 Jonson, *Complete Poems*, ed. George Parfitt (Harmondsworth, 1975), p. 259.

13 *Coryats Crudities* (London, 1611), p. 83. Subsequent references in text.

14 My reading of Coryate as a kind of bawd, bringing the reader to the courtesans, is similar to that of Ann Rosalind Jones, in her 'Italians and Others: Venice and the Irish in *Coryat's Crudities* and *The White Devil*', *Renaissance Drama* 18 (1987), 101–19.

15 See further, Brian Parker, 'An English View of Venice: Ben Jonson's *Volpone* (1606)', in *Italy and the English Renaissance*, eds. Rossi and Savoia, pp.187–201.

16 IV.i.22–31, quoted from *Volpone*, ed. Philip Brockbank (London, 1968). Subsequent references in text.

17 In *Tottel's Miscellany*, the source in which Nashe was most likely to have read Surrey, the sonnet 'From Tuskane came my Ladies worthy race: / Faire Florence was sometyme her auncient seate' is entitled 'Description and Praise of his Love Geraldine'.

18 The traditional identification of 'Geraldine' with Elizabeth Fitzgerald is nowhere attested by Surrey himself; it goes back to Richard Stanyhurst's 'Description of Ireland', printed in Holinshed's *Chronicles*.

19 Nashe refers to the incident in a nicely turned phrase: 'The French king, *Frances* the first, he kept in such awe, that to chaine his tongue he sent him a huge chaine of golde, in the forme of tongues fashioned' (II, p. 265).

20 See Richard Andrews, *Scripts and Scenarios: the Performance of Comedy in Renaissance Italy* (Cambridge, 1993), p. 67, where it is also pointed out that the language of Petrarchanism is mocked in the play's prologue.

21 On the Elizabethan taste for the elaborate artifice of Italian gardens, see Michael Leslie, 'Gardens of Eloquence: Rhetoric, Landscape, and Literature in the English Renaissance', in *Towards a Definition of Topos: Approaches to Analogical Reasoning*, ed. Lynette Hunter (Basingstoke and London, 1991), pp. 17–44.

22 'Thou Paradise of exiles, Italy!': Shelley, 'Julian and Maddalo'.

23 Compare G. K. Hunter's view that 'the "Italy" of Elizabethan and Jacobean tragedy is related to England in the same way as the abstract world of the Morality play is related to real life' – *Dramatic Identities and Cultural Tradition: Studies in Shakespeare and his Contemporaries* (Liverpool, 1978), p. 22.

24 On changing English attitudes to Italy in the period, see George B.

Parks, 'The Decline and Fall of the English Renaissance Admiration of Italy', *Huntington Library Quarterly*, 31 (1967–8), 341–57.

25 On this double image, see Felix Raab, *The English Face of Machiavelli* (London, 1964); for the way in which a respectful reading of Machiavelli was mediated into Elizabethan England via a reading of Guicciardini, see Hunter, *Dramatic Identities*, pp. 114–17.

CHAPTER 5

Tragic form and the voyagers

Philip Edwards

There are some comparisons to be made between patterns found in Elizabethan and Jacobean accounts of disaster on the high seas and patterns in fictional accounts of disaster performed in English theatres during the same period. I am not here concerned to trace the influence of voyage narratives on drama, or vice versa, although there certainly were interconnections. I approach two sets of writers as quite independent of each other. Each set confronts disaster, and creates narratives which attempt to organize and control it, without ever presuming fully to explain it.

One set, the tragic dramatists, invent their fictional disasters, or borrow them from mythology, or Italian *novelle*, or previous tragedies, or look for something purporting to be real in the pages of the chronicles or accounts of recent murders. The other set, the narrators of voyages, were participants in the actual happenings they write about. They are persons of the drama, and they have come home to write the story up in the shape they wish it to take. As though Edgar should sit down to give his version of the story of King Lear.

Both sets so pattern their narratives that, implicitly or explicitly, responsibility for disaster is attributed to, and apportioned between, a variety of agencies. The anger of God, for example, or the absence of God, or the interference of the devil, or the personality of the protagonists, the pressure of past events, the malice of opponents. The list of agencies, though long, is finite. The power of the story depends on the subtlety with which blame and responsibility are distributed and interwoven.

I am concentrating on voyage narratives because they are so little read by students of literature, whereas Elizabethan tragedy is

75

known to everyone; and I begin with the account by Edward Hayes
of the last voyage of Sir Humphrey Gilbert in 1583, printed by
Hakluyt in 1589.[1] It is understandable that this narrative of a
disastrous colonizing expedition has been generally misread,[2]
because the superficial view of it is carefully trailed before the
reader by Hayes himself. This view is of heroic failure in a great
and necessary enterprise, of failure in face of the power of the sea,
which is only less strong than the power of God, who will take the
sea's victims to Himself, because the advancement of the Christian
flag of England on the shores of America is His own cause.
Everyone knows the story of the homeward journey of the two
ships, Hayes in the *Golden Hind*, Gilbert in the little frigate, the
Squirrel. The weather was dreadful, the seas angry and high; but
they could see Gilbert 'sitting abaft with a booke in his hand',
'giving foorth signes of joy' and shouting to them, 'We are as neere
to heaven by sea as by land.'[3] But then, during the night, the lights
of the *Squirrel* went out. 'And withall our watch cryed, the Generall
was cast away, which was too true. For in that moment, the Frigat
was devoured and swallowed up of the Sea.'

So, wrote Hayes, 'it pleased the divine will to resume him unto
himselfe'. But what did he mean when, just before giving his
account of Gilbert's death, he wrote, 'I will hasten to the end of this
tragedie'?

Hayes believed in a God whose control of events was as tight
and unremitting as that of the gods in Kyd's *The Spanish Tragedy*.
He was a punishing God, chastising mortals for the least wrong
step, but then using such wrong steps in the ineluctable execution
of his preordained ends. The ending end was the extinction of
time, when Christianity, evermore rolling westward (but with a
slight northern tilt) had converted North America and so brought
history to its conclusion. The colonization and conversion of
North America is reserved for England; and it is interesting that
this is seen not as the commencement of a great new era but as
the end of a very old one. Englishmen must hold themselves
ready for the call. The right person, at the right time, will
succeed. God chooses both the person and the time. Englishmen
who offer themselves for the task cannot know beforehand
whether they are chosen by God; they can only know afterwards,

by their success or their failure. Gilbert failed; therefore he was
not chosen of God.

Hayes is at the same time presenting a national hero, and
someone who let God down by his temperament and his errors of
judgement and was punished by God as a lesson to others. It was of
primary importance to Hayes that North America should be
colonized by England, and perhaps his theology was subordinate
to his patriotism. He is giving reassurance to English contenders
that no one should be deterred by Gilbert's failure; he failed
because in the end, despite his qualities, he was not the right sort of
person. I do not think it was cynicism in Hayes to bolster his
patriotic fervour with a theological explanation of Gilbert's lack of
success, any more than it was duplicity in him to offer contrasting
and sometimes contradictory views of his hero. I think he was as
aware as a tragic dramatist would have been of the variousness of
the possible explanations, interpretations and judgements of
Gilbert and his fate. The overlaps are deliberate, and are a
recognition of the provisional and tentative nature of all explanation.

Tilt the narrative one way, and Gilbert is the Christian hero,
falling so that others may pick up the banner and succeed. Tilt it
another way, and Gilbert is a noble figure betrayed by unworthy
associates, who perseveres in an endeavour which he knows to be
doomed only because it would be dishonourable to retreat. In yet
another light, Gilbert is seen in true tragic-hero fashion collaborating
in his own downfall. Hayes makes strange use of Gilbert's
thoughtlessness or recklessness in retaining a crew of pirates in a
ship he had seized; this crew is represented as a continuing baleful
influence on the voyage, eventually by their irresponsibility in
carousing all night causing the loss of the expedition's major ship,
the *Delight*, after which the enterprise had to be abandoned.

Such contributory factors and alternative evaluations perplex
the narrative. The dominating view, however, is of a wilful and
selfish man whose obsessions and errors have parted him from God
and must lead to punishment. Hayes provides a sense of doom
from the start of his story, speaking of a voyage which 'begun,
continued, and ended adversly'. There is a sombre tragic irony in
that famous ending. Gilbert had obstinately insisted, against
advice, on remaining in the little frigate, which he had actually

made less seaworthy by overloading. In the most chilling way, Hayes wrote that 'as it was God's ordinance on him' nothing 'would divert him from a wilfull resolution of going through in his Frigat'. God had marked him out, and was using the man's own wilfulness to encompass His ends. When Gilbert cheerfully cried out, 'We are as neere to heaven by sea as by land', he did not know how far away from heaven he was. He was ignorant of his true condition and situation.

Hayes' narrative is a subtle undermining of its own celebration of Gilbert as hero, offering a contending variety of reasons why it was inevitable and necessary that Gilbert should fail, while never losing sight of his nobility. That 'God's ordinance' should be united with Gilbert's 'wilfull resolution' as the immediate cause of his death is very striking; the more striking in that the narrative was written not by a London dramatist but by a survivor of the expedition, who felt able to congratulate himself on God's protection, seeing that God had brought him into the same peril as others, 'in which he leaveth them, and delivereth us, making us thereby the beholders, but not the partakers of their ruine'.[4]

I have chosen for my second narrative one from which God is notably absent as the engineer of events: John Nicholl's *Houre Glasse of Indian Newes*, published in black letter in 1607.[5] This relates the misadventures of a group of colonists who were sent out in the *Olive Branch* to reinforce Charles Leigh's ailing colony on the Wiapoco river in Guiana, but never reached it. In his address to the reader, Nicholl wrote that he had published 'this pamphlet' in order 'to make knowne unto the world the greatnes and goodnes of God, miraculously shewed unto us'; but this, like many pious remarks about God's will in the course of the narrative, is a perfunctory gesture; his extraordinary story, which lacks a tragic hero as well as a god, is a story in which ill will and betrayal dictate the course of events, and in which (incredibly) the Spaniards take on the role of rescuing divinity.

The expected, desirable, reasonable unities of social life kept breaking apart. On board the *Olive Branch*, the sixty-seven settlers were already at odds with the seamen before the ship became hopelessly lost in the Caribbean. 'There was some heart-burning and malice one against another, which rested not onely in the common sort, but rather and most chiefly in our captaines, whose haughtie mindes not brooking contradiction on either side, had like to have grown to a daungerous discention.'[6] As for losing their way, Nicholl offers the reader three possible reasons in descending order of likelihood.

Whether it was our Masters want of knowledge that we fell not with the prefixed place, or that the current which our master alledged to be the reason, that setting verie strongly to the North-wards, put us so farre short thereof, or whither (as of all others that is most certaine) it pleased God in that place at that time, and in such a manner, to let us feele some part of his heavie displeasure, conceyved against us for our times formerly mispent...[7]

Touching at St Lucia, the settlers chose to stay on the island rather than continue at sea in discord and wrangling. But, when the Caribs appeared on the scene, the discord actually intensified into a shooting war between the two English parties, with the ship party (according to Nicholl) trying to get the Caribs on their side, 'telling them that we were bad people, and would take all they had from them, and would cut their throats'.[8] The first act ends with the seamen, having done their worst, sailing away.

In the second act, on the island, the settlers, struggling merely to survive, remain in unity. It is the Caribs who demonstrate the fatally fissile character of human society, with brother against brother. Nicholl calls the brothers Anthonio and Augramart, as though they were characters in a play. Each brother tried to convince the English that the other was really their enemy, and each brother tried to incite the English to murder the other. 'This,' wrote Nicholl, 'made us doubtfull which to trust to.' But hatred of the Europeans finally united the Caribs, and the leader of the settlers, Captain St John, was lured by a tale of gold in the mountains to set off with a prospecting party. They were never seen again.

Act III begins with carousal. The remaining Englishmen entertain the Caribs, with much aqua vitae flowing. Some of the party, who are beginning to suspect that the tale of gold in the mountains was a trap, suggest that since the Indians are now disarmed and drunk it would be a good time to kill them. Master Tench now comes to the fore. Although 'he had wont to bee a curious corrector of us in our merriments', he was so anxious for good relations with the Indians that he 'fell a singing of catches with the Carrebyes', and when he heard the whispered plot he opposed it,

saying: God woulde not bee pleased with such a bloudie Act agaynst such harmlesse people, and therefore willed us not to doe it without they gave us the first occasion; wherein hee wronged himselfe and us all, in seeking to save the lives of them, who within three houres after most cruelly murthered him.[9]

For the Indians were not as drunk as they seemed. They invited the English to go back with them, and led them into an ambush where they were massacred. A few survived and held out for some days before surrendering. They were astonished that their terms were accepted: namely, that if they could have a boat they would leave the island. So the nineteen survivors out of sixty-seven settlers got away, and after terrible privations and further loss of life, the remnant were rescued and nursed back to health by Spaniards.

No one will argue that Nicholl liked the crew of the *Olive Branch*, or the Caribs on whose good will they were absolutely dependent, but even so the even-handedness with which he apportions responsibility for what went wrong is astonishing. Captain St John was lured into a trap, but it was his eagerness for gold that betrayed him first. The responsibility accorded to Master Tench is fascinating. Here is an austere figure, something of a kill-joy, with strong principles about the relations between races which he rather ludicrously tried to demonstrate by singing catches with the Caribs. They had already planned the massacre, however, and by forbidding the Englishmen's pre-emptive strike as an offence against God, Tench precipitated the death of himself and his fellows. Tench was no doubt one of those 'plausible spirites. . .more addicted to unitie and peace' than to dissension, whom Tench praised for intervening in the shipboard disputes;[10] but in this case his good intentions only assisted the antagonisms he deplored. Nicholl's world is Conradian; a small niche ought to be found for him in the histories of literature.

Although Hayes and Nicholl were leading participants in the events they described, neither saw his role as that of tragic hero. At least two narrators certainly did see themselves in that light:

Thomas Cavendish and Sir Walter Ralegh.[11] Cavendish, trying in 1591 to be the first man to sail round the world twice, failed to get through the Magellan Straits, lost touch with his accompanying ships, and found himself with a recalcitrant crew heading back north in the Atlantic. He began to write his remarkable paranoid narrative of the expedition as a letter to Tristram Gorges, and he had almost certainly decided to take his own life as soon as he had written down his self-justification. That his death was indeed suicide is only inference, but it is hardly disputable. So his narrative is one that shapes itself towards a chosen tragic end. The self-pitying pattern is one of endless betrayal, and the determination that out of the wreck caused by the weakness, disloyalty and malice of others, he would at least emerge without dishonour.

But now I am grown so weak and faint as I am scarce able to hold the pen in my hand…But in truth I desired nothing more than to attempt that course, rather desiring to die in going forward than basely in returning backward again. But God would not suffer me to die so happy a man, although I sought all ways I could still to attempt to perform somewhat…

And now by this, what with grief for him [a kinsman] and the continual trouble I endured amongst such hell-hounds, my spirit was clean spent, wishing myself upon any desert place in the world, there to die, rather than thus basely to return home again…

I thank my God that in ending of me he hath pleased to rid me of all further troubles and mishaps…

Bear with this scribbling, for I protest I am scant able to hold a pen in my hand.[12]

The document is disordered. The seething resentment of thwarted pride and frustrated ambition bubbles up in syntactical chaos, interruptions battling with repetitions. It is a document that has its place within a tragedy, though it does not itself provide a tragic pattern. Cavendish's system of explanation is wholly inadequate, but his torrent of self-pity, as a crippled hero heading for the only conclusion that will salvage his honour, might have kindled a dramatist to provide a role in a tragedy for such role-playing.

Sir Walter Ralegh was, like Cavendish, proud, cruel and ambitious. But he was much more intelligent and much more interesting. It is quite impossible for us to sort out now the full responsibility for his downfall. But what we are concerned with is how Ralegh explained it in his narratives, particularly his *Apology* (the unpublished Apology of 1618), a document in which once again linguistic order breaks under the strain of total defeat and the struggle for self-justification.

Ralegh seeks the consolation of a theory of success and failure. The staggering simplicity of this theory is that success is a matter of luck. If the event were a measure of the abilities and personal qualities of the doer, we should all be doomed. If fortune deserts us, and leaves us to what Ralegh calls the trial of our virtues, we are quite helpless. Success is irrational and unpredictable. 'True it is, that as many things succeed both against reason and our best endeavours, so it is most commonly true that men are the cause of their own misery, as I was of mine.'[13] This handsome admission Ralegh immediately seeks to disprove by blaming everyone else for the failure of his Guiana expedition: the King, the Spaniards, his own colleagues, particularly the luckless Lawrence Keymis, who was unable to locate the gold-mine. This extraordinary exception of himself from his own recognition of human conduct and responsibility is characteristic of the man who could write the magnificent final paragraphs of *The History of the World*, in contempt of the vanity of human ambition, and still stake all on the mad bid for Guiana gold.

Cavendish wrote his narrative with his very private death firmly in his mind. Ralegh wrote his in a final attempt to avert the public death which he suffered. Both narratives, one may say, convert their own actions into theatre. But, as Ralegh wrote in his famous poem comparing life to a stage play, 'Thus march we playing to our latest rest, / Only we die in earnest; that's no jest.' The deaths in which both narratives terminate were real. The relationship of the theatre of the real to the theatre of the narrative is really beyond analysis. Both Cavendish and Ralegh devised plots which were acted out in distant waters, and which forced others to live out, or rather die into, the roles created for them. Lawrence Keymis had already committed suicide before Ralegh gave the written version of his activity.

It is different on the stage, where those who die rise to act another day. It is very surprising that there is no full study of patterns of accountability and responsibility in Elizabethan and Jacobean tragedy, no comparative study of what characters perceive to be the driving force in human affairs and what support the play as a whole seems to give to their perceptions. In an essay which concentrated on the extraordinary daring (in a Christian country) of Thomas Kyd's *The Spanish Tragedy*, in which all human effort is tied up and nullified in the strait-jacket of a non-Christian metaphysical system, I suggested that both Marlowe and Shakespeare in those early years joined Kyd in his subversive programme, and in their tragedies derided orthodox explanations of the direction of human affairs.[14] I wrote that *Titus Andronicus*, like *The Jew of Malta* and the two Tamburlaine plays, 'seem to me to be deeply speculative, ruminating with unbelievable freedom, considering the restraints of the time, on the relation of the willed activities of men and women to divine intervention and control'. What seemed to me particularly striking in these early Elizabethan tragedies was that all three dramatists recognized in the musings and assertions of their characters the untiring propensity of the mind to attribute the vicissitudes of life to the intervention of supernatural forces. None of this explaining activity was sanctioned with authorial support. On the contrary, the intervention of supernatural force, or pleas for it, was offered in almost parodic terms, as when Titus shoots arrows into the air to solicit the gods for their support, or when Tamburlaine falls fatally ill after burning the Koran.

Both Marlowe and Shakespeare moved on from their early libertinism. But *Doctor Faustus* is an extraordinarily hesitant play. (We must stick with the A-text and resist the insensitive interventions and omissions of the B-text.) There is a fundamental disproportion between the popular images of divine and satanic presence and the underlying debate about Faustus and his soul. As we waver and slide between profound theological searching and farcical clowning, we recognize that the discrepancy is intrinsic to the debate. Divine power and divine love, and the loss of divine love, are available to the audience only in images and metaphors which discredit them. This incongruity between idea and representation, so marked in the theatre, is itself a metaphor for the inability of the human imagination to find an appropriate language for its deepest needs and fears. There is certainly some mockery of conventional images of supernatural control in *Doctor Faustus*, but the dramatist mocks himself as well as others.

In *King Lear*, the constant attempts of the characters, particularly Albany, to set the ugly happenings within a cosmic theory are all shown to be inadequate. It is hardly possible that Shakespeare thought he was exposing an ignorance which he did not share. If we look at the supernatural machinery of the later tragedies and the romances – the Ghost in *Hamlet*, the witches in *Macbeth*, the masque in *Cymbeline* – we may feel we are in a dimension similar to that of *Doctor Faustus*. These theatrical images work towards both scepticism and faith. They are at the same time acknowledgements of powers beyond human will and the play of chance in shaping the direction of life, and also a recognition of the tawdrinesss, the shoddiness, of our imaginings of these powers. (And to believe in the real existence of these papier mâché puppets of our own creation is to set up a formidable new element in the forces directing affairs.)

In what spirit are we to take the machinery for the direction of human affairs in *The Tempest*? It is extremely difficult to conceive any level, literal or figurative, at which the magic of Prospero can be seen as a useful explanation of the way things happen in life. It is equally difficult to see it as satire. It belongs to the world of dreaming. And surely its dream-like nature, offering us faith in the benign outcome of all human troubles, is most evident in Prospero's on-off control of the power of the sea. In another late play, *Pericles, Prince of Tyre*, the sea is untameable. The director of affairs is Neptune, 'the god of this great vast', a wholly inscrutable god, impossible to buy off or control. In this play the unpredictable power of the sea is a measure of human helplessness, of the uselessness of trying to forecast or influence or explain the casual shower of blessings and disasters which make up human existence. Although *Pericles*, too, has its happy ending, with divine intervention restoring Pericles' long-lost wife to him, the contrast between the two plays as regards the sea is very great. It is sad that the one play, with its poor text never replaced, became a disowned waif while its illustrious companion starred as the opening play in the First Folio.

Stark though the contrast is between the hidden god Neptune and the very human Prospero, these two plays unite in that their action is wholly dependent on the power of the sea. Neither play is a tragedy, but they are among the final plays of a very great tragic dramatist. Although the ocean was to some extent brought under control by the technological ingenuity of capitalism, at this early stage in the history of European expansion, the sea was the great non-human power with which human striving had to contend. What was reality for the voyagers was a strong symbol for the writers of fiction.

Images of supernatural forces in Elizabethan tragedy are presented rather quizzically, inviting scepticism more than faith but refusing to invalidate faith. Elizabethan tragedy stresses unending human responsibility for situations which are not brought about by human control. That extra-human dimension, which ghosts, devils and witches on stage cannot satisfactorily embody, is better suggested by the power of the sea.

Those who were literally at the mercy of the whims of the physical ocean, and came home to write up their stories of disaster, seem to have shared the problems of the tragic dramatists when it came to the question of causality. Suggestions of supernatural intervention are confused or perfunctory or tentative, so jostled by alternative explanations that they cancel themselves out. What remains firm is human aspiration and strife, dwarfed and belittled by the power of the sea.

NOTES

1 I have published an extended study of this narrative in *Renaissance Studies*, 6 (1992) 270–86. There is a further study by Shannon Miller, 'Exchanging the New World: Production and Reproduction in the Newfoundland Enterprise', *Medievalia et Humanistica*, new series, 19 (ed. P. M.Clogan) (1993), 69–95.
2 For example, by Walter Ralegh in 'The English Voyages of the Sixteenth Century', in volume XII of the 1903–5 reprint of Hakluyt.
3 Hakluyt, *Principal Navigations*, 1903–5, VIII, p. 74.
4 *Ibid.*, p. 76.
5 A much edited and abbreviated version appeared in *Purchas His Pilgrimes* in 1625. There is a reprint of part of the text in *Wild Majesty*, eds. Peter Hulme and Neil L. Whitehead (Oxford, 1992), pp. 62–79.
6 *An Houre Glasse of Indian Newes* (London, 1607), fol. B4.
7 *Ibid.*, fol. B2 v.
8 *Ibid.*, fol. B4.

9 *Ibid.*, fol. C3 v.
10 *Ibid.*, fol. B2.
11 For the texts of their narratives , see my *Last Voyages* (Oxford, 1988).
12 *Ibid.*, pp. 77, 79, 80.
13 From the *Apology*. See *ibid.*, p. 229.
14 'Thrusting Elysium into Hell: the Originality of *The Spanish Tragedy*', in *The Elizabethan Theatre XI*, ed. A. L. Magnusson and C. E. McGee (Port Credit, 1990), pp. 117–132.

CHAPTER 6

Nationality and language in Thomas Kyd's 'The Spanish Tragedy'

J. R. Mulryne

Thomas Kyd's remarkable play *The Spanish Tragedy* acknowledges in its title a national identity other than its author's. Notoriously, its denouement presents a babel of languages – Latin, Greek, Italian, French – likely to have been unfamiliar, at least in colloquial form, to the great majority of its earliest audiences. Yet the play's critical record shows that with few exceptions modern interpreters have paid scant attention to the national politics of *The Spanish Tragedy*, or to the association of these politics with questions of linguistic difference. I want in this essay to sketch in the framework of political (and religious) associations that would attach to Spain and Spaniards in English minds of the 1580s, or a prominent faction among them at least, and to identify so far as I can how such associations might properly influence our understanding of the play. Much has been written about the play's immensely fertile treatment of revenge; about its wonderfully adroit structure of ironies; about its preoccupation with personal and social justice; about its melodramatic excitements and its hero's eloquent introspection (taken up and sophisticated in Shakespeare's *Hamlet*). I wish to take nothing away from any of these interpretations; I have indeed tried elsewhere to contribute to them.[1] I wish only to ask whether we can bring the play even more sharply into focus, and put ourselves more fully in touch with its original structure of feeling, if we attend to questions of nationality and language.

Popular interest in *The Spanish Tragedy* among Elizabethans, and after, was intense. By Jean Fuzier's count the play was performed under Philip Henslowe's auspices twenty-nine times between 1592 and 1597. It was taken up by no fewer than four of the Elizabethan acting companies, was issued in new editions at least nine times before 1633, had additions called for (like *Doctor Faustus*), and was referred to and parodied in literary texts on innumerable occasions (Claude Dundrap has listed 111 allusions).[2] Frazer and Rabkin, in the preface to their anthology, call *The Spanish Tragedy* 'the greatest theatrical success in the whole repertory of Renaissance drama'.[3] Such popularity may derive quite straightforwardly from the merits of Kyd's writing for the theatre. But it is tempting to think that the play touched a chord in Elizabethan sensibility (not a very creditable one perhaps) of jingoistic anti-Spanish prejudice.

We do not know when *The Spanish Tragedy* was written and first performed. It must have been written before 23 February 1592, because it was played on that date by Lord Strange's Men for Henslowe. It is unlikely to have been written earlier than 1582, since it adapts material from Thomas Watson's *Hekatompathia*, entered on the Stationers' Register in that year. We cannot pin the date down to narrower limits than these ten years, and scholars continue to disagree. Yet for present purposes this scarcely matters, for Hispanophobia was a strand in the English consciousness in the 1570s, and one that broadened and intensified as the 1580s led towards the Armada of 1588.[4] In the immediately following years, enmity between the nations increased rather than slackened. The sorry tale of the mythologizing of such prejudice, fuelled by accounts, true and fancied, of Spanish conspiracies against Elizabeth herself, has been eloquently told in William S. Maltby's *The Black Legend in England*.[5] Protestant opinion came to think of Spain and the Spanish not just in belligerent but apocalyptic terms; as Garrett Mattingly has it, to Englishmen in 1588 'the clash of the English and Spanish fleets in the Channel was the beginning of Armageddon, of a final struggle to the death between the forces of light and the forces of darkness'.[6] It is hard to think that Kyd's audience in the 1580s, at the Rose or elsewhere, was unaffected by such widely disseminated attitudes when attending a play set in the Iberian peninsula and called *The Spanish Tragedy*.

Two critics who have read *The Spanish Tragedy* in relation to current nationalistic views are Ronald Broude and Eugene Hill.[7] Broude argues that Kyd's play may be seen to turn on the fulcrum of Isabella's line (II.v.58):

> Time is the author both of truth and right.

He tells us:

Time as the revealer of truth and bringer of justice was a topos well known in Humanist circles...It was particularly prominent in English Protestant thought...During the ominous 1580's and 90's...the *topos* enjoyed special currency and seemed to promise not only that England would come through individual trials but that Divine Providence would guide English Protestantism through all its perils to ultimate victory.

The narrative of *The Spanish Tragedy*, Broude says, functions to reveal this humanist (but here sectarian) *topos* in action. Four narrative threads bind the play together in a series of revelations. Innocence is vindicated, calumny is unmasked, secret murder is revealed and avenged, and the wickedness of the Spanish royal house is brought to light. The play's ultimate catastrophe shows Time as not merely serial but providential. Broude takes this to mean that *The Spanish Tragedy* must have jingoistic appeal for its English audience:

While the Spain of Kyd's play cannot be taken literally as the historical Spain, it may certainly be understood as symbolic of a nation in which wickedness and depravity reign...The disaster which befalls Kyd's Spain is thus representative of the doom awaiting all nations in which the laws of God are ignored...Viewed in this way, *The Spanish Tragedy* must have offered welcome comfort to the English of the '80's.[8]

Eugene Hill's splendid essay 'Senecan and Virgilian Perspectives in *The Spanish Tragedy*' seeks to place Broude's insights (which he largely endorses) within a cultural nexus which takes in, as Broude does not, the framing action of Andrea and Revenge. For Hill, *The Spanish Tragedy* evokes, foregrounds and enacts 'a *translatio studii*, an historical rearticulation of privileged cultural models', these models being the creative insights associated with Virgil (in the framing action largely) and with Seneca. Recent studies, Hill argues, have recovered something of the Elizabethan Seneca as a writer who 'has no peer among classical poets in conveying the texture of evil in a hopelessly corrupt polity'. Virgil, by contrast, evokes in the *Aeneid* the burying of a regretted past, and the foundation of an enduring kingdom. 'In Seneca,' Hill writes, 'we observe with horror a hell-bent royal house, foundering in corruption. In Virgil we participate with wonderment in a rite of passage which inaugurates a new era of history.' The Senecan emphasis of *The Spanish Tragedy* is plain enough; the Virgilian perhaps needs some clarification. The Senecan prologue of the play, Hill explains, has been rewritten as an inversion of Aeneid VI:

in place of *pius* Aeneas. . .Kyd gives us proud Andrea. . .Aeneas is led into the underworld by the ever-vigilant Sybil. . .Andrea is taken from the underworld by Revenge, who falls asleep. Aeneas learns the glorious destiny of his Trojan line and sees the future Emperor of Rome; Andrea watches the downfall of the Spanish royal house. . .

Hill shows how such sentiments would chime with popular myth-making among the Elizabethans. Spain came to be regarded as a kingdom 'too arrogant to note that it is ripe for downfall', while England began to cherish imperialist visions of London as the new Troy (following Rome) and Englishmen as the new Romans. Thus anti-Spanish propaganda achieves in Kyd's play a culturally secure expression, making the energies of Senecan theatre expressively present for the Elizabethan popular stage.[9]

It is pertinent to ask what difference such interpretations make to our reading and performing of *The Spanish Tragedy*. Certainly, the horrors of act IV take on for informed readers and audiences a different kind of seriousness. The sense of absurdity with which it is tempting to greet Hieronimo's murderous play transforms itself to horror, or chauvinistic delight, as one realizes that what is at stake is the destruction of a kingdom and the collapse of its systems of government. The outcome may be read as minatory (England may go the same path if she neglects justice and privileges birth); but it must surely be understood in good part as a confirmation of the weakness at the heart of a hated if envied and (superficially) rich and powerful enemy. In Kyd's play, the King of Spain himself makes evident the historical parallel, and prompts the audience to indulge their fantasies at Spain's expense:

> What age hath ever heard such monstrous deeds?
> My brother and the whole succeeding hope
> That Spain expected after my decease!. . .
> I am the next, the nearest, last of all.   (IV.iv.202–8)

The dead march that ends the tragedy pays tribute to those killed in Hieronimo's playlet. But its rituals incorporate specifically the grief of the Spanish king and his Viceroy in Portugal, together with the political collapse of their kingdoms:

The trumpets sound a dead march, the KING of SPAIN *mourning after his brother's body, and the* VICEROY OF PORTINGALE *bearing the body of his son*

(IV.iv.217 s.d.)

The balance of emotions here is quite difficult to gauge. Conventionally, the grief that focuses on the death of the hero is mitigated by a sense of order restored, and the dawn of a new day. Here, we grieve for Hieronimo, and take pleasure in the sweeping-away of malice and corruption. We welcome too the avenging of Horatio. But the unease (familiar in the writing of critic after critic) with which the exacting of vengeance is greeted can only be allayed by taking the wider, the *historical* view, and subsuming unease within the gratified contemplation of a corrupt polity burning itself out. Hieronimo is displaced from the closing moments of the play – not only through death but through a diversion of attention – because, however heroic and sympathetic, his meanings are engulfed in a more comprehensive tragedy than his own; or perhaps in a greater comedy, for as Hill remarks 'a *Spanish* tragedy implies an *English* comedy'.[10]

There are further aspects of a historical reading of the play which are worth bringing to notice. Even those scholars who have touched on the matter have not sufficiently emphasized that the concluding masque is one given in honour of a dynastic marriage. Dynastic marriage was a prime instrument of political policy in the sixteenth century, and one not unknown to the Tudors. Entertainments to celebrate significant marriages were prominent public occasions. Kyd's play is emphatic about the importance of the intended marriage of Balthazar to Bel-imperia (whose very name must have been interpreted as allegory by some at least among the audience). Even with the restless presence of Hieronimo to interrupt him, the Portuguese ambassador manages to convey the high and solemn significance of the intended betrothal:

> Renowned king, he hath received and read
> Thy kingly proffers, and thy promised league,...
> First, for the marriage of his princely son
> With Bel-imperia, thy beloved niece

The news are more delightful to his soul,
Than myrrh or incense to the offended heavens.
In person, therefore, will he come himself,
To see the marriage rites solemnised;
And, in the presence of the court of Spain,
To knit a sure, inexplicable band
Of kingly love, and everlasting league,
Betwixt the crowns of Spain and Portingale.
There will he give his crown to Balthazar,
And make a queen of Bel-imperia.

(III.xii.32–50)

This set-piece diplomacy represents quite patently a bid for stability and political strength in an alliance between the states of Spain and Portugal. In the 1580s such an alliance would have particular meanings for an Elizabethan audience, a point to which I shall return. For the moment, it is enough to stress the dramatic irony of these high hopes: the 'kingly love, and everlasting league' which the alliance promises issues instead in a funeral procession mourning the collapse of both kingdoms' succession. Before that, Kyd takes the opportunity, on the Viceroy's arrival in Spain, to underline the weighty personal and political implications of the event:

KING
And now to meet these Portuguese,
For as we now are, so sometimes were these,
Kings and commanders of the western Indies.
Welcome, brave Viceroy, to the court of Spain,
And welcome all his honourable train.
'Tis not unknown to us, for why you come,
Or have so kingly crossed the seas:
Sufficeth it, in this we note the troth
And more than common love you lend to us.
So is it that mine honourable niece,
(For it beseems us now that it be known)
Already is betrothed to Balthazar,
And by appointment and our condescent
To-morrow are they to be married...

VICEROY
Renowned king, I come not as thou think'st,
With doubtful followers, unresolved men,

> But such as have upon thine articles
> Confirmed thy motion and contented me.
> Know sovereign, I come to solemnise
> The marriage of thy beloved niece,
> Fair Bel-imperia, with my Balthazar—
> With thee, my son; whom sith I live to see,
> Here take my crown, I give it her and thee;
> And let me live a solitary life,
> In ceaseless prayers,
> To think how strangely heaven hath thee preserved.
>
> (III.xiv.5–34)

This self-divesting together with the investiture of his son, followed by withdrawal into religion, should be the prelude to political order and religious peace. Of course, it is not.

I do not think criticism has sufficiently underlined how intense the ironic contradictions of dynastic anticipation and actual event really are. In Hieronimo's playlet the nominal bride, Bel-imperia, stabs to death, rather than embraces, the groom-to-be Balthazar. If this were not in itself sufficient to turn masque to anarchy, the improbable topic addressed by the marriage masque offers no less a mockery of conventional celebration. For *Soliman and Perseda*, Hieronimo's play, evokes the ancient conflict of Christian with Turk, but in a fashion scarcely appropriate, at least superficially, to the marriage alliance between Christian princes. Erasto, the Christian knight of Rhodes, becomes the victim of the Turkish emperor, Soliman, by the hand of his bashaw. Kyd makes Hieronimo explicit about the costume design for both actors: Erasto must wear 'a cross like to a knight of Rhodes' (IV.i.146); Soliman is arrayed in 'a Turkish cap' and 'a black mustachio' and carries the Turkish symbol of a 'fauchion' (a curved sword) (lines 144–5). Such patent emblems must stand out even more vividly in a kind of dumb show if the play was indeed performed in 'sundry languages', and was therefore incomprehensible to many of its audience. Simon Shepherd has noticed how a brief fashion for plays on Turks developed in the 1580s and 1590s, and furthermore how Protestant propaganda was inclined to 'describe the alleged cruelty of Catholics in general and Spaniards in particular as Turkish', a point Richard Bauckham amplifies by quoting Protestant apologists to the effect that 'the turke and antichrist differ not but as the devil differeth from hel'.[11] Shepherd offers an interesting discussion of *The Battle of Alcazar*, *Selimus* and *Tamburlaine*, but not *The Spanish Tragedy* (though he immediately turns to Kyd's play to discuss the topic of 'Fathers'). Yet the relevance of anti-Turkish prejudice to *The Spanish Tragedy*, and of the association of Turkish anti-Christianity with the perceived anti-Christianity of Spain, is I believe real – at least as a prevailing habit-of-mind within which Kyd's audience might interpret the *Soliman and Perseda* playlet.

As is well known, Kyd wrote a full-length play entitled *Soliman and Perseda* (or rather, a significant number of scholars regard him as the author). Whether this play precedes or follows *The Spanish Tragedy* is not certain – most commentators have thought it comes later – but it can arguably provide a near-contemporary frame within which the playlet may be understood. The printed play's title is given as *Soliman and Perseda, Wherein is laide open Loves constancy, Fortunes inconstancy, and Deaths Triumphs*, and indeed a heavy emphasis is given to death's eventual triumph through the framing action shared by Death, Fortune and Love. The play concludes with an *ubi sunt* spoken by Death:[12]

> Where is *Erastus* now, but in my triumph?
> Where are the murtherers, but in my triumph?
> Where Iudge and witnesses, but in my triumph?
> Wheres falce *Lucina*, but in my triumph?
> Wheres faire *Perseda*, but in my triumph?
> Wheres *Basilisco*, but in my triumph?
> Wheres faithfull *Piston*, but in my triumph?
> Wheres valiant *Brusor*, but in my triumph?
> And wheres great *Soliman*, but in my triumph?
> Their loues and fortunes ended with their liues,
> And they must wait vpon the Carre of Death.
> Packe, *Loue* and *Fortune*, play in Commedies;
> For powerful *Death* best fitteth Tragedies.
>
> (v.v.17–29)

Amusingly, and significantly, the one excluded victim is 'Cynthias friend', Queen Elizabeth herself, for

> Death shall die, if he attempt her end,
> Whose life is heauens delight, and *Cynthias* friend.

The play is not doctrinally extreme, for Soliman is allowed to be both honourable (in ceding Perseda to Erasto in acknowledgement of their love) and capable of remorse (after he has Erasto strangled on a false charge of treason). But the religious and political significance of his conquest of Rhodes *is* brought out quite emphatically:

> For by the holy Alcaron I sweare
> Ile call my Souldiers home from *Persia*,
> And let the Sophie breath, and from the Russian broiles
> Call home my hardie, dauntlesse Ianisaries,
> And from the other skirts of Christendome
> Call home my Bassowes and my men of war,
> And so beleager *Rhodes* by sea and land.
> That Key will serue to open all the gates
> Through which our passage cannot finde a stop
> Till it haue prickt the hart of Christendome,
> Which now that paltrie Iland keeps from scath.
>
> (I.v.7–17)

Soliman and Perseda would mean for Kyd's first audience, if we can take some guidance from the full-length play, not only a death-laden disaster, but a religious débâcle that struck at the very heart of Christendom – neither, on a superficial understanding, at all appropriate for a marriage alliance between two of the great Christian powers, Spain and Portugal.

I can best bring out – or perhaps exaggerate – the climate of association of the Turkish conquest of Rhodes (with Erasto standing for Rhodes) by referring to the most influential, without doubt, of all the Protestant polemicists, the martyrologist John Foxe. Foxe's *Acts and Monuments* inserts a lengthy digression into his Protestant martyrology, under the title 'The History of the Turks'. This is devoted to highlighting the Turks' 'cruel tyranny and bloody victories, the ruin and subversion of so many Christian Churches, with the horrible murders and captivity of infinite Christians'.[13] The most prominent of all the Turkish tyrants is Soliman, 'The Twelfth Emperor of the Turks'. Soliman's great deeds have been made possible by neglect of duty and doctrinal folly on the part of the Christian Church. In particular, the fault must be laid at the door of the Papacy:

the public church, standing in such danger as it then did, by the invasion of the Turk, reason would, nature led, religion taught, time required, that a good prelate, forgetting lighter matters, should rather have laid his shoulder to the excluding of so great a danger, as then was imminent both to himself, and the universal church of Christ. But now, his quarrel being unjust, and the cause of Luther being most just and godly, what is to be said or thought of such a prelate, who, forbearing the Turk, whom in a time so dangerous he ought chiefly to have resisted, persecuted the truth which he should specially have maintained? (p. 52)

The major outcome of such heinous neglect and wrong-headedness has been the conquest of the Isle of Rhodes:

This Rhodes was a mighty and strong island, within the Mediterranean sea; the inhabitants whereof, at the first, did manfully resist the Turk, sparing no labour, nor pains for the defence of themselves and all Christendom. But afterwards, being brought to extremity, and pinched with penury, seeing also no aid to come from the Christians, they somewhat began to languish in themselves...Thus Solyman, with his great glory, and utter shame to all christian princes, and also ruin of all Christendom, got the noble isle of Rhodes. (p. 53)

Foxe goes on to explore the manifest (to him) cause of such Christian reversals. He finds himself drawn to a discussion of the iniquities of Rome, and a comparison of Rome with Babylon:

The causes why we have so to judge, be divers: first, that the see of Rome hath been defended hitherto and maintained, with much blood; and therefore it may seem not incredible, but that it will not long continue, but be lost with blood again...Another cause is, the fulfiling of Apocalypse xviii., where it is written, 'That great Babylon shall fall, and be made an habitation of devils, and a den of unclean spirits, and a cage of filthy and unclean birds:'...What city this is, called Great Babylon, which, like a mill-stone, shall fall and burn, and be made a habitation of unclean spirits and beasts, let the reader construe. This is certain and plain, by these her kings and merchants standing afar off for fear, and beholding her burning, that the destruction of this city (what city soever it be) shall be seen here on earth before the coming of the Lord's judgment...by which merchants and kings of the earth, peradvanture, may be signified the pope, the rich cardinals, the great prelates, and the fat doctors, and other obedientiaries of the Romish see...And when they shall see with their eyes, and hear with their ears, the city of Rome to be set on fire and consumed by the cruel Turks, the sight thereof shall seem to them piteous and lamentable, to behold the great and fair city of Rome...so to burn before their eyes, and to come to such utter desolation, which shall never be re-edified again, but shall be made a habitation of devils and unclean spirits; that is, of Turks and heathen sultans, and barbarous Saracens, &c. (p. 77)

The only conclusion Foxe can reach is that we must think of Rome as we think of the Turks. His wonderfully prejudiced account culminates in a historian's pretended detachment that can only lead ultimately to a bracketing of Turk and Pope as figures for Antichrist:

Now, in comparing the Turk with the pope, if a question be asked, whether of them is the truer or greater Antichrist, it were easy to see and judge, that the Turk is the more open and manifest enemy against Christ and his church. But, if it be asked whether of them two had been the more bloody and pernicious adversary to Christ and his members; or whether of them hath consumed and spilt more christian blood, he with sword, or this with fire and sword together, neither is it a light matter to discern, neither is it my part here to discuss, who do only write the history and the acts of them both. (p. 122)

If we accept the Hispanophobic prejudice drawn out by Broude and Hill as pertinent to the play as a whole, then the relevance of the Turkish tragedy of Soliman and Perseda to the play's portrayal of the fall of the papist realm of Spain becomes obvious. The ironies of the play's structure extend to the choice of a marriage masque entirely appropriate to the dynastic ambitions of this corrupt papistical state. The masque, in other words, when aptly read *confirms* the betrayal of Christianity, Protestant-style, for which the play's Spain stands.

Several further specific ironies can readily be elicited from this adroitly-conceived anti-masque of Soliman and Perseda,[14] but the most inclusive irony lies in Hieronimo's own anticipation of his polyglot playlet's effect:

> Now shall I see the fall of Babylon
> Wrought by the heavens in this confusion.
> (IV.i.195–6)

– the confusion, that is, of the linguistically disordered playlet. S. F. Johnson has pointed out that in the Geneva Bible (a translation much favoured in Protestant circles in the 1580s) Babylon and Babel are represented by the same word, used interchangeably.[15] Bound with a 1586 edition of the Geneva Bible in the library of the

Shakespeare Birthplace Trust is a copy of *Two right profitable and fruitfull Concordances, or large and ample Tables Alphabeticall* 'collected' by R. F. H. The book is itself undated, but the preface is signed '1578'. Under the concordance entry for Babylon, one finds what amounts to a short essay on the significance (and the conflation) of Babel and Babylon in the compiler's mind:

Babel, and Babylon...so named of the confusion of tongues. Gene. 11.4,9...All nacio[n]s have drunken of the wine of the wrath of the fornications of Babylon. Reuel. 18.3. It is become the habitation of deuils, and the holde of all foule spirits. Reuel. 18.2. Her merchants were the great men of the earth, and all nations were deceiued with her inchantments. Reuel. 18.23. Utter destruction is prophecied against her, and her favourers [*many* references]...The Prophets and Apostles rejoyce at her destructio[n]. Reue. 18.20.

The proud and prosperous city whose 'inchantments' deceived the world, and whose lewdness led to a downfall greeted with joyful satisfaction by Prophets and Apostles, makes its appearance, as the compiler notes, throughout the Bible. But the principal appearances are in Isaiah (centred on chapter 13) Jeremiah (especially chapter 51) and Revelations (chapters 17 and 18). The Geneva Bible guided its readers' reading (like a modernist narrator) by marginal glosses. Taken together, text and gloss form a powerful interpretive alliance. I can quote isolated instances only, though the significant effect is cumulative. Take Isaiah 13, where the page heading (either side of the running title) is 'A thanksgiuing Against Babylon'. The first ten verses are occupied with prophecy, showing how 'the day of the Lorde cometh, cruel, with wrath and fierce anger to lay the land waste' (verse 9). Verses 11, 16 and 18–20 run as follows:

11 And I will visite the wickednesse vpon the world, and their iniquitie vpon the wicked, and I will cause the arrogancie of the provde to cease, and will cast down the pride of tyrants...

16 Their children also shalbe broken in pieces before their eyes: their houses shalbe spoyled, and their wiues rauished...

18 With bowes also shall they destroye the children, and shall haue no compassion vpon the fruit of the wombe, and their eyes shall not spare the children.

19 And Babel the glorie of kingdomes, the beautie & pride of the Chaldeans, shall be as the destruction of God in Sodom and Gomorah.

20 It shall not be inhabited for euer, neither shall it be dwelled in from generation to generation...

There are two marginal glosses to verse 11. The first (at 'the world') notes 'He compareth Babylon to the whole world, because they so esteemed themselves, by reason of their great empire.' It is easy to see how such a self-image could readily be associated with Spain and Portugal, who notoriously thought to part the whole world between them. The second gloss explains the word 'proude': 'He noteth the principall vice, whereunto they were most giuen, as are all y^t abound in wealth.' The association of pride, wealth and Spain was habitual. When the verses of the text go on to emphasize, as part of the desolation of Babylon, the loss of children and the coming emptiness of the city, it is difficult (with our present preoccupations) not to think of the ending of *The Spanish Tragedy*, and the King's lament for 'My brother, and the whole succeeding hope / That Spain expected after my decease!' One might expect a 1580s audience to recognize a suggestive analogy. The Geneva Bible and its commentators were content with no more than general application, when glossing the Prophets. Sectarian commentary is reserved for the marginal annotation of Revelations, and here combative candour is unrestrained. Verse 19 of Revelations chapter 16 runs:

And the great citie was deuided into three partes, and the cities of the nations fell: and great Babylon came in remembrance before God, to give unto her the cup of the wine of the fierceness of his wrath.

The first gloss (explaining 'the great citie') runs:

Meaning the whole of them that shall call themselues Christians, whereof some are so in deede, some are papists, and vnder pretence of Christ, serve Antichrist, and some are Newters, which are neither of the one side nor of the other.

The second gloss (attached to 'the cities of the nations') spells matters out equally plainly:

Signifying al strange religions, as of the Iewes, Turks and others, which then shall fall with that great whore of Rome, and be tormented in eternall paines.

Perhaps this is altogether enough; but the commentator reserves his plainest prejudice for the appearance of the whore of Babylon herself. Commenting on chapter 17 verses 5, 6 ('I saw a woman drunken with the blood of Saints, and with the blood of the Martyrs of Jesus') he lets any remaining mask of modesty fall right away:

The beast signifieth the ancient Rome: the woman that sitteth thereon the new Rome which is the Papistrie...

and of the woman herself:

This woman is the Antichrist, that is, the Pope with the whole body of his filthie creatures, as is expounded, vers. 18. whose beautie only standeth in outward pompe and impudencie, and craft like a strumpet.

Such a creative misreading must be one of the plainest instances on record of subjectivity in textual analysis. But it *was*, patently, a shared subjectivity, dispersed among a sectarian (and political) faction, at the least, in Elizabeth's court. For the reader, and the audience, of *The Spanish Tragedy*, we might expect Babylon and Babel to be braced together inseparably, with the polyglot confusion of Hieronimo's play signifying the downfall of the whore of Babylon, the papist church itself and its most prominent contemporary representative, the nation of Spain. Thus the Soliman and Perseda playlet, Babel and Babylon at once, serves as appropriately expressive dramatic inset for the play's account of a Spanish tragedy.

It has not been argued, I think, that the downfall of Spain amid Babylonian linguistic confusion is even more firmly tied to Protestant doctrine of the late sixteenth century. Yet, just as the Virgilian anti-type brings out for Hill the Senecan horrors of Spain's collapse, so the biblical anti-type for Babylon (or Babel) is itself a pertinent implicit contrast for an alert Elizabethan audience. Again, it is one that expresses itself in terms of diversity of languages. The biblical anti-type to Babylonian confusion for an Elizabethan churchman is the wonderful clarification of languages that came with Pentecost. The Epistle for Whitsunday (or Pentecost) as required by the Book of Common Prayer (Acts chapter 2 verses 1–12) tells how cloven tongues of fire sat on each of the Apostles, who 'began to speake with other tongues, as the Spirit gave them utterance'. Miraculously, among the multinational community of

Jerusalem 'euery man hearde them speake his owne language':

11 ...we heard them speake in our owne tongues the wonderfull workes of God.
12 They were all then amased...

The confusion of Babylon is healed. The Gospel for Whitsunday (John chapter 14 verses 15–end) promises 'another Comforter...Euen ye Spirit of trueth';[16] the Proper Preface at the Eucharist makes a connection with preaching the truth to all nations:[17]

Through Jesus Christ our Lord, according to whose most true promise the holy Ghost came downe this day from heauen, with a sudden great sounde, as it had bene a mighty winde, in the likenes of fiery tongues, lighting vpon the Apostles, to teach them, & to leade them to all truth, giuinge them both the gift of divers laguages, & also boldnes with feruent zeale, co[n]stantly to preach the Gospel vnto all nations, whereby we are brought out of darkenesse & errour, into the cleare light, & true knowledge of thee, of thy sonne Jesus Christ.

Such a missionary achievement as this might well be ringing in the minds of a Protestant audience as the fitting English comedy to complement implicitly the conclusion of *The Spanish Tragedy*.

There remains one further aspect of the play that invites comment here. Our discussion has so far assumed that *The Spanish Tragedy* is situated in a single court, the court of Spain. In fact, the Iberian history of the play is divided between the court of Spain and the court of Portugal (even the list of dramatis personae makes the division plain). The play begins from a battle between Spain and Portugal and it culminates in a disastrous marriage-masque intended to celebrate the final alliance between the two countries. Ambassadors from Portugal visit the Spanish court. The Spanish Viceroy in Portugal and his entourage make their way to Spain to grace the wedding ceremonies between the heir of Portugal and the niece of the Spanish King. Several major scenes are set in Portugal. Yet critics have been reluctant to consider whether Hispano-Portuguese relations of the 1580s may have influenced an audience's response to the tragedy. Some have wished the division of the courts suppressed partially or altogether: 'The Portuguese court,' writes Philip Edwards 'could have been introduced more economically and the relevance of theme is very slight.'[18] Patterns of irony have been identified to account for Kyd's inclusion of a second court; and a clear case can be made. But it is appropriate to ask whether a more contemporary and political relevance may have been apparent to a first audience, and one that will have intensified an Englishman's satisfaction at the destruction of the enemy Spain.

For those aware of the news from Europe (and, in a climate of gathering neurosis about Spain, almost everyone must have been) Portugal in the 1580s was perceived as at once Spain's enemy and Spain's possession. In 1580, Philip II annexed Portugal for Spain. He had some defensible title to the Portuguese crown, after the childless death of his nephew Sebastian I in the battle of Alcazarquivir (4 August 1578), and the brief reign of the aged Cardinal Henry (died 31 January 1580). Philip's hopes of constitutional succession were dashed by the Cardinal's inconveniently early demise, and he was forced to take Portugal with some brutality in the battle of Alcantara in August 1580. The union of Spain and Portugal that resulted was a matter, as J. H. Elliott puts it, of 'acute international concern',[19] and for English foreign policy a major source of anxiety, providing Spain, as it did, with maritime power of intimidating scope.[20]

A principal focus of opposition to Philip was Don Antonio, bastard son of the Duke of Braganza. Antonio had himself proclaimed King by a section of the ruling Cortes; first Santarem and then Setubal and Lisbon declared for him. After the crushing military victories of Philip he escaped to France and then the Azores. For the next ten or twelve years, he was a persistent irritant on the European scene, seeking alliances and financial support from France, England and elsewhere. In a climate of considerable political instability, he was far from entirely unsuccessful in such overtures. In 1582-3 the Dutch–French–English alliance provided him with ships and munitions for his assaults on the Azores; eleven of the ships were English. Antonio was a personable as well as plausible figure, a scion, if an illegitimate one, of the Portuguese royal family, fluent in several languages.[21] *The Calendar of State Papers, Domestic Series* of the 1580s bear testimony to the interest he stirred in England: there are numerous references from 1581 on, especially among communications to and from Walsingham – ever alert to potential conspiracies. On frequent occasions he is named as not merely pretender but *King* of Portugal, and generally taken seriously – though always with a sense that he was, after all, a dispossessed mendicant. Elizabeth certainly took him seriously, at least in terms of his potential as a pawn in the anti-Spanish cause. He was not only received at court (though the wary Elizabeth was inclined to play down the significance of this) but given financial backing – for example, an account of extraordinary payments from the Exchequer between Lady Day and Michaelmas 1587 records 'To King Antonio towards payment of his debts £1,000'.[22] His most prominent activities were those associated with the long-anticipated assault on Lisbon in May and June 1589, carried out by Drake and Norris; here the *State Papers Venetian* give especially eloquent testimony to the threat posed to Spain by Antonio, with the Venetian Ambassador sending up to three dispatches a day to the Consiglio di Dieci and the Doge.[23] There seemed a real possibility that the people of Portugal (if not the nobles) would rise and proclaim Antonio King; in the event they failed to do so, to Spanish relief and English disgust.

As Elliott remarks, wherever Don Antonio went 'he denounced the King of Spain and his wickedness, and managed to enlist widespread sympathy for his claims to the throne'.[24] It is scarcely conceivable that a play dealing so tendentiously as (we have argued) *The Spanish Tragedy* does with the matter of Spain and Portugal in the 1580s can have been unaffected by the stir he caused. There is one possible hint in the text that Antonio was not entirely absent from Kyd's mind. In the Portuguese court in I. iii, the Spanish Viceroy accuses the (honourable) figure of Alexandro:

> Was't Spanish gold that bleared so thine eyes...
> Perchance because thou art Terceira's lord,
> Thou hadst some hope to wear the diadem.
>
> (I.iii.76–8)

In the play, Alexandro is vindicated; Antonio had indeed some hope to wear the diadem; he was *not* Terceira's lord but in the *Calendar of State Papers, Foreign Series* there are numerous references that associate him with the island. For example, a letter from Cobham to Walsingham of 11 November 1581:

I am advertised as follows of the affairs of Portugal: that the Isles of Terceiras show themselves so affectioned towards Don Antonio that they have executed the King of Spain and the Duke of Alva by 'picture' after condemning them by their 'order of process' for tyrants.[25]

Terceira proved a power-base for Antonio. Plainly, Antonio is *not* the play's Alexandro, though in the manner of Elizabethan plays a passing compliment may have been intended. Nor is the history of the play the Hispano-Portuguese history of the 1580s. The play's initial battle is not Alcantara, and there was no dynastic marriage contemplated to correspond to the Bel-imperia/Balthazar marriage of *The Spanish Tragedy*. But the Portugal and Spain of the play perhaps bear a certain resemblance to the prejudiced English image of the international diplomacy of the decade – the Portuguese court, so fully compliant with the wishes of Spain, and under a Spanish Viceroy, may be thought to represent what Englishmen feared if, as the King of Spain in our play wishes it, 'Spain is Portugal, / And Portugal is Spain' (i.iv.132–3). The political prejudices of an Elizabethan audience (which of course included religious prejudices) may well have led to an understanding of *The Spanish Tragedy* as offering a commentary on the historical circumstances in which Englishmen found themselves in the 1580s and early 1590s.

NOTES

1 See the introduction to my edition of *The Spanish Tragedy* in the New Mermaids series, revised edition (London, 1989).

2 For documentation of the early record of *The Spanish Tragedy* see Arthur Freeman, *Thomas Kyd: Facts and Problems* (Oxford, 1967). See also the Revels Plays edition by Philip Edwards (London, 1959).

3 Russell A. Frazer and Norman Rabkin, eds., *Drama of the English Renaissance I: the Tudor Period* (New York and London, 1976), p. 13.

4 For a carefully documented account of Anglo-Hispanic relations in the period see R. B. Wernham, *Before the Armada: the Growth of English Foreign Policy 1485–1588* (London, 1966).

5 (Durham, NC 1971), *passim*.

6 *The Defeat of the Spanish Armada* (Harmondsworth, 1988), pp. 10–11.

7 Ronald Broude, 'Time, Truth and Right in *The Spanish Tragedy*', *Studies*

in Philology 68 (1971), 130–45; Eugene Hill, 'Senecan and Virgilian Perspectives in *The Spanish Tragedy*', *English Literary Renaissance* 15 (1985), 143–65.

8 Quotations from Broude *ibid.*, 131–2, 144–5.

9 Quotations from Hill, 'Senecan and Virgilian Perspectives', pp. 144, 146, 147, 150, 156.

10 *Ibid.*, p. 151.

11 Simon Shepherd, *Marlowe and the Politics of Elizabethan Theatre* (London, 1986), p. 144. The quotation is from E. Sandys, *Sermons* (London, 1585), p. 346. See Richard Bauckham, *Tudor Apocalypse* (Appleford, 1978) p. 97.

12 The quotations from *Soliman and Perseda* are taken from Frederick S. Boas ed., *The Works of Thomas Kyd* (Oxford, 1901).

13 The Revd. S. R. Cattley, ed., *The Acts and Monuments of John Foxe: a New and Complete Edition*, 8 vols., (London, 1841), IV, p. 18.

14 For an exposition of several of these ironies see Sacvan Bercovitch, 'Love and Strife in Kyd's *Spanish Tragedy*', *SEL* 9 (1969), 215–29.

15 '*The Spanish Tragedy* or Babylon Revisited' in *Essays on Shakespeare and Elizabethan Drama in Honor of Hardin Craig*, ed. Richard Hoseley (London, 1963), pp. 23–36.

16 Quotations are from the Geneva Bible (?1586).

17 From *The Booke of Common Prayer, with the Psalter or Psalms of David*, n.d. (signed in ink 1586, but perhaps 1578).

18 Philip Edwards, ed., *The Spanish Tragedy*, The Revels Plays (London, 1959) p. liii. Professor Edwards' more recent paper, 'Thrusting Elysium into Hell: the Originality of *The Spanish Tragedy*' (*The Elizabethan Theatre* 11 (1990), 117–32) takes a different view. The essay is a major contribution to the interpretation of Kyd's play.

19 J. H. Elliott, *Europe Divided, 1559–1598* (London, 1968), p. 278.

20 See, for example, J. H. Elliott, *Imperial Spain, 1469–1716* (Harmondsworth, 1970), p. 276, and R. B. Wernham, *Before the Armada*, especially pp. 356–7.

21 For relevant details of Spanish and Portuguese history in these years see Geoffrey Parker, *Philip II: a Biography* (London 1978), especially pp. 142–6; and H. V. Livermore, *Portugal: a Short History* (Edinburgh, 1973), especially ch. 4.

22 *Calendar of State Papers, Domestic Series, 1581–1590* (London, 1865), p. 427.

23 Horatio F. Brown, ed., *Calendar of State Papers and Manuscripts, Existing in the Archives and Collections of Venice 1581–1591* (London, 1894).

24 Elliott, *Europe Divided*, p. 281.

25 A. J. Butler, ed., *Calendar of State Papers, Foreign Series, January 1581–April 1582* (London, 1907), p. 361.

CHAPTER 7

Marlowe's Argonauts

Yves Peyré

Among the classical myths that were given new life in the Renaissance, the voyage of the Argonauts and the conquest of the Golden Fleece held pride of place. When as far back as 1429 Philip the Good, Duke of Burgundy, instituted the order of the Golden Fleece, he was deliberately invoking mythological patronage to promote a spiritual ideal, exalt the loftiest virtues of chivalry and consolidate his personal power.[1] This gave rise to numerous reworkings of Jason's adventures in honour of the house of Burgundy, such as Raoul Lefèvre's *Proheme de l'istoire de Jason* (*c.* 1460), translated by Caxton in 1477,[2] and the elaborate devices installed at the Château de Hesdin, which Caxton, in the prologue to his translation, proudly claimed to have seen. After the death of Philip's son Charles the Bold, the Golden Fleece passed on to his son-in-law Maximilian of Hapsburg, and was eventually handed down to his great-grandson Charles V: the Emperor's visit to London in June 1522 occasioned what seems to have been the first use of classical mythology in an English pageant.[3]

Besides glorifying both chivalric principles and supreme power, first ducal then imperial, the story of Jason soon came to be used, in a new historical context, to lend mythic aura to the discoverers of America. In Ariosto's *Orlando Furioso* (1516), Astolphus wonders, as he journeys back home after escaping from Alcina's palace, whether any ship has ever ventured over the seas beyond India and whether it is possible, by sailing eastwards from India, to return to France or England. Andronica's reply echoes Virgil's fourth Eclogue (34–5), which announced the advent of Augustus' reign, when 'Alter erit tum Tiphys, et altera quae vehat Argo / Delectos heroas', [There will be another Tiphys; a new Argo, / Bearing chosen heroes]; she prophesies new discoveries by Andrea Doria and Fernando Cortez, those 'nuovi Argonauti e nuovi Tifi'[4] of Charles V's reign, before going on to praise the Emperor's achievements at length. In his translation of Ariosto (1591), Sir John Harington felt that he had to qualify this eulogy by condemning the Emperor's overreaching ambition:

It was thought that Charles meant to conquer all the world, and then to enter into religion and become Pope and Emperor both...but it was but a vaine conceit of some idle head.[5]

He made the text more agreeable to English readers by noting that

for the Indian voyages we need not so much admyre the captaines of forren nations, having two of our owne nation that have both as forwardly adventured, and as fortunately performed them; namely sir Francis Drake...and young master Candish. (p. 119)

It was precisely in Sir Francis Drake's honour that Geoffrey Whitney had devised one of his emblems (1586), in which he demonstrated the knight's superiority over Jason: the latter, after all, succeeded thanks to Medea and her enchantments, whereas it was *auxilio divino*, 'By helpe of power devine', that Drake found 'the goulden mine':

Let *Graecia* then forbeare, to praise her *Iason* boulde?
who throughe the watchfull dragons pass'd, to win the fleece of goulde.
Since by *Medeas* helpe, they weare inchaunted all,
And *Iason* without perrilles, pass'de: the conqueste therfore small?
But hee, of whome I write, this noble minded Drake,
Did bringe away his goulden fleece, when thousand eies did wake.
(A Choice of Emblemes, p. 203)

In the entertainments at Elvetham in 1591, Queen Elizabeth accepted a jewel from 'gould breasted India' before naming a pinnace Bonadventure; under such favourable auspices, the ship was bound to sail to success and might even 'dare attempt a golden fleece'.[6] Just as India had been present at Elvetham, six tributary Indian kings attended Medea and Jason in Anthony Munday's *The Triumphs of the Golden Fleece* (1623), which was given in honour of the Lord Mayor.[7]

Jason's priceless spoil did not merely symbolize overseas conquests, however. The Fleece may have been far less precious to Ronsard than a lock of his mistress's blond hair –

> Si blond, si beau, comme est une toison
> Qui mon deuil tue et mon plaisir renforce,
> Ne fut oncq l'or, que les toreaux par force
> Aux champs de Mars donnerent à Jason.[8]

> [So blond, so fair, so like a fleece
> Which kills my woe and quickens my joy
> Never so was the gold, which bulls forcefully
> Yielded to Jason on the fields of Mars.]

– but in *The Merchant of Venice* its gold transforms Portia into an exquisite prize:

> the four winds blow in from every coast
> Renowned suitors, and her sunny locks
> Hang on her temples like a golden fleece,
> Which makes her seat of Belmont Colchos' strond,
> And many Jasons come in quest of her.
>
> (I.i.168–72)

As an image for a peerless object of desire, the Fleece even characterized the Queen, to whose love many pretenders aspired: in a show presented at the Tilt-yard on Whitsun Monday 1581, four champions, the Foster Children of Desire, laid siege to the fortress of Beauty, 'venturing to win the golden fleece without Medea's helpe'. On realizing that it is in the nature of Perfection to frustrate Desire, they submitted to Elizabeth and withdrew from the contest. This was intended to impress the French Ambassadors, who had crossed the Channel to seek the Queen's hand in marriage on behalf of the Duke of Alençon.[9] The French party's hopes came to nothing, but remained memorable, and after the Queen's death a laudatory poem chuckled over the failure of 'That brave French Monsieur who did hope to carry / The Golden Fleece, and faire Eliza marry'.[10] James VI of Scotland proved more successful when, in spite of 'the conspiraces of witches, and such devilish dragons', he undertook 'to saile to Norway, and, like a new Jason, bring his Queene, our gracious Lady, to this kingdome'.[11]

Be it to conquer a wife or newly discovered lands, the difficulties involved required courage and determination. In the dedicatory Epistle to his translation of Ovid's *Metamorphoses* (1567), Arthur

Golding understood 'The good successe of Jason in the land of Colchos' to mean

> That nothing is so hard but peyne and travell doo it win,
> For fortune ever favoreth such as boldly doo begin.[12]

For Henry Peacham, 'The Dread-nought Argo' which 'cuts the foaming surge, / Through dangers great, to get the golden prize' is there to remind us that we should 'undertake with pleasure, any paine, / Whereby we might our wealth, or honour gaine'.[13] Fraunce had reached a similar conclusion:

Iason was many wayes endangered, before he could atchieve the golden fleece: there is no man that can attayne to any excellency, without extraordinarie labour. The golden fleece noteth either great riches and treasure, or fame and immortality.[14]

Readings of the myth that extolled the spirit of adventure and enterprise did not prevent a powerful counter-current of negative ones too. Seen from the point of view of Aeëtes, whom Jason deprived of the Fleece, the Argonauts were rapacious plunderers: this was the line the inhabitants of Rouen chose to take when Henry IV received the Order of the Garter in 1596. One of the tableaux in his honour featured a shorn lamb to illustrate the city's plight before the King brought the religious wars to an end:

> O, King! your Lambe, before our wretched broile,
> Was wont to beare uppon her humble backe
> The golden fleece, like that of Colchos Ile;
> But certaine new-come, Argonauts (alacke!)
> Have her oft-times so barely cut and shorne,
> That on her body poore and all forlorne,
> You scarce with paine can find at all to pull,
> One simple fleece, or little lock of wooll.[15]

In his commentary on Ovid's *Metamorphoses* (1555), Georg Schuler (Sabinus) listed a variety of divergent interpretations. The idealistic vision came first:

Argonautarum expeditio in Cholcos admonet generosos animos, ut ad gloriam excitentur, eamque magnis et illustribus rebus gerendis quaerant.

[The Argonauts' expedition to Colchos incites noble-hearted men to seek out and achieve glory by means of great and memorable feats.][16]

The historical dimension followed, with Philip the Good's Order, then the alchemical version, which was rounded off by Schuler's conclusion that the myth illustrated nothing more than 'greed for gold':

Quare non dubium est, Iasonem aut bello repetivisse thesauros...; vel auri gratia intulisse bellum Colchis, quemadmodum nostro tempore Hispani, qui eadem de causa in Indiam navigarunt, ut videlicet aurum inde auferrent.

[Which is why it is obvious that Jason obtained the treasure as a result of war..., or brought war to Colchos because of his greed for gold; thus in our time the Spaniards who travelled to India for the same reason, that is, to bring gold from hence.][17]

One of the most negative visions of the Argonauts' voyage was to be found in a classical text, the second Chorus of Seneca's *Medea*, which deplored the recklessness of the first navigators:

> Ausus Tiphys pandere vasto
> carbasa ponto
> legesque novas scribere ventis (318–20)

John Studley's translation, with the choice of the more emphatic 'hoysted' for 'pandere' ('unfold'), the addition of 'bould', and the enjambment throwing 'new lawes' into strong relief, makes Tiphys' enterprise seem even more hubristic:

> Yet Typhys bould on open seas durst show
> His hoysted sayles, and for the wyndes decree
> New lawes.[18]

This first pilot was breaking a natural order of things and putting an end to a state of innocence,[19] a transgression which had to be paid for, hence the dangers that beset the Argonauts, and all for nothing but a paltry prize:

> Quod fuit huius
> pretium cursus? Aurea pellis
> maiusque mari Medea malum,
> merces prima digna carina (360–3)

How deerly was that wicked journey bought?
Medea accurst, and eke the golden Fleece,
That greater harme then storme of seas hath wrought
Rewarded well that voyage first of Greece.

(Studley, fol. 127r)

The Chorus' lament ends on the prospect – which may well have seemed prophetic in the sixteenth century – of new worlds waiting to be discovered:

The wandring World at will shall open lye.
And *Typhis* will some newe founde Land survay
Some travelers shall the Countreys farre escrye,
Beyond small Thule, knowen furthest at this day.[20]

Similarly, the Argonauts' first appearance in Marlowe's works takes place in a negative context, amid much lamenting about the first act of navigation. Catullus had made the birth of Peleus and Tethys' mutual love coincide with the launching of the Argo (*De Nuptiae Pelei et Thetidis*, lines 1–22); in contrast, the eleventh elegy in Ovid's second book of the *Amores* is dedicated 'Ad amicam navigantem': the Lover who remains on shore while his mistress embarks on a voyage to distant lands is bound to wish that the first expedition overseas had never taken place:

The lofty Pine from high mount *Pelion* raught
Ill waies by rough seas wondring waves first taught,
Which rashly twixt the sharpe rocks in the deepe,
Caried the famous golden-fleeced sheepe.
O would that no Oares might in seas have suncke,
The *Argos* wrackt had deadly waters drunke.[21]

The Argonauts' venture is the distant cause of separation and loss, and hence of the lover's frustrated desire; *Dido, Queen of Carthage* dramatizes a parallel situation, with Aeneas having to choose between love in Carthage and glory beyond the seas. The sea as separation constitutes the fatal backcloth of *Hero and Leander*, against which ironies are built up. Leander urges Hero to become a ship sailing on the ocean of love:

A stately builded ship, well rig'd and tall,
The Ocean maketh more majesticall:
Why vowest thou then to live in *Sestos* here,
Who on Loves seas more glorious wouldst appeare?

(1.225–8)

As for the experience of love, it is described not only as an assault against a well defended citadel but also in terms of maritime discovery; Leander first scales 'the rising yv'rie mount', which the Poet also calls a 'globe', thus associating erotic desire and the exhilarating exploration of 'some newe founde Land': 'a globe may I tearme this, / By which love sailes to regions full of blis' (II.275–6). This metaphorical voyage ironically contrasts with his actual swimming across the Hellespont, in the course of which he arouses Neptune's desire, a desire that must be frustrated – or, if satisfied, lead to the swimmer's death. From the outset, Marlowe's description of Leander casts the young man in the role Ronsard gave his mistress as an object of his desire:

> His dangling tresses that were never shorne,
> Had they been cut, and unto *Colchos* borne,
> Would have allur'd the vent'rous youth of *Greece*,
> To hazard more, than for the golden Fleece.
>
> (I.55–8)

Plot and situation would seem to cast Hero, as object of a quest and longed-for prize, in the role of the Golden Fleece, and Leander, who must cross the Hellespont to win her, in that of Jason and the Argonauts. Yet the reader's expectation is deliberately frustrated; desire tugs in two opposite directions that threaten to neutralize each other. For when, later, 'The god put *Helles* bracelet onto his arme' (II.179), the reader is reminded that Leander arouses as much desire as the Fleece. The whole story of the Golden Fleece started with Helle trying to cross the Hellespont – to which she gave her name – on the back of the Golden Ram; she fell, drowned, and eventually became Neptune's bride (Ovid, *Fasti*, lines 851–76). By giving Helle's bracelet to the wearer of the Golden Fleece, Neptune ironically conflates beginning and end in an inconclusive circle; a wished-for quest is constantly suggested, but simultaneously left suspended and unfulfilled, perhaps not unlike the poem itself: Desunt nonnulla...[22]

Desire is much more forcibly expressed in the two parts of *Tamburlaine*, though not without similar ironies and ambiguities. When Cosroe is about to seize power in Persia with Tamburlaine's help, Meander tries to reassure Mycetes that the attack will easily

be repulsed: undisciplined and eager to disperse for spoil, Cosroe's
and Tamburlaine's soldiers will soon be at one another's throats:

> Like to the cruell brothers of the earth,
> Sprong of the teeth of Dragons venomous,
> Their carelesse swords shal lanch their fellowes throats
> And make us triumph in their overthrow.
>
> (*1 Tamb.*, II.ii.47–50)

The comparison is ironically misapplied. Mycetes is no Jason
about to conquer the Golden Fleece. It is not Tamburlaine's army,
but Persia, that is divided against itself, brother fighting brother.
Developing Ovid's 'Civilique cadunt acie' [they fell in a civil war
(*Met.* VII.142)], Schuler explained that

Per sementem intelligenda sunt intestina Colchorum dissidia, quae
Argonautis bono et commodo fuerunt.

[By this sowing [of dragons' teeth] one should understand the internal
conflicts of Colchos, which were a boon to the Argonauts.][23]

Whatever Meander says or wishes to believe, the new Jason,
prompt to take advantage of internal brawls, is Tamburlaine. And
indeed, having conquered Persia, the Scythian shepherd crowns
his enterprise, in the first part, by capturing Damascus, which he
assures his soldiers will yield up spoils as rich 'as was to Jason
Colchos golden fleece' (*1 Tamb.*, IV.iv.9). Tamburlaine gilds his
enterprise by using the myth whereby the inhabitants of Rouen
were to express the rapaciousness of plunderers; the image also
brings together and catalyses numerous references to maritime
expeditions which seem to haunt Tamburlaine's imagination:

> The Galles and those pilling Briggandines,
> . . .
> Shall lie at anchor in the Isle *Asant*,
> Untill the Persean Fleete and men of war,
> Sailing along the Orientall sea,
> Have fetcht about the Indian continent:
> Even from *Persepolis* to *Mexico*,
> And thence unto the straightes of *Jubalter*:
>
> (*1 Tamb.*, III.iii.248–56)

The route of the Persian fleet boldly runs across the Pacific to the western coast of Mexico then back to Gibraltar across the Atlantic in a circular voyage which, although merely conjured up in words, already seems to make Tamburlaine master of the world, in a flight of fancy which Harington, writing about Charles V, was to call madness. Tamburlaine's dreams are full of the exhilaration of vastly expanding space; the world reaches out to the southern hemisphere ('We meane to traveile to th'Antartique Pole, / Conquering the People underneath our feet', *1 Tamb.*, IV.iv.136–7), and is enriched with new countries which do not yet exist on maps:

> I will confute those blind Geographers
> That make a triple region in the world,
> Excluding Regions which I meane to trace,
> And with this pen reduce them to a Map,
> Calling the Provinces, Citties and townes
> After my name and thine *Zenocrate*.
>
> (*1 Tamb.*, IV.iv.75–80)

Tamburlaine is here imitating a practice frequently adopted by the explorers of the New World, most famously in Virginia.[24] In his words, it consists in denying a conquered land its intrinsic reality by 'reducing' it to a map,[25] so as to impose one's own identity upon it. The thread of overseas exploration that runs through Tamburlaine's imagination interweaves with his mention of Jason's Golden Fleece under the walls of Damascus to suggest that the enthusiastic urge to discover new territories hides a somewhat less noble thirst for gold. West Indian – in the Elizabethan sense of South American – gold-mines had become proverbial. They are among Tamburlaine's objectives:

> Ile make the Kings of *India* ere I die,
> Offer their mines (to sew for peace) to me.
>
> (*1 Tamb.*, III.iii.263–4)

The play's constant, underlying fascination with the discovery and conquest of a new world waiting to be plundered is made clear in Orcanes' reference to

> faire *Europe* mounted on her bull,
> Trapt with the wealth and riches of the world
>
> (*2 Tamb.*, I.i.42–3)

and it finally surfaces in Callapine's promise to bestow upon Almeda

> Armados from the coasts of *Spaine*,
> Fraughted with the golde of rich *America*.
>> (*2 Tamb.*, 1.ii.34–5)

This, however, is merely the lure of wealth which, for Almeda, remains an unfulfilled ambition. Tamburlaine's dreams are similarly unsatisfied. He dies without having rounded off his task. In his final survey of the lands he leaves unconquered, South America figures prominently:

> Looke here my boies, see what a world of ground,
> Lies westward from the midst of *Cancers* line,
> Unto the rising of this earthly globe,
> Whereas the Sun declining from our sight,
> Begins the day with our Antypodes
>> (*2 Tamb.*, v.iii.145–9)

What frustrates him most is the thought of all that untapped wealth:

> Loe here my sonnes, are all the golden Mines,
> Inestimable drugs and precious stones,
> More worth than *Asia*, and the world beside
>> (*2 Tamb.*, v.iii.151–3)

At the end of part one, Tamburlaine had been forced to concede that even 'The highest reaches of a humaine wit' are powerless to express beauty to the full and must be content to leave 'One thought, one grace, one woonder at the least, / Which into words no vertue can digest' (*1 Tamb.*, v.i.172–3). Here, at the end of part two, he is expressing the ultimate futility of his unquenchable desire to annex ever more territories. His anguished, indignant cry – 'And shal I die, and this unconquered?' – ironically emphasizes his sense of failure before an audience whose contemporaries thought they were laying hands on the spoils Tamburlaine had been unable to grab. While his imagination pictures conquest in terms of maritime adventure, he himself, his anger a storm, appears as the sailor's enemy; in his presence, Agidas feels

> As when the Sea-man sees the *Hyades*
> Gather an armye of Cemerian clouds,
> (*Auster* and *Aquilon* with winged Steads

All sweating, tilt about the watery heavens,
With shivering speares enforcing thunderclaps,
And from their shieldes strike flames of lightening)
And fearfull foldes his sailes, and sounds the maine,
Lifting his prayers to the heavens for aid,
Against the terrour of the winds and waves.

(*1 Tamb.*, III.ii.76–84)

This identification of Tamburlaine with a violent storm, strengthened
and deepened in turn by the identification of the storm with a
battlefield, suggests that his 'sea venture' bears the seeds of its own
destruction.

One of Cosroe's grievances against his ineffectual brother
Mycetes was that he had lost 'Indian Mines' to the Christians (*1
Tamb.*, II.v.41–2). It is partly from the same mines, 'That trade in
metall of the purest mould', that Barabas fortune derives. In *The
Jew of Malta*, 'The wind that bloweth all the world' is 'Desire of
gold' (III.v.3–4). The precious metal, as Ferneze contemptuously
assures the Turkish Bashaw, is not to be found in Malta but 'in the
Westerne Inde' (III.v.5), or South America. The Governor's breach
of promise is just one of many in a web of treacheries and inverted
alliances: winds in Malta are contrary; passions criss-cross and
cancel each other out. Thirst for gold drives Bellamira to arouse
Ithamore's desire; ironically enough, in his declaration of love,
with its upside-down appeal to '*Dis* above' (IV.ii.97), he is trying to
act upon someone who is in fact acting upon him:

we will leave this paltry land,
And saile from hence to *Greece*, to lovely *Greece*,
I'le be thy *Jason*, thou my golden Fleece

(IV.ii.88–90)

The image is reversible; what Ithamore has in mind is the amorous
interpretation, but the context reveals that what Bellamira is intent
on is the gold of Ithamore's master, whom she intends to fleece
properly. At the same time, Ithamore unwittingly reverses the tale
of glorious adventure and discovery, cancelling it out by substituting
Greece for Colchos, or the point of departure for the goal to be
attained. In *Tamburlaine*, the sheer power of Jason's desire drives the
hero onwards with an irresistible energy that finally burns itself up
in a feeling of frustration; in *The Jew of Malta*, the driving force

explodes in a host of conflicting desires which ironically invert their energies; while in *Edward II*, it is the negative of an Argonautic myth that seems to be suggested.

On landing in England, Gaveston imagines that he might have 'swum from *France*, / And like *Leander* gaspt upon the sande' (1.i.7–8), thus foreshadowing with intimations of death the outcome of his relationship with Edward II. The King, for his part, welcomes him with another image of death by drowning:

> Not *Hilas* was more mourned of *Hercules*,
> Then thou hast beene of me since thy exile.
>
> (1.i.144–5)

Hercules, one of the most famous Argonauts, had abandoned the glorious quest for the Golden Fleece and set out in search of his minion Hylas, whose beauty was such that water nymphs fell in love with him (as Neptune had done with Marlowe's Leander) and enticed him to the bottom of a pond, where he drowned. Like Hercules in that episode,[26] Edward II gives up affairs of state for private pursuits. Instead of leading his subjects in an exhilarating discovery of distant lands, he would let his own country drift aimlessly like an unrigged boat:

> Ere my sweete *Gaveston* shall part from me,
> This Ile shall fleete upon the Ocean,
> And wander to the unfrequented *Inde*.
>
> (1.iv.48–50)

While Jason made himself master of the seas and fomented civil strife in Colchos to win the spoil he coveted, Edward causes England to be divided by 'civil broiles' (iv.iv.6) and 'betrays' his own land 'to spoyle' (iv.iv.11).

The self-conflicting nature of desire and the tug of war between its various forms result in ambivalence and indeterminacy. Mortimer senior takes up the image of Hercules' love for Hylas (1.iv.393), seeing in it a relationship which may be condoned, not very far removed from Spenser's image of ideal friendship (*The Faerie Queene*, iv.v.27); yet derogatory suggestions lurk below the surface.[27] The suggestion of inordinate, unhealthy desire is at odds with the melancholy mood the image draws from its conventional use in elegiac poetry.[28] For Seneca, Hylas deserved to die –

The rash attempting *Argonautes* deserved all the death
That *Hylas* whom *Alcides* lost bereft of fading breath
That springall which in sowsing waves of waters drowned was.

(Studley, fol. 132v)

– while Erasmus saw in Hercules' tears and calls for Hylas an instance of unproductive grief:

Hylam inclamas. De frustra vociferantibus, aut in genere, de nihil proficientibus.

['To cry for Hylas' is said of those who clamour in vain and, more generally, of that which achieves nothing.][29]

The evocation of tears superimposed on that of drowning emphasizes dissolution as the end of Edward's desire. Floating adrift towards annihilation, Edward is an inverted Argonaut, in appearance only the opposite of Mortimer who, '...as a traveller, / Goes to discover countries yet unknown' (v.vi.65–6); in both cases the end of the journey is the same: the unexplored country is that of death.

It is left to Doctor Faustus, who descends a step further in the corruption of desire, to carry out the exploration of death. The quest of the Argonauts lent itself to religious interpretations. According to Petrus Berchorius, since the Golden Fleece could be understood to mean temporal wealth, 'and more especially' that of the Church, Jason represents any 'good prelate...who aspires to an ecclesiastical prebend'.[30] The *Ovide Moralisé* offers a more spiritual reading: the Golden Fleece refers to Christ's incarnation and to his sacrifice as 'the holy lamb':

> Jason prist la toison doree:
> Jhesu en la vierge honnoree
> Prist char et humaine nature.
> C'est la toison, c'est la courture
> Dont Diex, douz moutons, fu couvert,
> Qui dou glaive ot le cors ouvert
> Pour home, et fu sacrefiez
> Et pendus et crucefiez.

[Jason took the Golden Fleece: / Jesus in the honoured Virgin / Took on flesh and human nature. / 'Tis the Fleece, 'tis the hide / That covered God the gentle lamb / Whose body was cut open by the spear / For mankind; who was sacrificed / And hanged and crucified.][31]

Spiritual interpretations still lingered in Marlowe's time; Johannes Sprengius, for instance, wrote that 'Colchidos instinctu ceu vellera portat Iason, / Sic aeterna Dei dona parantur ope' [As Jason needs [Medea's] instigation to carry away the fleeces of Colchos, so eternal gifts are acquired with God's help].[32] In contrast, Valdes mingles mythical and modern conquests when promising Faustus the help of spirits:

> From *Venice* shall they drag huge *Argosies,*
> And from *America* the Golden Fleece,
> That yearely stuffes old *Phillips* treasury
>
> (1.i.157–9)

With characteristic anti-Spanish feeling, the mythological allusion conveniently brings together the plundering of South America and the order of the Golden Fleece which had passed on to Philip II at the death of his father Charles V. The promise echoes Faustus' own dreams:

> I'le have them flie to *India* for gold;
> Ransacke the Ocean for Orient Pearle,
> And search all corners of the new-found-world
> For pleasant fruites, and Princely delicates.
>
> (1.i.109–12)

The purely materialistic attraction which Faustus finds in the modern Argonauts' voyages may be contrasted with Donne's later use of the same discoveries in his address 'To Mr Tilman after he had Taken Orders'[33] or in his 'Hymn to God, my God, in my Sickness'.[34] Not only is Faustus' dream a betrayal of the world of the spirit, it is also an enterprise carried out, not by oneself but by servant spirits, as in Walsingham's interpretation of the fiendish charms Medea used to help Jason.[35] Like Valdes' promises, Faustus' words retain the sense of intense excitement conveyed by the myth of the Golden Fleece and the modern discovery of new countries, albeit with a hint of the grasping rapaciousness that Seneca, and more recently Schuler, had deplored. Simultaneously, Faustus' enterprise is corrupted from the outset; a spiritual quest is debased and reduced to a pursuit of materialistic greed and sensual indulgence which carries its own seeds of destruction, as is later suggested by another, clearly fateful, naval expedition, when

Faustus is enraptured by 'the face that Launcht a thousand ships /
And burnt the toplesse Towers of Ilium' (v.i.1768–9).

   Faustus' frantic scramble after futile goals suggests that desire for
its own sake matters more to him than its object, hence a possible
fear of fulfilment, which would bring about the death of desire.
According to Edward A. Snow,

Ultimate fulfilment or satiety can be the most fearful prospect of all for a
self that suspects it has created itself out of nothing (in order to protect
itself from nothingness), and can thus only sustain itself in the 'conceited'
space between desire and possession.[36]

The tensed thrust of desire constantly threatens to melt, like Icarus'
wings, into nothingness, transforming Jason's 'horizontal', active
quest into the 'vertical', passive agony of drowning. Ironically,
Doctor Faustus thought that he could get bold divers to 'Ransacke
the Ocean for Orient Pearle'; instead, it will not even be granted to
him to have the pearl of his soul 'chang'd into little water drops, /
And fall into the Ocean, ne're be found' (v.ii.1977–8) – and thus
find total annihilation. Like Marlowe's other Argonauts – especially
in *Hero and Leander* and *Edward II* – Doctor Faustus is faced with the
anguishing discovery of an unsuspected kinship between resolution
and dissolution.

The Renaissance appropriated the culture of Antiquity to explore
the potentialities of its own present. The malleable nature of the
myth of the Argonauts, together with its inexhaustible adaptability,
enabled it to encapsulate within a single image suggestions of
conflicting quests for love, material riches, noble adventure and
spiritual discovery. The brutal contrasts thus created between
idealism and materialism, between a triumphant extolling of glory
and a satirical denunciation of greed, added to the jarring
conjunction, in one single quest, of love and money, massacre and
glory, God and gold, provided unlimited scope for irony which
could be developed in a dramatic interplay between enthusiasm for
new discoveries and conquests, contempt for paltry ambitions, and
distaste for the human cost involved. Beyond the dramatic conflict
of divergent quests, Marlowe's stirring rhetoric and thematic
inversions exploit fragments of the myth of the Argonauts in an

exploration of the tragically self-defeating nature of desire. Between 1586 and 1588 Thomas Cavendish sailed 'round about the circumference of the whole earth': his fleet was composed of the *Hugh Gallant*, the *Desire* and the *Content*. At about the same moment Marlowe was launching Desire, Frustration and Fear of Fulfilment on the London stage.

NOTES

1 See Lucie Marignac, 'Philippe le Bon et l'ordre de la Toison d'or: les enjeux d'une référence mythique', *Razo, Cahiers du Centre d'Etudes Médiévales de Nice* 12 (1992), 87–112; Jean-Philippe Lecat, *Le siècle de la Toison d'or* (Paris, 1968).

2 Raoul Lefèvre, *Histoire de Jason*, ed. G. Pinkernell (Frankfurt, 1971); William Caxton, *The Historie of Jason*, ed. John Munro, *Early English Text Society*, extra series 111 (London, 1913 (for 1912), rpt. Millwood, NY, 1973).

3 Jean Robertson, 'L'entrée de Charles Quint à Londres, en 1522', in *Les fêtes de la Renaissance*, ed. Jean Jacquot (Paris, 1960), 11, pp. 169–81.

4 *Orlando Furioso* xv.21, *Opere di Ludovico Ariosto*, ed. Adriano Seroni (1961, rpt. Milan, 1968), p. 268. Natale Conti considered that, for all its glory, the Argonauts' expedition paled besides the far greater ventures of contemporary Spanish discoverers: *Mythologiae* (Frankfurt, 1584), p. 598.

5 *Orlando Furioso in English Heroical Verse* (London, 1591), p. 114, marginal note.

6 Jean Wilson, *Entertainments for Elizabeth I* (Woodbridge, 1980), pp. 96–118.

7 *Pageants and Entertainments of Anthony Munday*, ed. David M. Bergeron (New York, 1985), p. 137–42. Munday had already used the myth in *Metropolis Coronata* (1615)

8 *Amours de Cassandre*, ccxi, *Oeuvres complètes*, ed. Gustave Cohen (Paris, 1950), 1, p. 91.

9 Jean Wilson, *Entertainments*, pp. 61–85.

10 'A Chaine of Pearle' (1603) in *The Progresses and Public Processions of Queen Elizabeth*, ed. John Nichols (London, 1823), 111, p. 643.

11 *A True Accompt of...the Baptism of...Prince Henry Frederick, by the Grace of God Prince of Scotland...*, ed. Nichols, *Progresses*, 111, p. 367.

12 *The XV Bookes of P. Ovidius Naso, entytuled Metamorphosis*, ed. W. H. D. Rouse (London, 1961), p. 4.

13 *Minerva Britanna* (London, 1612), p. 54.

14 Abraham Fraunce, *The Third part of the Countesse of Pembrokes Yvychurch: Entituled, Amintas Dale* (London, 1592), fol. 47r.

15 Nichols, *Progresses* III, p. 403.
16 Schuler, *Fabularum Ovidii Interpretatio, Ethica, Physica, et Historica, tradita in Academia Regiomontana à Georgio Sabino* (Cambridge, 1584), p. 256 for p. 255.
17 *Ibid.*, 256.
18 John Studley, *Medea*, in *Seneca His Tenne Tragedies*, ed. Thomas Newton (London, 1581), fol. 126v.
19 The translator, whose imagination is caught by the evocation of that pristine state of innocence, widely amplifies its description, incorporating into it memories from Ovid's description of the Golden Age. In Virgil, *Eclogue* IV. 38–48, the return of the Golden Age is associated with the end of navigation.
20 Studley, *Medea*, fol. 127r. Studley used a Latin text giving 'Typhis' instead of 'Tethys', hence his translation of 'detegat' ('will display') by 'will survay'; this version emphasizes discovery and is more apt to be taken as a presage of modern exploration.
21 *Ovid's Elegies* II.xi, 1–6. All line references to Marlowe's works are to *The Complete Works of Christopher Marlowe*, ed. Fredson Bowers (Cambridge, 1973).
22 On the discussion about the state of completion of the poem, see W. L. Godshalk, '*Hero and Leander*: the Sense of an Ending', in *A Poet & a filthy Play-maker: New Essays on Christopher Marlowe*, eds. Kenneth Friedenreich, Roma Gill and Constance B. Kuriyama (New York, 1988), pp. 293–314. In '*Desunt nonnulla*: the Construction of Marlowe's *Hero and Leander* as an Unfinished Poem', *Journal of English Literary History* 51 (1984), 241–68, Marion Campbell argued 'that the poem "intends" to frustrate, not fulfill, readerly expectations, and that Marlowe's poem can be accounted for as a deliberate reversal of a famous story', p. 263.
23 Schuler, *Fabularum Ovidii Interpretatio*, p. 260. A similar interpretation was given by Boccaccio in his *Genealogie Deorum Gentilium Libri*, XIII.xxvi, ed. Vincenzo Romano (Bari, 1951), and developed by Joachim du Bellay in *Les Antiquités de Rome*, x, trans. Spenser, *The Ruines of Rome*, x.
24 'Our general named sundry islands, mountains, capes and harbours after the names of divers noblemen and other gentlemen his friends', *The second voyage of Master Martin Frobisher, made to the west and northwest regions, in the year 1577*, in Richard Hakluyt, *Voyages and Discoveries*, ed. Jack Beeching (Harmondsworth, 1972), p. 194.
25 This was first noted by Stephen Greenblatt in 'Marlowe and Renaissance Self-Fashioning', *Two Renaissance Mythmakers: Christopher Marlowe and Ben Jonson*, ed. Alvin Kernan (Baltimore, 1977), pp. 41–69, later reprinted in *Renaissance Self-Fashioning from More to Shakespeare* (Chicago, 1980).
26 Theocritus had noted that 'Thus came…the heroes to gird at

Heracles for a deserter because he wandered and left the good ship of the thirty thwarts', trans. J. M. Edmonds in *The Greek Bucolic Poets* (London, 1912), p. 163.

27 Compare with Beaumont and Fletcher, *The Scornful Lady*, ii.ii.7; *Philaster*, ii.iv.19; see also the trick played by M. Thomas on Hylas in *Monsieur Thomas*.

28 Theocritus, *Idylls*, xiii; Propertius, 1.20; Spenser, *Faerie Queene*, iii.xii.7. In Virgil, it becomes matter for a song in *Eclogs* vi.43–4, but set alongside the monstrous love of Pasiphae (to which Marlowe also alludes to in connection with Edward's loves in i.iv.13), sung by Silenus, it is a symbol of inordinate desire.

29 Erasmus, *Adagia*, chil. i, cent. 4, prov. 72, quoted from *Opera Omnia* (Lyon, 1703), ii, fol. 173 C.

30 Petrus Berchorius, *Ovidius Moralizatus*, vii, ed. J. Engels (Utrecht, 1962), fol. 54 a-b.

31 *Ovide Moralisé*, vii.799–806, ed. C. de Boer, Verhandelingen der Koninklijke Akademie van Wetenschappen te Amsterdam, Afdeeling Letterkunde Nieuwe Reeks Deel xxx (Amsterdam, 1931), iii. The *Ovide Moralisé* was transferring on to Ovid's fable the traditional typological interpretation of Gedeon's fleece.

32 *Metamorphoses Ovidii...expositae* (Paris, 1570), fol. 78 r.

33 'Or, as a ship after much pain and care, / For iron and cloth brings home rich Indian ware, / Hast thou trafficked, but with far more gain / Of noble goods, and with less time and pain?', *John Donne: the Complete English Poems*, ed. A. J. Smith (Harmondsworth, 1971), p. 331.

34 '...this is my south-west discovery / *Per fretum febris*, by these straits to die, / I joy, that in these straits, I see my west', *ibid.*, p. 348.

35 *De Archana Deorum*, vii.iii, ed. Robert A. van Kluyve (Durham, NC, 1968), pp. 108–109.

36 Edward A. Snow, 'Marlowe's *Doctor Faustus* and the Ends of Desire', *Two Renaissance Mythmakers*, pp. 70–110, p. 71.

CHAPTER 8

Pirates and 'turning Turk' in Renaissance drama

Lois Potter

Probably the best-known pirate incident in Renaissance drama is the interception of Hamlet's ship by 'a pirate of very warlike appointment' (IV.vi.14–15)[1] which becomes the means by which he gets back to Denmark while Rosencrantz and Guildenstern sail on towards England. Nineteenth-century readers were so troubled by this coincidence that several of them, independently, came to the conclusion that Hamlet had prearranged the interception as part of his revenge plot.[2] In fact, few events could have seemed less unlikely to an Elizabethan audience than an attack by a pirate ship. For one thing, there was a long literary tradition, deriving from the Greek romances, in which pirates were, as Jacques Lezra puts it, 'established agents of unexpected intrusion'.[3] Pirates were also, of course, a genuine threat, as indeed they still are.[4] It is the relation between the traditional and topical status of these characters that I propose to explore in this essay. I shall focus in particular on that aspect of piracy that was new to the seventeenth century: the brief period during which it was not only a means of cross-cultural exchange but also a threat to traditional English values.

The pirates of classical history and literature are often sympathetically presented: indeed, Thyamis in Heliodorus' *Æthiopica*, the apparent prototype of the 'Egyptian thief at point of death' (*Twelfth Night* v.i.116) who tries to kill his mistress so that no one else shall have her, has turned to piracy because his younger brother had usurped his role as hereditary priest of Memphis.[5] In due course, he is reunited with his family and restored to his rightful rank, much like the Banished Duke of *As You Like It*. Other classical pirates are portrayed, like Robin Hood, as exemplifying a kind of justice that cannot be found in supposedly civilized society. In a widely quoted anecdote (*De Republica*, III) Cicero had described a pirate's retort to Alexander the Great: 'For when that king had asked the man what he meant by keeping possession of the sea, he answered with bold pride, "What thou meanest by seizing the whole earth; but because I do it with a petty ship, I am called a robber, whilst thou who dost it with a great fleet art styled emperor."'[6] In the *Offices*, Cicero makes a similar point: describing the Illyrian pirate Bardylis or Bargalus as someone who 'got a great power by the fame of his justice in dividing the prey', he suggests ironically that justice, if it is admired even in pirates, must surely be still more valued in a state.[7] This comparison/contrast between piracy and government clearly stuck in Shakespeare's mind. In *2 Henry VI*, IV.i, a scene heavily loaded with classical references, a pirate bitterly attacks the Duke of Suffolk for his corruption of the country and the Duke replies with a scornful comparison of his accuser to Bargalus (105–7). Against this background, the fact that 'Suffolk dies by pirates' (138) is clearly meant to be rough justice.[8] Both York (in *2 Henry VI*, I.i.223–30) and Margaret (in *Richard III*, I.iii.158–9) compare their enemies to pirates who, in Margaret's words, 'fall out / In sharing that which you have pilled from me' (that is, England): the image recalls the striking opening of the Heliodorus romance, where Thyamis and his followers come upon the remains of a banquet that was brought to a bloody end by such a fight. The inspiration for Hamlet's encounter with the pirates is thus, like much else in Shakespeare, literary rather than topical; it is in keeping with the classical tradition that Hamlet describes the pirates as 'thieves of mercy' (*Hamlet* IV.vi.19), and that their action, however involuntarily, furthers his cause.[9] But the episode may also have some topical aspects. Nothing is said about the nationality of the pirates; the sailors in IV.vi. do not appear to be foreign, and the 'good turn' that Hamlet says he will do for them is presumably a request for their pardon, which would make sense only if they were his compatriots. The classical pirate rarely has any compunction about attacking his own countrymen but, after years of Elizabethan legalized privateering, the status of robbery at sea was a highly topical issue at the beginning of the seventeenth century.

By the time James I came to the throne, the English already had a reputation as the fiercest pirates in the Mediterranean and

Atlantic oceans. Much of what they did could be justified by the state of war with Spain and thus considered piracy only by their victims. But one of the first acts of James I's reign was the making of peace with Spain in 1604. Historians differ as to whether this peace actually lessened the activities of English pirates; one suggests that in fact 'their operations were continuous throughout the period'.[10] However, the peace with Spain was *perceived* as a blow to legitimate plunder and therefore something of an excuse for piracy. The view is not expressed directly, of course, but it is easy to read between the lines of, for instance, one Captain Harris, who in 1609 quoted the arguments that won him to a career of piracy:

> our most royall Soueraigne, and his prudent and graue counsell, on approoued considerations best knowne to his grace and the state, and not requisite for us that are subiects to enquire, hath lessend by this generall peace the flourishing imployment, that we seafaring men do bleede for at sea.[11]

A similar oblique criticism of the peace can be found in the popular spokesman Thomas Heywood. His *Troia Britannica*,[12] a verse account of the Trojan war, was published in 1609, the year of James' proclamation against pirates and the mass execution of nineteen of them, including the above-mentioned Captain Harris. The poem, in what may well be a last-minute addition, compares the end of Jupiter's wrath against the Trojans with James I's making peace with Spain (VI. 49, p. 124) – and attributes this change of heart to Ganymede's persuasion!

In his plays, of which the dates are less certain, Heywood also reflects the sense that the rules had somehow been changed unfairly. *Fortune by Land and Sea*, which he wrote with William Rowley, clearly relies on the existence of a recognized enemy. The hero, who has fallen on hard times, puts to sea and is chosen captain of a ship that has lost its own commander. The principles by which he and his crew operate are carefully distinguished from out-and-out piracy: 'We seek for purchase, but we tak't from foes, and such is held amongst us lawful spoyl; but such as are our friends & countrymen we succour with the best supply we have of victuals or munition being distrest' (sig. E2).[13] By contrast, the pirates Purser and Clinton prey on their own countrymen, justifying themselves on the ground that 'since our country have proclaim'd us pyrats and cut us off from any claim in *England*, we'l be no longer now call'd English men' (sig. E1 v). The hero captures the two pirates in a fair fight, and is rewarded with a knighthood. But Purser and Clinton are allowed to die not only courageously but patriotically. Purser's last speech can even be described as elegiac:

> But now our Sun is setting, night comes on, the watery wilderness ore which we raign'd, proves in our ruins peaceful, [Merchants] trade fearless abroad as in the rivers mouth, and free as in a harbor, then fair *Thames*, Queen of fresh water, famous through the world, and not the least through us, whose double tides must o'rflow our bodies, and being dead, may thy clear waves our scandals wash away, but keep our valours living. (sig. F3)

Fortune by Land and Sea was not published until 1655, though there are records of its performance in 1617 and it is dated 1607–9 in *Annals of English Drama*.[14] However, the historical Purser and Clinton were executed in 1583, so the play, however contemporary in its appeal, seems intended to appeal to nostalgia for an age of simpler values.[15] For the same reason, although part I of Heywood's *Fair Maid of the West* is usually dated between 1597 and 1604, I think that it is actually a Jacobean work.[16] Its heroine, Bess Bridges, is unperturbed when she hears that the four sea-captains drinking in her tavern may be pirates: 'No matter; we will take no note of them. Here they vent many brave commodities by which some gain accrues. Th'are my good customers, and still return me profit' (II.i.54–6). Bess can express such amoral views precisely because the play evokes a past era, less sophisticated but more straightforward, when English seamen were famous the world over and Spaniards were still fair game.

The polarities of Heywood's plays are simple ones. Against James I's policy of assimilation and conciliation he sets an image of Englishness defined chiefly as anti-Spanish. It is nationalistic rather than religious in its emphasis: anti-Catholic references apply only to Spain, and when the scene is North Africa, as at the end of part I and the beginning of part II of *The Fair Maid*, the nature of the Moors' religion is hardly raised, while their colour is made the subject of many offensive jokes. Similarly, when the action shifts to Italy in part II, the Catholicism of the Duke of Florence is as irrelevant to the play as his nationality. Though Bess is never called a pirate, and she ostensibly flies the black flag in mourning for her lover's supposed death rather than as a symbol of her trade, it is significant that the two rulers who most admire and reward her (after the inevitable attempts on her invincible virtue) are the King of Fez in Marmora and the Duke of Florence–both of them notorious patrons of pirates.[17]

Another feature of Heywood's cross-cultural contacts is that foreigners are consistently overwhelmed by the nobility of the English, to the point where this alone serves to convert them to Christianity. A characteristic example occurs in part II of *The Fair Maid* when a noble Moor, after vainly trying to compete in nobility with the Christians, finally gives in to their superior virtue:

> Such honor is not found in Barbary.
> The vertue in these Christians hath converted me,
> Which to the world I can no longer smother.
> Accept me, then, a Christian and a brother.
>
> (v.iv.184–7)

The reality behind these plays was far different. While many ships from England and other North European countries were indeed putting into North African ports in the early seventeenth century, they were not treated like honoured guests and allowed to reprieve their fellow-countrymen from bondage; they were servants of the state, which fixed the price of their prizes and connived at their notorious debauchery in exchange for the right to dispose of their spoils. It was pirates from the North who, by instructing the local sailors in the art of sailing larger ships, enabled Muslim pirates to penetrate to waters outside the Mediterranean. Moreover, the effect of Christian–Muslim contact on their respective religions was exactly the opposite of what Heywood envisaged. As N. I. Matar says, in 'The Renegade in English Seventeenth-Century Imagination', 'While Christians converted to Islam, Muslims did not redress the demographic imbalance and convert to Christianity.'[18]

The part of the North African coast containing the harbours of Algiers, Tunis, and Sallee was known collectively as Barbary. That its inhabitants are referred to in the drama both as Moors and as

Turks is understandable, since all three countries were Turkish regencies ruled by Viceroys sent from Constantinople, though with more autonomy than most other parts of the Turkish empire.[19] Like Venice, the cities inhabited by the pirates were cosmopolitan and relatively tolerant of other cultures, as long as their presence was profitable. The intermediaries who sold pirate booty were normally Jews, of whom there were considerable colonies in North Africa. Those who specialized in ransom and prizes were 'French Jews' or 'Christian Jews' from France or Leghorn, better treated than other North African Jews and under the protection of the French Consul.[20] The fact that Turks and Jews were 'both circumcized' is stressed by Barabas in *The Jew of Malta* (II.iii.215),[21] but George Sandys' *Relation of a Journey* (1613) notes that, despite this and other resemblances, 'the *Turkes* will not suffer a *Iew* to turne *Mahometan* vnlesse he first turne a kinde of Christian'.[22] So, in this curious triangulated relationship, the Jew was a commercial middleman between Christian and Muslim, while the Christian was, equally, a middleman in the process of conversion to Islam.

It was the extent of Christian apostasy, on a scale unprecedented since the period of the Crusades, that was most shocking to English readers. While some converts to Islam were captives, slaves who wanted to improve their treatment and their chances of eventual freedom, others had actually come to Barbary with a view to making their fortunes: 'Christian renegades were treated better than any other non-Turk in Barbary, and as members of the sect of *hamafi*, the sect of the Turkish ruling class, could enter the army and the highest posts in the government.'[23] The extent of these conversions is uncertain, but contemporaries perceived it as enormous. William Davies, a barber-surgeon who had visited Tunis, claimed in 1614 that Turkey and Barbary contained more renegades than native Turks.[24] His book includes an account of the ceremony by which the renegade publicly renounced Christianity:

He is put upon a horse with his face towards the tayle, and a Bow and an Arrow in his hand, then the picture of Christ is carried before him with his feete upwards, at the which he drawes his bow with the Arrow therein, and thus he rideth to the place of Circumcision, cursing his father that begate him, and his mother that bore him, his Country,' and all his kindred. (sig. B3 v)

The most famous of the English renegades was the pirate John Ward. Evidence about his early life is vague – to the point where one historian thinks that his story may be an amalgalm of tales about several different men.[25] His name became widely known only when he was already about fifty, after his greatest exploit, the seizing of a rich Venetian argosy in 1607. James I's proclamation against pirates, dated 8 January 1608–9, gave specific mention to the 'diuers great and enormious spoiles and Piracies heretofore committed within the Straits of *Gibraltar* and other places by Captain *Iohn Ward* and his adherents'. The proclamation adds that he is 'harbored in Tunis and Argiers', and urges English ships to be on the lookout for him but not to trade with him in any way. Ward quickly became a legendary figure: Donne's Elegy 14 gives, as an example of a conversational commonplace, the question 'whether Ward / The traffique of the Inland seas had marr'd'; two ballads and two pamphlets on him appeared in 1609.[26] In these, he is linked with another historical figure, the Dutch pirate Dansiker,[27] who is generally credited with transforming the North African navy. He had also been in the news recently because of an attempt to play Muslims and Christians off against each other: in 1609 he arrived in Marseilles, and offered, if allowed to fly the French flag, to turn against his recent base, Algiers, and put his galleys at the disposal of the French King.[28]

This is the material that went into the making of *A Christian Turn'd Turk, or, The Tragicall Liues and Deaths of the two Famous Pyrates, Ward and Dansiker* (1612). Its author, Robert Daborne, is probably best known to scholars for his begging letters to Philip Henslowe, which give a blow-by-blow account of an author at work. In what seems to have been his first play, he was writing for a children's company, the King's (or Queen's) Revels, of which he had just become the manager. This fact explains the play's surprising references to some of the characters as 'boys' and, perhaps, its allusions to *The Jew of Malta* and *The Spanish Tragedy*, plays that had been revived by child actors not long before.[29] The play, at least in its final form, cannot be much earlier than the year of its publication. In particular, it refers to one very recent event, the execution of Dansiker by the Dey of Tunis in 1611 – an event of importance precisely because pirates so rarely received official punishment. However, the event that clearly inspired the play was not Ward's piracy (which, the prologue suggests, may have been the subject of another play, now lost), but the reports, in 1610, that he had become a Muslim.

It is fair to say that *A Christian Turn'd Turk* is less bad than it will seem to anyone who reads it in the edited or unedited facsimiles which are the only currently available texts.[30] It must have been printed from papers nearly as foul as the hero: the list of dramatis personae is incomplete, crucial stage directions are missing, speeches are misattributed, and the awkward prose of the author's self-righteous preface does not help matters. Nevertheless, the story is fast-moving and interesting, and there is, in the beginning at least, some attempt to make Ward's character worth watching: he is brave, rough, but capable of reflection, although inclined to dismiss his better thoughts with a fatalism that is clearly condemned by the author. (Daborne soon after went into the Church.) However, the play is striking for its refusal to romanticize piracy as a profession. In the opening scene, two young men who have come on board Ward's ship to gamble realize to their horror that the pirates have hoisted sail and are carrying them out to sea. Ward and his lieutenant attempt, in language very like that used to Captain Harris (see above, p. 126), to persuade them that their country has been ungrateful in failing to provide them opportunities for action. To this, they reply that piracy is *not* action but 'theft, most hatefull'; the truly daring man is the merchant

> whose manly breast
> Scorning base gaine at home, puts to the maine
> With hazard of his life and state, from other lands
> To enrich his owne...
>
> (sig. B2)

After this opening sequence off the coast of Ireland, the scene shifts to Tunis, where Daborne effectively sketches in the rowdy community of English expatriates and Jewish middlemen that he could have read about in the pirate pamphlets and travel literature of the period. This interesting gathering includes a receiver of stolen goods, Benwash, a Jew who has turned Turk in order to keep his wife from being prostituted to others. This character, especially in his relationship to his comic and equally villainous servant, owes a lot to Marlowe's Barabas; he and his servant also refer specifically to 'the play of Pedringano' in *The Spanish Tragedy*, the classic example of a double-cross of servant by master, which is repeated at the end of the play. Unfortunately, once the characters are assembled at Benwash's seedy establishment, the play turns into a series of predictable sexual intrigues.[31] Benwash's wife has an affair with the pirate Gallop, and both are eventually murdered by the jealous husband; Voada, sister of the 'Crossman' (Cara Osman, leader of the janissaries and the most powerful man in Tunis), falls in love with Ward's page, who is actually a woman in disguise; and Ward becomes infatuated with Voada. It is through his passion for her, not through any serious discussion of Islamic beliefs, that he is persuaded to change his religion. The ceremony of 'turning Turk' is depicted in dumb show and described by a Chorus. Other characters try to dissuade Ward before the event and discuss his actions with horror afterwards. The renegade soon suffers losses at sea, through the burning of the pirate fleet (this event, which really took place in July 1609, is here attributed to Dansiker and depicted as heroic). Voada promptly deserts Ward and betrays him to his enemies, and Ward falls in with the general view of women as devils that has been expressed by most of the other characters. Through a complicated series of double-crosses, which appear to have satisfied the company's taste for intricate plotting,[32] most of the characters are destroyed. Ward himself recognizes his awful fate as a just punishment. In his last words he curses the Turks, hopes that a reunited Christendom will lead a crusade to free Jerusalem, and warns 'All you that liue by theft and Piracies' to take warning from him. (sig. I4 r-v)

Daborne's preface makes it clear that 'this oppressed and much martird Tragedy' was unsuccessful in the theatre, and claims that his main intention in printing it is to 'publish my innocence concerning the wrong of worthy personages, together with doing some right to the much-suffering Actors' (A3). If audiences did not simply object to the blasphemy of the scene in which Ward renounces Christianity, the play's failure may have been due to its giving personal offence. The most obvious persons to be offended would be those who knew what liberties Daborne had taken with the ending, since Ward, far from expiring with curses on his lips, went on living comfortably in Tunis, where he died of the plague in 1622. Dekker's *If This Be Not a Good Play, the Devil is In It* (also published 1612) may have set out to answer this particular inaccuracy in its final scene. Hearing that the devils have brought 'Soules, for whose comming all hell long hath sought', Pluto excitedly asks whether this means Ward and Dansiker. (v.iv.82–3).[33] He is told that Dansiker has just arrived but that 'Ward is not ripe for damming yet' (94):

> The Merchants are not pilld nor pulld enough,
> They are yet but shauen, when they are fleade [flayed]
>   hee'le come.
> And bring to hell fat booties of rich theeues,
> A crew of swearers and drinkers the best that liues.
>
>   (90–3)

That Ward should be mentioned with such prominence, in a scene that features the punishments of the arch-traitors Guy Fawkes and Ravaillac, indicates the horror with which the dramatist regarded his turning against his own country and religion. At the same time, the tone of the passage is curiously flippant by contrast both with its treatment of the other traitors and with Daborne's portrayal of Ward's apostasy in *A Christian Turn'd Turk*. It is more in keeping with a throwaway line that occurs earlier in the play: 'I thought the diuell was turnde Merchant, theres so many Pirates at Sea' (iv.ii.58–9). This uncertainty of tone results from the clash between the romantic treatment of piracy, with its accompanying satire on supposedly respectable merchants, and the horror inspired by the specific case of Ward.

There are other reasons why the play might have been considered offensive. Baldwin Maxwell has suggested that the Verney family may have recognized in another of the play's characters, the pirate Francisco, an allusion to Sir Francis Verney, who became a pirate in 1608 or 1609 and was reported in 1610 as having turned Turk along with Ward.[34] Another possibility is that some may have seen the story as an attack on Daborne's immediate predecessor as patentee of the King's Revels company at the Whitefriars, Lording Barry. Barry took over the already struggling company in 1607, and wrote a play for it: *Ram Alley, or Merry Tricks*.

A combination of bad luck (the plague) and bad management led to a rapid decline in the theatre; Barry was jailed for debt, released on bail, and, in a merry trick of his own, fled the country. By August 1608 he had become a pirate. Most of those with whom he consorted were hanged in 1609 but he escaped this fate (possibly because of his status as a gentleman) and survived to conduct a successful career as a shipowner on the edge of the law. Given the number of literary figures with whom he had been associated during his brief period in theatrical management (Michael Drayton was one), it is unlikely that any enthusiastic theatregoer would have been unaware of Barry's history. C. L'Estrange-Ewen, who (in two privately printed monographs) traced both Ward's history and Barry's shady career through the Admiralty records, noted that the abduction in the opening episode of *A Christian Turn'd Turk* actually resembles an episode with which Barry was charged by one of the pirates hanged in 1609.[35] Barry himself never turned Turk. His career was more like that of the profligate Count Lodovico in Webster's *The White Devil*, who is banished, rumoured to have become a pirate, and then pardoned.[36] However, given the number of tradesmen who were probably ruined by Barry's abandoning of his creditors, and Daborne's obvious sympathy with hard-working respectable men, it is quite possible that he intended Ward's career to be seen as an analogy to Barry's.

Verney died in 1615, but Barry was still known as a pirate in 1614–15, at which time his lieutenant was said to have been 'a player in England.'[37] Their stories show the extent to which piracy had become part of everyday experience in the first decades of the seventeenth century. Thus, it is evident that Bianca's casual question in *Women Beware Women* (1620–7, published 1657) – 'What news now of the pirates; any stirring?' (III.i.153) – is not as inane as it looks:[38] the Duke of Buckingham had become Lord Admiral in 1619 and it was hoped that he would make a vigorous effort to stamp out piracy.[39] It clearly remained an interesting topic for another twenty years, but the figure of the English renegade is less prominent; Massinger's *The Renegade*, a much more serious treatment of the Christian–Muslim conflict than Daborne's, is based on Spanish sources.[40]

I have already said that, for Shakespeare, the topicality of piracy was less important than its literary heritage. He generally uses the phrase 'to turn Turk' in a purely metaphorical or proverbial sense, as when Hamlet asks Horatio to consider his chances of making a successful career as an actor, 'if the rest of my fortunes turn Turk with me' (III.ii.269–70). To turn Turk, in this context, was to be as cruel as Turks were purported to be, whereas when Antonio speculates that Shylock will 'turn Christian' it is only in the sense that 'he grows kind' (*Merchant of Venice*, I.iii.174). There is, however, a difference when Othello raises his idea of the unthinkable horror: 'Are we turn'd Turks?' (II.iii.161). Like the use of the cliché 'it was Greek to me' in *Julius Caesar* (I.ii.281), when someone has in fact spoken Greek, the phrase has a literal as well as a metaphorical meaning in this play where the Turks are as much internal as external to the characters.[41] Othello's elopement with Desdemona is as dubious as the actions of some English privateers. Brabantio regards him as a 'foul thief' (I.ii.62) but Iago sees that all depends on the government's attitude:

> he tonight hath boarded a land-carrack.
> If it prove lawful prize, he's made forever.
>
> (I.ii.50–1)

The real pirate is of course Iago himself, who sails under false colours, telling Roderigo that 'I must show out a flag and sign of love, / Which is indeed but sign.' (I.i.156–7) Othello is a converted Moor like Joffer (though we never learn the motives for his conversion), but Iago claims that Desdemona could use her sexual power to make him 'renounce his baptism' (II.iii.334). Even the sight of her dead body makes her uncle Gratiano reflect that she might have been an agent of damnation for her father, if he were still alive (v.ii.205–10). Despite the angelic and even divine images so often used of Desdemona, this theme of the renegade led astray by a *femme fatale* haunts the play.

In *Antony and Cleopatra*, of course, the theme is made explicit. Perhaps the Egyptian setting of Plutarch's history recalled the Egyptian atmosphere so important to the Greek romances. The historical pirates who appear in the Shakespeare play – Sextus Pompeius, Menecrates and Menas – are typical both in their willingness to turn respectable by betraying other pirates (in the treaty Pompey accepts in II.vi.34–6) and in their flirtation with the idea of putting to sea while their guests are feasting on Pompey's galley. They are also analogues for the queen who, 'when she first met Mark Antony,...pursed up his heart upon the River of Cydnus' (II.ii.186–7). Like the renegades, Antony adopts the luxurious and sensual eastern life, rejecting the Roman values of Octavius and Octavia which, as depicted here, resemble the solid, puritanical virtues stressed by Heywood and Daborne. Like Othello, however, he is a renegade in reverse, since what he abandons is not Christianity. Ward, in Daborne's play, sounds almost like Antony when, having fallen in love with Voada, he abruptly decides that 'If there be any Divinity, it hath / His seate in beauty' (sig. E4 v). His view is of course condemned by, and in, the play. By contrast, his classical sources empowered Shakespeare to evoke, as Daborne and others could not do, not only what the renegade loses but the real attractions of what he gains.[42]

NOTES

1 Shakespeare's plays are quoted from the relevant Arden editions.

2 See the note on this passage in the Furness Variorum, also D. J. Snider's essay of 1873 (quoted in the appendix, II, p. 184). D. S. Savage, *Hamlet and the Pirates, an Exercise in Literary Detection* (London, 1950) adds the suggestion that the episode also satirizes those who had pirated the text of the play itself. Most editors dismiss the conspiracy theory; see, for example, Harold Jenkins in the Arden edition (London, 1982), III.iv.207–11, n., and IV.vi.19, n.

3 Jacques Lezra, 'Pirating Reading: the Appearance of History in *Measure for Measure*', *ELH* 56 (1989), 255–92, quote p. 266. Though the purpose of Lezra's witty essay is different from mine, his notes provide some useful sources on piracy in the early seventeenth century.

4 See Gérard A. Jaeger, ed., *Vues sur la piraterie des origines à nos jours* (Paris, 1992), which includes modern piracy and highjacking. I should like to thank Madame Ulane Bonnel for bringing this work to my attention.

5 Heliodorus, *An Aethiopian History*, trans. Thomas Underdowne, The Tudor Translations, (London, 1895), I, p. 29. The suggestion that the lines in *Twelfth Night* refer to him was first made by Theobald in 1733.

6 Quoted Augustine, *City of God*, IV, iv, in *St Augustine: the Political Writings*, ed. Henry Paolucci (Washington, DC, 1962), pp. 29–30. The same story is told in Villon's Testament (xvii–xx), possibly via John of

Salisbury's *Polycraticus*; see the note on 'Diomedès' in François Villon, *Œuvres*, ed. André Mary, Classiques Garnier (Paris, n.d.). I owe the Villon reference to the useful chronological table in Jaeger, ed., *Vues*, p. 444. Compare the Pirate King in W. S. Gilbert's *Pirates of Penzance*: 'I don't think much of our profession, but, contrasted with respectability, it is comparatively honest' (*The Complete Plays of Gilbert and Sullivan* (New York, n.d.), I, p. 145).

7 Marcus Tullius Cicero, *Cicero's Offices*, trans. Thomas Cockman, introduction by John Warrington, Everyman's Library (London and New York, 1909, rpt. 1966), II.xi, p. 89.

8 For Shakespeare's possible alteration of the Quarto text to create an allusion to Cicero, see Andrew S. Cairncross' introduction to the Arden edition (London, 1957), p. xliv. Illyria was famous for piracy in classical times and the sixteenth century – a fact that may influence the treatment of Antonio in *Twelfth Night*. See Alberto Tenenti, *Piracy and the Decline of Venice 1580–1615*, first published as *Venezia e i Corsari*, (Bari, 1961), trans. Janet and Brian Pullen (Berkeley and Los Angeles, 1967), pp. 3–15.

9 Harold Jenkins has plausibly suggested that the episode recalls Plutarch's Life of Julius Caesar. See Arden *Hamlet*, p. 104.

10 Sir Godfrey Fisher, *The Barbary Legend: War, Trade and Piracy in North Africa 1415–1830* (Oxford, 1957; Westport, CT, 1974), pp. 140–3.

11 *The Lives, Apprehensions, Arraignments, and Executions, of the 19. late Pyrates. Namely: Capt. Harris, Iennings. Longcastle. Downes. Haulsey. and their companies*, printed for John Busby the elder (London, 1609), sig. B1 v.

12 *Troia Britanica: or, Great Britaines Troy. A Poem Deuided into XVII. seuerall Cantons*, W. Jaggard (London, 1609).

13 *Fortune by Land and Sea. A Tragi-Comedy*, (London, 1655). Much of the play, as here, is verse but printed as prose.

14 *Annals of English Drama*, ed. Alfred Harbage, rev. Samuel Schoenbaum (1964); 3rd edn rev. Sylvia Stoler Wagonheim (London and New York, 1989). Dates given for plays are based on this book.

15 A pamphlet about Purser and Clinton (*A True Relation of the Lives and Deaths of the Two Most famous English Pirates...*), was published in 1639, possibly to take advantage of the interest aroused when an English captain seized the port of Sallee, a pirate stronghold, in 1637. It is possible that Heywood wrote this too: both play and pamphlet contain a comic episode (a proclamation repeated in garbled form by a clown) that goes back at least to the Wakefield mystery play of *Abel*.

16 I quote from the edition of *The Fair Maid of the West, parts I and II*, by Robert K. Turner (Lincoln, NE, 1967). The explicit references to Essex and the naming of Ralegh, which Turner and others have seen as evidence that part 1 followed closely on their Cadiz and Islands

expeditions of 1596 and 1597, seem to me, on the contrary, unlikely in the lifetimes of the persons mentioned.

17 See for example, Fisher, *Barbary Legend, passim.*

18 *Studies in English Literature*, 33 (1993), 489–505, quote, p. 501.

19 See, apart from the works already mentioned, Christopher Lloyd, *English Corsairs on the Barbary Coast* (London, 1981); Peter Earle, *Corsairs of Malta and Barbary* (London, 1970), and Pierre Boyer, 'état pirate ou état corsaire: les Barbaresques', in Jaeger, ed., *Vues*, pp. 61–9.

20 Earle, *ibid.*, p. 75.

21 *The Complete Works of Christopher Marlowe*, ed. Fredson Bowers, 2 vols, (Cambridge, 1973).

22 *A Relation of a Journey begun An. Dom. 1610*, four books, 2nd edn, London, 1615 (Amsterdam and New York, 1973), book 3, p. 147. Martin Wiggins has suggested that Sandys refers to the need to find an equivalent for the ceremony of circumcision that accompanied a Christian's acceptance of the Islamic faith.

23 Earle, *Corsairs*, p. 30.

24 *The True Relation of the Travailes and most miserable Captivitie of William Davies, Barber-Surgion of London, under the Duke of Florence* (London, 1614), sig. B3 v.

25 Fisher, *Barbary Legend*, pp 160–1.

26 C. L'Estrange-Ewen, *Captain John Ward, 'Arch-Pirate'*, printed for the author, 31 Marine Drive (Paignton, October 1939), p. 2.

27 Also spelled Danseker, Danziger, etc., in the various works where he is mentioned. I have arbitrarily normalized the spelling.

28 Tenenti, *Piracy*, pp. 84–5.

29 Matar suggests ('The Renegade', 492–3) that the main influence is *Dr Faustus*; Ward sells his soul for lust and material rewards. An epigram by Samuel Rowlands puns on his name: 'Perpetuall flames is reprobates Re-warde' ('To a Reprobate Pirat that hath renounced Christ and is turn'd Turke', in *Complete Works of Samuel Rowlands, 1598–1628* (1880, rpt. New York, 1930), II, sig. B2, quoted by Matar, 495).

30 I quote from the photocopy of the original 1612 edition produced by the Da Capo Press, Theatrum Orbis Terrarum Ltd. (Amsterdam and New York, 1973). The play has been edited by A. E. H. Swaen, *Robert Daborne's Plays*, in *Anglia* 20 (1898), 153–256, also reprinting Daborne's interesting letters and the two ballads about Ward. But his is an old-spelling edition, not much easier to read than the original and, in these days of photofacsimiles, no easier to obtain.

31 Baldwin Maxwell argues that Daborne's habit of starting a new play before he had finished the one he was working on resulted in a repetition of the plot of *The Poor Man's Comfort*. Baldwin Maxwell,

'Notes on Robert Daborne's Extant Plays', *Philological Quarterly* 50 (1971), 85–98, quote p. 96.

32 One of the few other plays known to have been written for this group, John Mason's *The Turk* (*c.* 1607), brags on the title-page of its second edition (1610) that it is 'full of interchangeable variety, beyond expectation'. Its title may also indicate a current fashion for Turkish subjects, since the play is, in fact, more about Italy than Turkey.

33 Fredson Bowers, ed., *The Dramatic Works of Thomas Dekker* (Cambridge, 1958), III. This was a Red Bull play; Daborne was writing for the Red Bull at this period and may therefore have had a hand in this part of the play.

34 Maxwell, 'Notes on Robert Daborne's Extant Plays', 97–8. The only objection to this view is that Francisco is several times referred to as a boy, and is depicted earnestly pleading with Ward not to renounce his religion. However, Daborne may have altered the printed text in an attempt to undo the damage he had done.

35 C. L'Estrange-Ewen, *Lording Barry, Poet and Pirate* (privately printed, 1938), p. 9. Elsewhere, L'Estrange-Ewen refers to an unpublished book on Robert Daborne – which, unfortunately, appears to have remained unpublished – in which he explains that Daborne's father had suffered much at the hands of pirates. See his *Captain John Ward*, 'Arch-Pirate', p. 1. Claims of having been abducted by pirates were common in the period: a number of the pirates hanged in 1609 claimed this as the cause of their induction into crime. Sir Henry Manwaring, a reformed pirate himself, confessed in 1618 that he and other pirates sometimes arranged fake kidnappings for the benefit of those who wanted to join him, thus providing 'cover' in case they might later want to return to respectability. See *The Life and Works of Sir Henry Manwaring*, ed. G. E. Manwaring, Navy Records Society 2 vols. (vol I. 1920, vol II.1922), II, pp. 22–3. For Manwaring's life, see I, pp. 12–46.

36 As F. L. Lucas points out, the historical Lodovico was a pirate and Venice was much troubled by them in this period; see the introduction to his edition of the play (London, 1927, rev. 1958), p. 31. The play might also allude to the commission of 1610, intended to take the pirate Peter Easton, who was said to have forty ships under him; Manwaring, who was appointed one of the captains in this expedition, had himself turned pirate by 1612. See Manwaring, I, pp. 7–31.

37 L'Estrange-Ewen, *Lording Barry*, p. 14, n.

38 Thomas Middleton, *Five Plays*, eds. Bryan Loughrey and Neil Taylor (London, 1988).

39 Lloyd, *English Corsairs*, pp. 66–7.

40 See Colin Gibson's introduction to the play in *Plays and Poems of Philip*

Massinger, eds. Philip Edwards and Colin Gibson (Oxford, 1976), ii, pp. 2–4.

41 For 'the Turk' as a metaphor for the barbarian in both Othello and Iago, see the essay by Alvin Kernan prefaced to the Signet edition of *Othello* (New York, 1963, rpt. 1986), pp. xxxii-iii.

42 I should like to thank my research assistants, Pamela Vasile and Mark Netzloff, for their help with various stages of this essay.

CHAPTER 9

The wrong end of the telescope

Brian Gibbons

At the beginning of *Utopia* Sir Thomas More offers to justify presenting yet another traveller's tale. Nothing, says More, 'is more easy to be found, than be barking Scyllas, ravening Celaenos, and Laestrygonians, devourers of people, and such like great and incredible monsters; but to find citizens ruled by good and wholesome laws, that is an exceeding rare and hard thing'.[1] More gains his ironic effects through straight-faced parody. In the account of Utopia the narrative conventions of the traveller's tale are preserved, and with them the usual anticipation of the exotic and marvellous; only in place of barbaric rites comes a description of a society which uses – of all things – reason as a basis for social organization. Since the name of the narrator, Hythloday, in Greek means 'dispenser of nonsense', a Lucianic intention has been shrewdly suspected here, although commentators differ in their assessment of how far the Lucianic influence goes. On the one hand, there are those like Douglas Duncan who argue the case for *Utopia* as wilfully provocative, in the Lucianic spirit of serious play, seeing More's intention as to highlight problems, 'not to test perception of a "true" point of view so much as to enforce awareness of difficulty'.[2] On the other hand, are those like Paul Turner, believing that the book does attempt to solve the problems of human society.[3]

Thomas More combines diverse elements in *Utopia* – the political, (going back to Plato), the paradisaic and the traveller's tale – and he adds the precious but risky innovation of topicality. *Utopia* is a mirror of European conditions, rather than a lens through which remote Otherness might be perceived, yet by directly alluding to the voyages of Amerigo Vespucci, More reminds his readers that to hold up a mirror to Europe's faults now, in 1516, in the great age of exploration and colonization, is directly to address that global enterprise, and the ideological debate that accompanied it. Furthermore, an analysis as intellectually sharp and radical as *Utopia* constitutes an original contribution to anthropology.

One result of More's hybridization and irony is to modify the effect of the several elements. The potential weakness of the debate format – with its artificially one-sided emphasis and advocacy – is overcome. At the same time the full imaginative power of another element, the traveller's tale, is here qualified: *Utopia* does not imaginatively convey that fundamental disorientation which is the most feared – and desired – aim of the explorer, and which justifies his traditional, symbolic preoccupation with the monstrous. Not that in *Utopia* More freed the mode from monsters, only that the monstrous is present there in the form of oppressive social and bureaucratic systems. As subsequent works in the Utopian tradition show, it is one of the strengths of its hybrid make-up that it invites a variety of possible emphases. In a Utopian fiction the theme of disorientation is always a potential centre; for instance, it resurfaces with extraordinary power at the beginning of Conrad's *Heart of Darkness*. There, on board the yawl *Nellie*, anchored in the sea-reach of the Thames, Conrad assembles five practical men of affairs – a lawyer, an accountant, a company director and two mariners – a somewhat droll choice for a symposium.

Gazing at the broad sea-reach of the Thames as dusk falls, Conrad's narrator, himself an old salt, succumbs to Victorian sentiment and conjures up a patriotic pageant featuring the Thames as loyal servant to the British empire:[4]

It had known and served all the men of whom the nation is proud, from Sir Francis Drake to Sir John Franklin, knights all, titled and untitled – the great knights-errant of the sea.

As the purple prose swells, Conrad finds the temptation to parody irresistible:

They had sailed from Deptford, from Greenwich, from Erith – the adventurers and the settlers; king's ships and the ships of men on 'Change; captains, admirals, the dark 'interlopers' of the Eastern trade, and the commissioned 'generals' of East India fleets. Hunters for gold or pursuers of fame, they had all gone out on that stream, bearing the sword, and often the torch, messengers of the might within the land, bearers of a spark from the sacred fire.

This, incidentally, seems to have proved too much for T. S. Eliot, judging by the ironic echo in part III of *East Coker*:

> O dark dark dark. They all go into the dark,
> The vacant interstellar spaces, the vacant into the vacant,
> The captains, merchant bankers, eminent men of letters,
> The generous patrons of art, the statesmen and the rulers,
> Distinguished civil servants, chairmen of many committees,
> Industrial lords and petty contractors, all go into the dark,...

Certainly it is too much for the other mariner of the group, Marlow, who remarks that 'The conquest of the earth, which mostly means the taking it away from those who have a different complexion or slightly flatter noses than ourselves, is not a pretty thing when you look into it too much.' Marlow offers an alternative historical perspective, of nineteen hundred years ago. He visualizes the Thames through the eyes of the first Romans as they arrived. For them it must have been 'the very end of the world' – 'Sand-banks, marshes, forests, savages, precious little to eat fit for civilised man'. As Marlow continues, he succumbs to a different (if no less typically Victorian) compulsion: 'marsh' metamorphoses into 'swamp', 'forest' metamorphoses into 'jungles' – 'all that mysterious life of the wilderness that stirs in the forest, in the jungles, in the hearts of wild men'. A moment later this transforms itself into unnamed 'mysteries', the 'incomprehensible', and 'abomination'. To Marlow, as dusk falls and outlines blur, time and distance no longer provide security for civilization, and the Thames reflects both a history and a prophecy of barbarity. Conrad's narrator bluffly plays down Marlow's Ancient Mariner propensities, explaining him as atypical, a seaman but a wanderer too, in contrast to most seamen 'whose minds are of the stay-at-home order'.

Conrad's tale is an example of the dark end of the spectrum of Utopian writing, something which should not be overlooked in Elizabethan treatments of Utopian themes. The Elizabethans associated More with a deceptiveness in which genuine gravity was combined with a taste for practical jokes, and with a propensity to use humour as a serious philosophical tool. At the same time, in his special, equivocal mingling of engagement and detachment, there is, ultimately, something disturbing about the tradition More bequeathed.

This may provide a useful context in which to consider the interrelations of some plays concerned with ideas about a commonwealth: a first pair written in the same year, 1599, *King Henry V* and *The Shoemaker's Holiday*; a second pair, *The Tempest* and *Bartholmew Fair* (1610 and 1614); and in between, *Eastward Ho!* of 1605.[5]

Shakespeare's *King Henry V* (1599) is a play concerned with ideas of commonwealth, with a voyage of conquest and colonization, and the attendant concern with cultural contrasts. I start from the proposition that the play's concerns are with English society: the expedition to foreign parts allows an anatomy of Britain, and it is so little interested in France that the chief impression conveyed by the episodes representing the French is that they are designed to stress English prejudices, to demonstrate that chauvinism is as English as Tewkesbury mustard.

This is Shakespeare's fourth play about the Bolingbrokes, father and son, and like the last movement of a quartet it offers in presto time a reprise of motifs from earlier movements, and with a certain effect of distancing: the exclusion of Falstaff, like the addition of the Chorus, points to Shakespeare's interest in individuals as they represent issues; short shrift is given to them as they face their personal fate. The play's design presents exemplary groups through whose interplay the political discourse is dramatized, and this is a feature parallelled in *The Tempest* and *Bartholmew Fair*.

King Henry V is a play about English society, but in wartime, when instability sets all on hazard, especially allegiances and identities. Wartime makes chances for the quick-witted – court factions, gentlemen, the prelates, the common people. Representatives from the outlying parts of Britain – Wales, Ireland and Scotland – are prominent, and their regional accents implicitly signal their long tribal history of antagonism to the central power England, and mark their past history of disruption, and indicate their potential future if once again marginalized. Early on in the action, Henry V deals with devious prelates and a failed putsch at court, but it is only when he threatens the citizens of Harfleur that he directly confronts uncontrollable violence. The border between civilization and anarchy now looks decidedly provisional:

> What rein can hold licentious wickedness
> When down the hill he holds his fierce career?
> We may as bootless spend our vain command
> Upon th'enraged soldiers in their spoil
> As send precepts to the Leviathan
> To come ashore. Therefore you men of Harfleur,
> Take pity of your town and of your people
> Whiles yet my soldiers are in my command,
> ...
> If not, why, in a moment look to see
> The blind and bloody soldier with foul hand
> Defile the locks of your still-shrieking daughters,
> Your fathers taken by the silver beards,
> And their most reverend heads dashed to the walls,
> Your naked infants spitted upon pikes. (III.iii.22–9, 33–8)

The tactical intention of this rhetoric is plain, to terrify the citizens, but it also constitutes a less controlled, imaginative enactment by Henry V, in advance of the real thing, of sheer immersion in violence.

By showing battle scenes and the preparation for battle, Shakespeare directly relates the power of the King to his common soldiers. The doctrine of the King's two bodies is put in testing contexts, whether hand-to-hand combat or man-to-man debate at night in the camp. The night scene before Agincourt is not in Holinshed, Shakespeare invents it, taking the desacralization process far into Machiavellian territory. In flat contradiction of this, however, Agincourt itself is endowed with mythic status: Shakespeare suppresses reference to Henry's use of hidden archers and protective stakes – a 'politike invention' as Holinshed calls them – which played a crucial part in the historical victory. Thus Agincourt is made to appear to be a victory against impossible odds and is felt and claimed as miraculous, although elsewhere Machiavellian principles are shown producing modern, scientifically planned success for Henry V. This ambivalence is typical of the play's general dialectical mode. It disconcerts in reminding its Elizabethan audience, in 1599, of England's long equivocal history of great possessions won but then lost in France. The sea-borne

expedition described by the Chorus might remind an audience of
the recent English armada led by Essex to crush revolt in Ireland,
but talk of naval invasion could equally well remind an Elizabethan
audience that invasions had been incoming as well as outgoing.
Recent expeditions further afield might also come to mind – across
the Atlantic, never mind the Channel or the Irish Sea – although
the record of Tudor colonization in Virginia was one of failure.
Henry V's proposed expedition to France is seen from disconcertingly
multiple aspects: the new King is personally challenged from home
as well as abroad, so that chivalric and patriotic attitudes are starkly
juxtaposed to politic calculation and acquisitive opportunism. To
the end the play offers a double perspective. The Chorus reminds
us that after Henry V's success, France would be lost and England
itself would eventually unravel in a civil war – 'Which oft our stage
has shown'. Every kind of border would then crumble:

> For those do hold or break,
> As men are strong or weak

– as Marvell's bleak words insist.

   In the same year as Shakespeare's *King Henry V*, Thomas Dekker
offered a rival account of Henry V's commonwealth – in *The
Shoemaker's Holiday*. Dekker's play shows that he recognized clearly
the ironic and dialectical elements of Shakespeare's play *King Henry
V*, and as clearly opposed them: he presents a pageant-style
approach to political drama; he elides the dark central concerns of
Shakespeare, and offers an agreeable populism to paper over the
cracks which Shakespeare deliberately exposes.

   Dekker's narrative frame is simple, concerning the rise to wealth
and fame of a modest tradesman to Lord Mayor of London. The
implicit parallel between this bourgeois success story and that of
Shakespeare's King is made explicit in act v when Dekker's Henry
V makes an appearance to give his blessing. In place of Shakespeare's
wide geographical and social panorama, Dekker confines the
action to the City of London. King Henry V's war is referred to,
but only to be made the occasion for London pride. We never see
France or even a Frenchman. Patriotism is expressed through a
local hierarchy of family, trade, guild, mayor and corporation. The
vicious aspects of the nation's economic and class systems are

localized in terms of the trials of a single individual, a journeyman shoemaker, called up, sent to war, returning crippled and only rescuing his wife from a well-born gentleman in the nick of time. Dekker ensures that his King Henry V appears only at the very end, an isolated royal icon, apparently untainted by his connections with the upper classes and enjoying relations of mutual esteem with the tradesmen.

Dekker relies on Morality conventions, but he fails to avoid recycling their parochial ideology. Dekker's deference to the City of London unintentionally exposes the gap between its public image and its actual practice. In recasting the design of *King Henry V* for *The Shoemaker's Holiday* Dekker divides the action, making a conventional sub-plot for the story of the journeyman who goes to war. This effectively subdues the real imaginative centre of *King Henry V*, the confrontation with the violence which every civilization seeks to appease by codes of law and religion.

Eastward Ho! (1605) a collaborative work by Jonson, Chapman and Marston, is from the first moments an obvious burlesque of *The Shoemaker's Holiday*. Its authors follow Dekker in confining the dramatic action to London, but their alterations to pace and tone completely change the emphasis. They exaggerate the parable scheme of Dekker's story. The tradesman is now given two apprentices, one industrious, named Golding, one prodigal, named Quicksilver. The success story is taken to extremes, as are the didactic implications: the industrious apprentice wins a reward almost on a par with the miraculous victory of Henry V, is given meteoric promotion to Alderman on the very day he completes his apprenticeship, while coincidentally Quicksilver is locked up in the Counter prison. In principle the parable of the prodigal is composed of a simple set of narrative elements: moral desert is encoded as material reward. In *Eastward Ho!* it only takes a little further exaggeration of Dekker to make his simplistic adaptation of the prodigal theme appear ludicrous in relation to the complex of social issues he offers to address.

Besides this general burlesque of *The Shoemaker's Holiday*, the title itself, *Eastward Ho!*, signals allusion to City Comedies even closer at hand. Scholars have tended to leave it at that. But what about the connection to *King Henry V*, the play that lies behind Dekker? Two of *Eastward Ho!*'s authors, Chapman and Jonson, had classical interests, and it seems reasonable to suppose they had their reservations about Shakespeare's 'epic' style in *King Henry V*. All three of *Eastward Ho!*'s authors, as writers of City Comedy, would have taken an appreciative interest in Shakespeare's bitingly ironic reuse, in his story of Prince Hal in *King Henry IV* and *King Henry V*, of the old-fashioned Tudor dramatic schema of the Prodigal. In *Eastward Ho!* we also see (though in outright parodic style) a moralizing father anxious about his heir and the future of the family business, a titled prodigal, tavern scenes, a comic treatment of fashionable ladies and sordid financial deals preceding a voyage of colonial adventure. It is obvious that *King Henry V* is not the exclusive, consistent object of parody in *Eastward Ho!*[6] nor would one expect it to be, given the way Jacobean dramatic parody usually works; but the parodic connections between the two plays do seem to me worth exploring.

Henry V, receiving the insulting gift of a tun of royal tennis balls, elaborately extends the Dauphin's conceit:

> When we have matched our rackets to these balls
> We will in France, by God's grace, play a set
> Shall strike his father's crown into the hazard.
>
> (I.ii.261–3)

(At the same time, such an offer to turn the Dauphin's balls to stone does strike one as more appropriate to the Parc des Princes than the All England Club at Wimbledon.) In *Eastward Ho!* also, sporting metaphors express a view of international affairs, although in a somewhat less high-falutin tone of voice –

I shall be a merchant forsooth, trust my estate in a wooden trough as he does! What are these ships but tennis-balls for the winds to play withal? Tossed from one wave to another: now under-line, now over the house; sometimes brick-walled against a rock, so that the guts fly out again; sometimes struck under the wide hazard, and farewell, master merchant!
(II.ii.58–64)

The speaker is Quicksilver, setting out on a heroic career Jacobean-style: get rich quick from a voyage to Virginia, then buy favour at court. His mistress warns him 'the seas you say are uncertain; but he that sails your court seas shall find 'em ten times fuller of hazard' (II.ii.65–7). Security the banker chips in with Wall Street wisdom: 'all trades complain of inconvenience, and therefore 'tis best to have none' (II.ii.86–7). A following wind for one ship is a head-wind for another, a good harvest means 'corn will bear no price', the manufacturing sector is always worrying about a recession – 'Where we, that trade nothing but money, are free from all this'. Merchants may complain their traffic is subject to much uncertainty and loss, but after all it is 'other men's substances' they expose to the risk of shipwreck while they double their money. Innocent bankers such as this one, meanwhile, 'honest men as live by lending money, are content with moderate profit – thirty or forty i'th' hundred – so we may have it with quietness' (II.ii.94–6).

King Henry V's French expedition, like Sir Petronell Flash's Virginian expedition, needs money. The Church lends Henry money. As the bishops see the situation, if Henry succeeds, the Commons bill to sequestrate their property gets nowhere. If he fails, his expedition will have been a distraction and a further 'scambling and unquiet time' will win the Church breathing-space. How can they lose? The banker Security lends Petronell Flash money. If the voyage succeeds, it may yield untold sums. If it fails, Security gets a whole country estate. How can he lose? No wonder he exclaims 'We have too few such knight adventurers' (II.ii.156–7).

It is when Sir Petronell Flash's voyage is actually about to begin in *Eastward Ho!*, however, that the ironic analogy to *King Henry V* is most interesting. The Captain gives a glowing account of their destination. Virginia is, exactly, like More's *Utopia*: 'Why man all their dripping-pans and their chamber-pots are pure gold': and what it lacks is equally attractive – no sergeants, courtiers, lawyers or intelligencers. There is just one disadvantage. It does have some Scots – come to think of it, says the Captain, 'I would a hundred thousand of 'em were there…we should find ten times more comfort of them there than we do here' (III.iii.44–5). The Captain and Sir Petronell, now styled Colonel, arrange a farewell 'aboard Sir Francis Drake's ship, that hath compassed the world'. Military expeditions, voyages of discovery, merchant adventures, piracy – Drake's example reminds one that the categories are not exactly mutually exclusive. Still, a famous voyage must have a fitting ceremonial send-off. Shakespeare's Chorus for act III covers the great naval operation from Hampton Pier to Harfleur in only seventeen lines, and declares that only a spectator deficient in manhood could forbear to cheer:

> For who is he whose chin is but enriched
> With one appearing hair that will not follow
> These culled and choice-drawn cavaliers to France?
>
> (*King Henry V*, III.0.22–4)

But where Shakespeare goes to great lengths to stress the Christian piety of Henry V's dedication of his expedition, here Francis Drake the freebooter is Sir Petronell's guiding spirit, and a drunken orgy is the appropriate ceremony, on board Drake's old ship. What with the drink and the storm, none of these voyagers even get as far as their own ship. Petronell and the Captain are swept away in a small boat and washed up on the Isle of Dogs, which they imagine is the French coast. The Chorus in this play takes the farcical form of a butcher's apprentice. He shins up a pole, from where he gives a running commentary on the 'furious tempest' as it engulfs the drunken voyagers (IV.i). These would-be cavaliers cannot keep in the saddle: 'Lord, what a coil the Thames keeps! She bears some unjust burden, I believe, that she kicks and curvets thus to cast it…the bit is out of her mouth, I see' (IV.i.12–16). A woman passenger is literally flung out of her boat and the Thames takes the chance to be 'rude' and take up her clothes. Contrast the high style of the Chorus in *King Henry V*, inviting us to visualize the fleet in feminine terms, beribboned with silk,

> Breasting the lofty surge. O do but think
> You stand upon the rivage, and behold
> A city on th'inconstant billows dancing.
>
> (III.0.13–15)

Eastward Ho! takes Shakespeare's point that the journey to France in *King Henry V* is an occasion for inspecting British national and personal issues, not for discovery of the remote and foreign French. In a great court scene Henry V's expedition is officially justified by the claim that France is in fact English. The nonsensical element in this claim is then made clear by the decisive language barrier, not least in the complete ignorance of English which even a French princess displays. A basic comic idea exploited by Pistol is that to speak French is a ridiculous aberration, given the obviously preferable alternative of English, and as Pistol hears it French is no more than garbled English anyway. But then the audience is shown that the diversity of dialects is actually a problem not of the French but of the 'English' camp. It is among the 'English' that it makes for misunderstanding and prejudice and embodies a history of tribal antagonism. In *Eastward Ho!* the joke is varied when the drunken survivors of the shipwreck suppose they have landed in France, address the inhabitants in Franglais and are mocked by being greeted with Scots, the barbarous language of the new King of England, James I. The episode ironically alludes to *King Henry V* but it also looks forward, to *The Tempest* and Stephano's amazement at a monster that can speak English – and at both ends! Both episodes have the Utopian concern to present a critical, defamiliarized version of the home country.

The parallels between *Eastward Ho!* and *The Tempest* begin right away with the shipwreck, and associated puns on drinking and drowning: Antonio asserts that the boatswain is drunk, and this is followed up by the arrival ashore of Trinculo and Stephano with his bottle. As a parallel to *Eastward Ho!*'s goldsmith, Touchstone, we have Prospero the magus. *The Tempest*'s first scene presents the ship itself, but there are also contrasting Choric accounts of the shipwreck, by Miranda and by Ariel. Then the shipwrecked mariners come severally ashore. Gonzalo's pieties are so trite they almost recall the ironic Security in *Eastward Ho!*:

> our escape
> Is much beyond our loss. Our hint of woe
> Is common: every day some sailor's wife,
> The masters of some merchant, and the merchant
> Have just our theme of woe.
>
> (II.i.2–6)

To Gonzalo it may be a miracle, but to Antonio it is a golden opportunity for political assassination, (so Menas views the drunken revel on another ship, Pompey's galley, in *Antony and Cleopatra*) while to Stephano the island presents an excellent get-penny:

A strange fish! Were I in England now, as once I was, and had but this fish painted, not a holiday fool there but would give a piece of silver: there would this monster make a man; any strange beast there makes a man: when they will not give a doit to relieve a lame beggar, they will lay out ten to see a dead Indian. (II.ii.28–34)

The shipwreck is presented from diverse points of view and in diverse styles, but these all converge in the explicit Utopian discourse of Gonzalo in II.i. Gonzalo's is an illustration of specious, one-sided advocacy: his ideal commonwealth accords exactly, but negatively, with European civilization. The civilized world-system is named, part by part, then each is cancelled, a rhetorically enacted dismantling:

> Letters should not be known; riches, poverty,
> And use of service, none; contract, succession,
> Bourn, bound of land, tilth, vineyard, none;

The pattern, thus established, runs on:

> . . .
> All things in common Nature should produce
> Without sweat or endeavour: treason, felony,
> Sword, pike, knife, gun, or need of any engine,
> Would I not have, but Nature should bring forth
> Of it own kind, all foison. . .

> (II.i.146–59)

But although he does not mean to, Gonzalo sounds as if he is saying nature will produce treason and felony – his negative – 'Would I *not* have' – comes so late it cannot cancel the effect. A few minutes later the play's action will insist on the grim truth that to dismantle civil order naturally breeds violent anarchy, when Antonio and Sebastian attempt murder on the sleeping Gonzalo.

Shakespeare's presentation is ironic and skewed, in the Utopian tradition. As we listen to Gonzalo's extreme, one-sided view, we observe his companions Antonio and Sebastian, obvious evidence to the contrary. They do not even try to disguise their vicious cynicism. The confrontation dramatically comments on the gap between political theory and political practice, but as a piece of theatre it is a highly formalized set-piece. Shakespeare suspends the narrative action and explicitly marks the episode out as exemplary. There is every reason to see this discourse as functioning in a parallel manner to the night scene on the eve of Agincourt – *King Henry V* IV.i. – when the King goes disguised among his men, and is obliged to debate issues at the centre of the play's dialectic.

The Tempest dramatizes in succinct terms the mundane truth that power corrupts, though its special concern is with the improbable and the inexplicable, the fantastic. Again and again the fantastic is endowed with a supremely vivid sensory immediacy, yet this is prone to dissolve at any moment. *The Tempest*'s manner is extraordinarily intent on undermining its own medium. It is a kind of dramatic palimpsest, in which a number of discrepant codes are laid one across another. Whichever code happens to be legible at a given moment, there is continuous awareness of the others, and it is this which constitutes the unique quality of the play.

One layer is the Prospero story: there he is on a desert island with his daughter, exiled, and with a few books, while over there in Italy lies his dukedom and over there Tunis. And over there, Asia. Or – and at the same time – over there, to the West, lies Virginia, and there to the East, England. The island itself is a palimpsest. It is simultaneously Mediterranean and Bermudan. It is a desert wilderness which has to be civilized, it is an unspoilt natural paradise that yields abundance without labour. It is full of violence, it is governed by irresistible benevolence. The only native of the island, Caliban, resembles an American Indian, but unlike the real American Indians, his racial and territorial claim is dubious – the island had been uninhabited until his mother, the witch Sycorax, was set ashore shortly before his birth. The references in the play to Naples and Tunis suggest a concern with current European politics; but jokes about 'widow Dido' remind us of Virgil, and make us recall that the Mediterranean is criss-crossed by ancient, medieval and Renaissance literary romances as well as trade routes and wars. And now the Atlantic, opened up by discoveries, reflects the same European patterns. These two kinds of history are brought together. The past is ironically connected to the present. Shakespeare takes pains to create and at the same time to uncreate his island. He makes you believe it, and then he reminds you that you can't believe it. The shipwreck spills on to the island the cast for a Jacobean satiric court play by John Webster or Thomas Middleton, which Prospero can then rewrite.

Shakespeare's island is, like a ship, a model of a state, and is also like More's *Utopia*, an ironic and satiric model for how men might live, how alas men do live, and how the past seems fatally to predetermine the future. When Shakespeare wrote *The Tempest* in 1610 the matter of discoveries was as multifaceted as his play. In that same year Sir Walter Ralegh, imprisoned by James I in the Tower, was writing his *History of the World*, undaunted in his belief that the golden half of the world, across the Atlantic, was there to be taken.

Given Jonson's allusions to Shakespeare's war plays and their 'three rusty swords', the 'Chorus that wafts you o'er the seas' and to his Romances, 'tales, tempests and such-like drolleries', it is clear that Shakespeare was a positive irritant in Jonson's mind. Meditating on a new play in 1614, Jonson showed wit worthy of a disciple of Erasmus and More. He seized on the paradoxical conceit of siting a Utopian 'island' right in the heart of the City of London, choosing Smithfield since it acquired special legal autonomy for the duration of the annual Fair of 24 August – thus resembling, in miniature and for a brief moment, an independent state. A play about the Fair could afford comic festivity, but also could license a critical representation of social types and attitudes.

In *The Tempest* the first scene, a realistic shipwreck, makes explicit allusions to the issue of monarchy and rebellion: 'What cares these roarers for the name of king?' Jonson, the chief author of the Jacobean masque, must have recognized that in *The Tempest* Shakespeare's borrowing of masque elements also involved their redirection to an ironic, not adulatory, view of autocratic rule. Did Jonson sense some implicit rebuke from Shakespeare? If there is a comic parallel between Jonson's Justice Overdo and Shakespeare's Prospero, I would go further and see *Bartholmew Fair* as Jonson's showing how to do it properly – how to make the masque form yield a true comedy – by giving the anti-masque its head. *Bartholmew Fair* presents the City as anti-masque, its grotesques having broken bounds to fill a whole five acts; and furthermore, (so the ironic implication would run) with fairgoers and stall-holders like these, who needs a monster from Bermuda?

The discovery that London, if viewed with truthful objectivity, must appear as strange and exotic as any new-found land, is basic to the scheme of *Bartholmew Fair*. Jonson makes the point backhandedly, in the induction, where the obstreperous Stage-keeper remarks that the spectators 'were e'en as good go to Virginia' as expect to recognize Smithfield in what they are about to see. While accommodating the neo-classical rule that comedy excludes Kings and confines itself to ordinary urban persons and settings, Jonson contrives to make the play a kind of British social microcosm, and as in *King Henry V* there is a range of national accents, from northern to cockney and including Welsh, Irish and Scots (from Bristle, Whit and Haggis respectively).

While Rabelais and Jonson are fascinated by the extreme effects of magnification and miniaturization, it is the naturally fluctuating complexities of perception which they chiefly celebrate – with an explorer's hunger but a philosopher's awareness. Jonson's poem 'The Famous Voyage' is a Rabelaisian scatological mock-heroic on the subject of great voyages. Instead of going around the world, his voyage is, though extremely ordurous, ludicrously short, within the City of London, up Fleet River from Bridewell to Holborn. It is depicted in terms of classical mythology since London's rivers can equal any river of hell for filth, horrors and noise. The absurdly foreshortened distance is combined with a no less disorientating magnification of scale for the vulgar City sights and – beginning with 'that ugly monster, Ycleped Mud' – for London's unbelievable stench, which here achieves fabulous proportions.

Jonson's chief method in *Bartholmew Fair* is Rabelaisian: the metamorphoses, although verbal and imaginative, not physical, all contribute to the same effect of distortion and defamiliarization: change the lens, and anything may look monstrous. The human beings are not only magnified – being compared to bears, whales and horses – they are also miniaturized by being likened to the smaller creatures attracted by this high summer Fair – calves, chickens, hawks, dogs, polecats, mice, wasps, hornets, bees, flies, daddy longlegs, spiders, grasshoppers, crickets, fleas – and in the same process these creatures are magnified to grotesque effect. There is a gallant who is said to go sniffing around for widows like a mongrel at a butcher's stall – 'there cannot be an ancient tripe or trillibub i'the town but thou art straight nosing it'. He is warned that caressing an old widow will be like scrubbing a piece of buff leather or a horse's carcase, and that after a month's marriage his virility will be sucked dry: he will have the legs of a spider and the voice of a cricket.

It is not a proper Fair if it does not display monsters, although there are in fact rival claimants in *Bartholmew Fair* to the role of chief monster. The obvious candidate may seem to be Mistress Ursula, seller of roast pork and bottle ale, and herself an embodiment of pink flesh and explosiveness. To rival her, Jonson presents a newly discovered monster who has a horrible name, Zeal-of-the-Land Busy, and makes a horrible noise: 'But the fleshly woman, which you call Ursla, is above all to be avoided, having the marks upon her of the three enemies of man: the World, as being in the Fair; the Devil, as being in the fire; and the Flesh, as being herself.' Busy is a hypocrite devotee of extreme Puritanism. His rapacious selfishness finds its political equivalent in tyranny. He is first described as violently gorging in secret, 'fast by the teeth i' the cold turkey-pie i' the cupboard, with a great white loaf on his left hand, and a glass of malmsey on his right' (1.vi.32–4). He ends a failed revolutionary, but Jonson gives proper weight to his exemplary significance: Busy's vision grossly distorts the world, yet his passion to force the world to correspond to his monstrous fantasy is palpable. He represents a real danger. Given power, he would create real barbarism.

The presence of the Fair's own Justice, in disguise, ironically parallels Shakespeare's observing rulers Henry V and Duke Vincentio, as well as Prospero; it also alludes to a celebrated episode in the life of Sir Thomas More.[7] Justice Overdo, the Puritan, has an obsession with discovering 'enormities' in the Fair to put in his black book, but what he calls 'enormities' are seen, from a corrected focus, to be tolerable, whereas he overlooks the real menace of bad law and its victims, such as Troubleall or Grace Wellborn. Overdo is the perennial tourist, at once suspicious and gullible, mistranslating foreign cultural signals, and when he is most superior making the biggest fool of himself. He considers the Fair to be an area of darkness, and he sets out to discover it as if there were no difference between a Puritan Tudor interlude and reality:

Look upon me O London, and see me, O Smithfield! the example of Justice, and Mirror of Magistrates;

Nevertheless, Overdo cannot resist the appeal of the real New World voyages: he knows the narrow lanes near Charing Cross are nicknamed the Straits or the Bermudas and he announces his final triumph like this:

Harken unto my labours and but observe my discoveries; and compare Hercules with me, if thou dar'st, of old; or Columbus, Magellan, or our countryman Drake of later times. (v.vi.31–6)

Jonson the dramatist is certainly daring in choosing to make a strictly plotted comedy and then half-submerge it in a Fair, the most shapeless kind of festival; he is no less ironic in choosing a Fair, where social and economic relations are at their most ungoverned, as a medium for an essentially serious debate about the equivocal relationship of civilization to oppression, of festive consumption to exploitation, of property to theft. Jonson's dramatic debate tests the principle of tolerance as severely as that of discipline.

The plays share an idea, associated with the More of *Utopia*, that the narrative of a voyage to remote and foreign places can be a means to reflect attitudes and issues at home in Britain. Something in each play invites but also frustrates a clear resolution, whether intellectual or generic: an episode of knock-about farce is as likely as a solemn utterance of public pieties suddenly to confront us with unexpectedly awkward, ironic, serious questions. As I would argue, this typical feature of the plays is owed to the influence of *serio ludere*, the risky mode practised by Sir Thomas More, with its strategies of ironic simplification to manoeuvre the unwary into untenably extreme or obnoxious positions. The voyaging impulse includes a fascination with the dark, the feared and the forbidden. It is important to stress this dark aspect in these plays, since their ironic conception requires that serious concerns should be deceptively masked. Here in the Elizabethan period we already perceive, though not to its full extent, the dark end of the Utopian spectrum.

These plays require us to keep our wits about us, to discriminate scrupulously, since the dramatists' ironic mode involves the utterance of extreme views, whether racist, colonialist, anarchic or jingoistic. Some audiences may not perceive any irony, may positively applaud such views, and then the writer's sense of satisfaction at hitting a target must be mixed with anxiety at the sheer power of those irrational impulses he attacks – a sobering truth that applies to the mode of irony in general, to writers as various as Jonathan Swift and the Conrad of *Heart of Darkness*. Swift's pamphlet *A Modest Proposal*, read ironically, is a righteous assertion of humane values, but it gains its force precisely because there are people who might think such things without a hint of irony: because we know this is how an actual *Endlösung* would be set out.

Sir Thomas More's skill in anticipating his opponents' moves is recognized. Reason may be a cornerstone of western philosophy, but the idea in *Utopia* of a state systematically based on reason might appear, however theoretically desirable, quite decidedly unrealizable in practice. More seems to leave himself wide open to this obvious line of attack, but if we take it we risk humiliation: we may rapidly find ourselves arguing for the power of tribal totem and taboo in our European customs, as surely as in those of the anthropophagi.

NOTES

1 Quotation from the first English translation by Ralph Robynson 1551. I have modernized the spelling. See the useful bi-lingual edition, *The Utopia of Sir Thomas More*, introduction by J. H. Lupton (Oxford, 1895).
2 Douglas Duncan, *Ben Jonson and the Lucianic Tradition* (Cambridge, 1979), p. 69.
3 Thomas More, *Utopia*, trans. Paul Turner (Harmondsworth, 1965), introduction, p. 12.
4 Quotations from Joseph Conrad, *Youth, Heart of Darkness, and The End of the Tether*, the collected edition (London, 1946), pp. 47–51.
5 Quotations from the following editions: J. H. Walter, ed., *King Henry V* (The Arden Shakespeare, 1954). C. G. Petter, ed., *Eastward Ho!* (The New Mermaids, 1973). G. R. Hibbard, ed., *Bartholmew Fair* (The New Mermaids, 1977). F. Kermode, ed., *The Tempest* (The Arden Shakespeare, 1954).
6 There are several obvious joke-allusions to other Shakespeare plays. These display *Eastward Ho!*'s characteristic mode of exuberant burlesque: for example, Security, having got drunk at the farewell party, shouts 'A boat, a boat, a boat! A full hundred marks for a boat!' (III.iv.4–5). Potkin, a tankard-bearer, rebukes a footman: ' 'Sfoot, Hamlet, are you mad?' (III.ii.6). In his excellent study *Ben Jonson's Parodic Strategy*

(Cambridge, Mass., 1987, pp. 81–2), Robert N. Watson discusses the pattern of parodic allusions to other plays, referring to *Hamlet*, *The Four Prentices of London*, *The Legend of Whittington*, *The Story of Queen Elenor*, *If you Know not Me*, *A Looking Glass for London and England* and *The Glass of Government*, and notes that the goldsmith Touchstone visualizes his son's successful future in terms 'clearly derived not from reality but from such plays as *The Legend of Whittington*, and that his story will be "played i' thy life-time by the best company of actors, and be called their get-penny"'.

7 See G. R. Hibbard's note to *Bartholmew Fair*, III.v.98–100. Robert N. Watson, *Ben Jonson's Parodic Strategy*, pp. 167–8, offers further grounds for relating Overdo to Prospero and notes that *Bartholmew Fair* was performed at court on 1 November 1614 – which is, to the day, exactly three years later than *The Tempest* – and that the performance would probably have been preceded by the service of All Saint's Day Evensong. Watson sees allusions in both *The Tempest* and *Bartholmew Fair* to the two prescribed scriptural readings for that service, passages emphasizing the reassertion of God-given authority.

CHAPTER 10

'Travelling hopefully': the dramatic form of journeys in English Renaissance drama

Peter Holland

We tend rather glibly to talk of a play as a journey. The critical cliché to describe the central character's progress through an action suggests an easy compatibility between the form of a drama and a bit of travelling. Even the word 'progress' carries, to the ears of Renaissance scholars, the overtones of royal wanderings usually to the accompaniment of interminable speeches of welcome by figures in a variety of mythological and allegorical guises. Fletcher's *The Sea-Voyage* ends with Sebastian defining what constitutes a good trip:

> when a while
> We have here refresh'd ourselves; we'll return
> To our several homes; and well that voyage ends,
> That makes of deadly enemies, faithful friends.[1]

But for all the play's eerie and complex rethinking of *The Tempest*, it is not interested in charting a voyage so much as an arrival at a point of cultural and geographical limbo, an opposition of two islands, sterile and fertile, of enforced Amazonianism and masculine greed. Sebastian himself spends most of the play off the island, having escaped by stealing the boat that brings the others to his isle of shipwrecked misery, as if Prospero had used the availability of Alonso's ship to nip back to Milan and abandon the others to their several fates. The hungry confrontation with a hostile environment and the impossibility of suppressing heterosexual desire are the play's main concerns, not the route by which someone gets to that space. The title is, in effect, a misnomer, for the play is not concerned about the sea and the voyage to any substantial extent, except the voyage between the two islands.

Placing a voyage on stage is, of course, a direct route to

dramaturgical difficulty. The readiest way to demonstrating the limitations of the stage is to try to move spaces. For all the vaunted flexibility of the Elizabethan stage's response to place it is always liable to appear only too well aware of its own limitations when a journey is at issue. Take, for instance, the Chorus' awkward attempts in *King Henry V* to describe the movements of the King's cross-Channel ferrying: 'But, till the King come forth and not till then, / Unto Southampton do we shift our scene'[2] or, in the Chorus to act v, 'Now we bear the King / Toward Calais: grant him there; there seen, / Heave him away upon your winged thoughts / Athwart the sea' (6–9). In the latter case, though, in spite of the brilliant narration of the King's triumphal entry into London, the Chorus has to end by moving the action back to France again, its description of Henry's *nostos* only an interlude before

> Henry's back-return again to France:
> There must we bring him; and myself have play'd
> The interim, by remembering you 'tis past.
> Then brook abridgement, and your eyes advance,
> After your thoughts, straight back again to France.
>
> (41–5)

King Henry V shares with most plays of journey a reliance on a Chorus to define the stages of the progress and, if none of the other plays I shall look at make of the Chorus such an extraordinary representation of the gap between what can be described and what shown, they share the same anxiety about what can be 'digested in a play'. Thomas Heywood's Chorus in *The Fair Maid of the West* is reduced to a lame apology for the theatre's handicaps:

> Our stage so lamely can express a sea
> That we are forc'd by Chorus to discourse
> What should have been in action.[3]

and immediately goes on to use the word that, more than any other, demonstrates the problem: 'Now *imagine*.'[4] Imagine this, suppose that, think the other: the vocabulary of the unactable journey comes easily to the Renaissance dramatist's own imagination.

Yet in the greatest of all Elizabethan plays of travel, Marlowe's *Doctor Faustus*, the use of a choric form is a deliberate part of the play's shaping, its careful adoption of a five-act form in which the journeying to the heavens, to Rome or to the court of the Duke of Vanholt, marks further stages down the road which defines the limitations of Faustus' ability to imagine, his failure to find more things to ask for from the devil. Mephostophilis' diabolic generosity only serves to increase our sense of the human brilliance and metaphysical poverty of Faustus' imaginings.

The journeyings of Marlowe's Tamburlaine are constricted by the limitations of terrestrial geography; even then, his travels mark an expanse of the world distant from the London of the audience, though at times approaching it at high speed through the machinations of the European Christian monarchs in part II. The journeyings of Faustus have no such limitation: their boundary is unimaginable, 'Even to the height of *Primum Mobile*',[5] and certainly theatrically unrepresentable. There can be no transition here from saying to showing, from sound to sight. The court of the Duke of Vanholt can be shown, the heavens cannot. Marlowe's play is the object-lesson in the limitations of representation of place.

It is striking that George Hunter's excellent account of the play's structure, the form which links the geographical mobility to the order of topics in a system of knowledge, should have been collected into a volume called *Dramatic Identities and Cultural Tradition*,[6] a volume much concerned with defining the nature of English Renaissance culture's creation of its identity through the definition of others as Other, foreigners in general, blacks and Italians in particular. For journey plays make particularly acute the sense of the originating culture, using the concept of the journey's end, the other place, as a means of redefining the journey's origin, just as the heart of darkness in Conrad's novel is initially posited as lying behind Marlow as he faces downstream away from London.

But travel plays are also centrally and structurally concerned with a relation between geography and recognition. In its most acute Shakespearean example, Pericles' wanderings, the epitome of aimless travel, cannot be resolved until the moment of recognition gives a purpose for a journey, until, that is, the reunion with Marina can lead directly on to the divine instruction to make a journey to be reunited with Thaisa. It is not only a cheap critical remark to suggest that Pericles' journey is a search for identity, a form of self-definition that may make it sound like a moment of

1960s West Coast hippydom, but which is reformulated in proper Renaissance style by defining identity in terms of family structures and royal responsibility. Vast tracts of travel plays are obsessed with, premised on and structured out of the search for another person, as Heywood's Bess Bridges sails the seas in search of her Spencer. But equally vast expanses of dramatic time are spent failing to recognize the other person whom one has been seeking. It has always struck me as odd that, in *The Comedy of Errors*, Antipholus of Syracuse, who has been travelling for years in search of his twin brother, does not seem to guess for a moment the real reason why everyone in Ephesus seems to know his name; by contrast, Viola in *Twelfth Night* perceives instantly though cautiously one likely solution to Antonio's calling her Sebastian for 'Even such and so / In favour was my brother' (III.iv.372–3).

In the wanderings across Europe towards Jerusalem that constitute the dramatic geography of Thomas Heywood's *The Four Prentices of London* the four noble youths, Godfrey, Guy, Charles and Eustace and their sister Bella-Franca, seem positively wilful in their inability to recognize each other. So convinced is each one by the reports that the other three brothers have drowned and that their sister must be safe at home that they seem able to spend weeks of time and whole acts of the play in each other's company without doing more than wondering with mind-numbing frequency how like x is to y. Here, chosen at random, is Godfrey looking at a newcomer on to the stage:

> Had not young *Eustace* in the seas been drown'd,
> I should haue said, he treads vpon this ground.
> And but none scap'd the dangerous seas saue I,
> This *French-man* I should thinke my brother *Guy*.[7]

It is not even as if the audience is confused or bewildered, other than by Godfrey's overweening trust in his own swimming ability. Costumes and helmets may disguise the brothers from each other but the audience is always perfectly clear who is who. This is one Elizabethan play whose staging demands seem to me insuperable and the labour of recovering the codes of costuming and disguise that would be needed to make the play work beyond our labours.

As the four brothers explore various corners of Europe – including a memorable stop by Eustace in Ireland – they converge on Jerusalem and the moment of mutual recognition, ending with an extraordinary verse line split between the four brothers and an extra-metrical shout for all four together:

> GODFREY. My brother *Eustace!*
> EUSTACE.   *Godfrey!*
> CHARLES.   *Guy!*
> GUY.   And *Charles!*
> ALL. Brothers!
>
>   (sig. I4a)

The action of the play depends on an endlessly reshaping symmetry, a view, remarkably like a child's kaleidoscope, of the virtues of pattern. Adding to the four brothers two other males, Robert of Normandy and Tancred, Heywood diagrammatizes the play's journeyings as, for instance, both Guy and Eustace end up being banished for fighting each other, something the brothers are usually praised for but not at moments where diplomacy and a certain show of unity seems in order.

Significantly the symmetries break down in the confrontation with women. There is only one sister for both Robert and Tancred to fall for and only one French lady for the brothers to marry. The male patterning collapses in the play's limited inclusion of the possibilities of marriage. I am not, of course, suggesting that Heywood should have included four more women, preferably sisters, to complete the diagram but rather that the shapeliness of the male world in its conflicts and alliances, its journeys and battles, cannot be repeated in a female form when women's progress through the play necessitates a continual anxiety about gender: both women at different times dress up as page-boys to enable them to pursue their loves.

Heywood is properly anxious about how the play can be shaped at all, how it can cover its material, converting it into dramatic form. The play is already well under way when he introduces a Presenter:

> Now to auoide all dilatory newes,
> Which might with-hold you from the Stories pith,
> And substance of the matter wee entend:

> I must entreate your patience to forbeare,
> Whilst we do feast your eye, and starue your eare.
> For in dumbe shews, which were they writ at large
> Would aske a long and tedious circumstance:
> Their infant fortunes I will soone expresse,
> And from the truth in no one point digresse.
>
> (sigs. B4b–C1a)

Together with the chorus, these plays recurrently make use of dumb show, using the chorus as rapid explication of the compressed drama of mute display. Gower, the chorus of *Pericles*, promises 'To glad your ear, and please your eyes' (Chor.i.iv).[8] He repeatedly offers event to the spectators' eyes for consideration, 'But tidings to the contrary / Are brought your eyes; what need speak I' (Chor.ii.15–16), or, memorably,

> And what ensues in this fell storm
> Shall for itself itself perform.
> I nill relate, action may
> Conveniently the rest convey.
>
> (Chor.iii.53–6)

At times he has to offer to link the silence of the show with his explanation: 'What's dumb in show I'll plain with speech' (Chor.iii.14) or 'Like motes and shadows see them move awhile; / Your ears unto your eyes I'll reconcile' (iv.iv.21–2).

These structural devices, non-recognition, chorus and dumb show, in Heywood's play take on the further powerful structural control of a cultural clash. Robert and Tancred, French Duke and Italian Prince, may have some overtones of their cultural specificity, but all such distinctions pale before the confrontation between East and West. This play – and others – explore a form of orientalism that is the crucial determinant on the identification of the unity of western culture. As Richard Marienstras observes of voyage narratives,

What is discovered at the end of the voyage is not really other worlds: rather, different moments of our own. The voyage brings together places formerly far apart, the far becomes the near, indeed becomes so dangerously near that it invariably proves necessary to recreate familiar distances to separate the far-off world from the world of Christian civilisation.[9]

If the problem is there in travel literature it is even more acute in drama and it is most often formulated through that vaguely conceptualized agglomerate of Persia and Turkey, the Sultan and the Sophy. Though our interest in *The Tempest* has tended to make us look west across the Atlantic, most travel plays move east, towards the Middle East at least.[10]

Heywood's prentices end their play triumphant, the pagans driven from the Holy City and Guy elected King of Jerusalem. It is an accomplishment of mythic heroic proportions but then Heywood's play belongs to a mythic past. *The Travels of the Three English Brothers* (1607), a collaboration between John Day, George Wilkins and William Rowley,[11] is tussling with an all-too immediate present, a narrative that had, as yet, no conclusion.

By 1607 the travels and travails of the three Sherley brothers, Thomas, Anthony and Robert, had been the subject of at least three pamphlets: *A True Report of Sir Anthony Sherlies Journey* appeared in 1600 and was quickly suppressed; William Parry's *A New and Large Discourse of the Travels of Sir Anthony Sherley, Knight* appeared in 1601; Anthony Nixon's *The Three English Brothers* seems to have been commissioned by the family at the time of Sir Thomas Sherley's return in 1607 from three years' imprisonment in Turkey. The playwrights may have had access to Nixon's narrative in manuscript but they might just as easily have spent time talking with Sir Thomas himself. Many more pamphlets would appear in the next decade to narrate further stages of the brothers' extraordinary adventures.[12]

It was conventional in comments on the play to deride the playwrights for their inventiveness. Bullen in his edition of the play remarks that 'Nixon stated what facts were known to him, and then drew on his imagination; but the playwrights deliberately distorted the truth';[13] Boies Penrose, in slightly more complimentary vein, identifies Nixon and Parry as Day's sources 'but he did not let either book interfere with his imagination'.[14] But the playwrights were confronted with the sheer difficulty of shaping their material. Parry, Nixon in manuscript or Sir Thomas Sherley in conversation are not essentially dramatic forms. Nixon, for instance, deals with each brother in turn in order of seniority while Parry, for all the incidental delights of his narrative style, provides very little in the way of dramatic conflict, the materials for an action.

Like Heywood, the trio of playwrights are anguished about the process of shaping what they call in their dedication 'this Idea and shape of honor' (sig. P1a). As the prologue, spoken by Fame, explores it,

> should our tedious muse
> Pace the perticulers of our trauellers,
> Fiue daies would breake the limmits of our Sceanes
> But to expresse the shaddowes

and their conclusion is to

> Present you with the fairest of our feast,
> Clothing our truth within an argument,
> Fitting the stage and your attention

(sig. A2a)

Day and Co make use of all the predictable devices for providing a dramatic solution to this problem of compression. There are choruses aplenty and numerous dumb shows. The play unwinds itself through a series of non-recognitions and chance meetings. All the devices of Heywood's *Four Prentices* reappear in different guises. Yet the play does not meander. Neville Davies, in the only substantial study of the play to have appeared, suggests a scenic form of symmetrical design, even while noting that the form is easier to draw than to perceive, obscured by the disproportion of the parts and the way 'other elements smudge the schematic sharpness'.[15] Davies identifies an incompatibility between the play's potential for formal pattern and its failure or refusal to achieve this. Noting the effective use of dumb show, he sees that

there is no attempt. . .to stylise the play's episodic structure by introducing recurrent dumbshows at the punctuation points. Indeed, the authors do what they can to prevent such patterning, and their management of the story by allowing it to pass freely between narration, mime, and spoken drama is part of that endeavour.[16]

Davies goes on to complain of this 'unsystematic mixing of the media', finding it 'unsettling'. Yet it is so only if the search for formal pattern is of prime concern. Heywood's *Four Prentices* stood, in effect, for Day and his collaborators, as a warning against the

need to pattern too much and *The Travels of the Three English Brothers*
achieves a fluidity and fluency that Heywood's play clearly lacks.

Day and the others are caught between the shapeless indeterminacy (that is the consequence of responding to the pressure of
realist history) and the shapeliness of drama. What they achieve is a
dramatic form dependent much less on the articulation practicable
through choruses and dumb shows, drums and trumpets, processions
and scenic forms and much more on a remarkable creation of an
articulated series of confrontations between opposing cultural groups.

The play opens with Sir Anthony's first meeting with the Sophy
in Casbin (Qasvin). Day dramatizes the event, so often commented
on in the pamphlets, when the Sophy graciously stopped Sir
Anthony from kissing his foot. But he then invents a competing
display of battles, a Persian battle in which 'the one halfe driue out
the other, then enter with heads on their swords' (sig. A3b) and a
'Christian battell showne betweene the two Brothers, Robert
driuen out, then enter S. Anthonie and the rest with the other part
prisoners' (sig. A4a). Though the scene will go on to identify
Persian primitivism by their reaction to cannon-fire ('*Mahomet*, it
thunders...Sure 'tis a Diuell' (sig. A4b)), it is much more significant
that these two *shows* of battles – deliberately not battles themselves – should articulate the Persian astonishment at the whole
idea of taking prisoners. The contrast between the Sophy's proud
explanation, 'Then are we sure our enemie is dead, / When from
the body we diuide the head' (sig. A3b), and his enquiry about the
Christian prisoners, 'Why do they liue?' (sig. A4a), defines a
cultural gap across the notion of honour. Sir Anthony explains the
prisoners both as a mark of clemency and as a source of ransom for
'our friendes life' or 'for Gold, and that hardens valour, / When he
that wins the honour, gets the spoile', evoking from the Sophy the
statement 'We neuer heard of honour vntill now' (sigs. A4a–b).

This may well be crude but it is also an attempt to provide a
thematic centre for the rest of the play. Again and again the
treatment of prisoners and the definition of honour will be the
means for cultural distinction: Robert arguing with Hallibeck over
prisoners taken in the fight with the Turks; Robert initially
intending to kill thirty Turkish officers because 'We are now here
the *Persian* substitute, / And cannot vse our Christian clemencie'

(sig. E1a) and then keeping them to ransom Thomas; Robert, again, forgiving Hallibeck for his plots against Anthony but the Sophy condemning him to have his hands and tongue cut off before execution. It will also contrast with the treatment of Sir Thomas as a prisoner in Constantinople and the recurrent near-imprisonments of Sir Anthony.

This opposition between Persian and Christian practices is finally resolved by the Sophy standing as godfather at the christening of Robert's child and allowing him to erect a church and arrange for Christian children to be separately educated. As John Cartwright commented in 1611, writing, I suspect, of Nixon's pamphlet rather than Day's play,

> But that hee should haue a child in *Persia*, and that the King...should bee the God-father; this certainly is more fitte for a Stage, for the common people to wonder at, then for any mans more priuate studies.[17]

But if this provides a dramatic ending to the action it does not mark the end of the play. Instead, in Fame's epilogue, the gulf between what the stage can do and what the brothers in reality cannot do is depicted in a way that is both imaginative and rather moving.

> Vnhappy they (and haples in our Sceanes)
> That in the period of so many yeares,
> That destinies mutable commandresse
> Hath neuer suffer'd their regreeting eyes
> To kisse each other at an enterview:
> But would your apprehensions helpe poore art
> Into three parts deuiding this our stage:
> They all at once shall take their leaues of you
> (sigs. H4a–b)

After which the final dumb show is performed, the three brothers coming on stage 'three seuerall waies' as if in Persia, Spain and England,

> Fame giues to each one a prospective glasse, they seeme to see one another, and offer to embrace, at which Fame parts them and so: Exeunt. (sig. H4b)

This distant embrace across the known world, using telescopes, re-creates the geographical space that the play's action has circumvented. In its expression of distance and the grief of separation and in its recognition of the unresolved nature of the brothers' journeys, it is a remarkable moment.

I have been suggesting the gap between Christian and Persian civilizations as an articulating force in the play. Yet, since part of Sir Anthony's aim – and hence the aim of a play dedicated to the Sherley family – was a Perso-Christian alliance against the Turk, the play is far more sympathetic to the Persians than, say, Nixon, who describes them as 'all *Pagans*, and *Infidels*, *Sodomites* and Liars'.[18] The play goes on to explore a whole series of cultural divides. Where, in Heywood, Persian and Turk are united against the Christians, Day's Sophy spends much of his play fighting the Turks and enlisting Sir Anthony's help. The triangle of cultures, Persian, Turkish and Christian (and this is a play remarkable in its sympathetic depiction of the Papacy as the embodiment of Christianity – Sir Anthony had converted to Catholicism) is expanded further in a series of scenes in Venice where Sir Anthony is at the mercy of a villainous Jewish usurer, Zariph. Self-evidently profiting from the example of Shylock, Day deliberately discards Parry's account of a wicked Friar – no room for disunity in the Christian ranks in this play – and Nixon's account of the kind Jew who helped Sir Thomas in prison.[19] Zariph is both dramatically effective and thematically appropriate, marking the Jews as a further cultural group.

The two scenes with Zariph frame a final cultural conflict, perhaps the most remarkable in the play and one which, according to Davies' diagram, would appear to occupy a structural centre for the play, a meeting between Will Kemp and an Italian Harlequin. Kemp, of course, stands for the tradition of English wit and theatre practice of which Day's play is a part, as if the reappearance of a popular actor was bound to please the Red Bull audience. But Harlequin and Kemp spend most of their dialogue debating the presence in Harlequin's tiny acting company of his wife. Two great improvisatory traditions meet and disagree about the presence of women. The refrain of the controversy is 'the custom of the country' and the joke that Harlequin's wife must be promiscuous since she plays the part of a whore. The two styles of performance clash irreconcilably, albeit with the play siding inevitably with

Kemp. The theatre itself becomes the one area of cultural difference within the sphere of Christian countries, a difference focused on the implications of actresses.

If the confrontation between West and East is conceived of in *The Travels* as a process amenable to recuperative assimilation, perhaps through religious conversion, then the problem of gender and travel was always acute. As early as 1575, in a translation of Jerome Turler's Latin text as *The Traveiler*, the accusation that travel for women is necessarily bound up with the uncontrollability of female desire is linked directly to drama:

Whereupon the Tragicall and Comicall Poets, when they bringe in any far traueiling Woman, for the most parte they feine her to be incontinent. Semblably, frantique and furious Persons are unfit to traueill. (p. 9)

To be mad or a woman makes travel unsuitable. In both parts of Heywood's *The Fair Maid of the West* Bess Bridges' chastity, her undeviating commitment to her beloved Spencer, is the point of certainty against which all other behaviour is measured. Bess's intransigent virtue necessitates the sudden introduction in part II (one of Heywood's more desperate dramatic manoeuvres) of Tota, Queen of Fez, desperate for Spencer's body, parallelling, equally awkwardly, the sudden slip back to uncontrollable desire for Bess that Mullisheg, the King of Fez, seemed to have sorted out perfectly happily by the end of part I – one should always be wary of a dramatist having a character return to an emotional state that had been adequately resolved earlier in the play. The symmetries of a double bedtrick which leaves King and Queen in bed together, mental adultery and bodily chastity, is too neat after the energetic shapeliness of travel in part I, as if the play is seeking a form that it cannot otherwise attain. It parallels the awkward manoeuvre in part II which splits the play geographically in two, the move from Fez to the court of the Duke of Florence, with its recapitulation, yet again, in a slightly different key of Bess's unassailable virtue, her mislaying of Spencer somewhere around the Mediterranean and eventual mutual recognition and resolution in the nick of time.

But if Bess answers Turler, (a woman can go in for transcontinental travel without being 'incontinent'), the play construes cultural difference in very peculiar forms. Mullisheg's lust for Bess may

seem a conventional form of using desire as the basis for action but
it is not premised on his cultural otherness; such desire is not typed
as geographically Other even if it is morally Other – indeed it also
seems less objectionable than the English class mockery of Bess the
barmaid which led Spencer to kill a man in a pub and have to flee
the country at the beginning of part I. Fez is remarkably Western in
its codes of behaviour: honour, the recurrent definition of Englishness
seems equally central to the culture of Fez. Over and over again
characters register amazement that Bashaw Joffer is so noble in his
actions. Joffer himself has to enunciate this otherness as a form of
connection:

> Sir, think me, though a Moor,
> A nation strange unto you Christians,
> Yet that I can be noble
>
> (part II.vi.33–5)

and in an eerie passage the perspective is reversed as Mullisheg
doubts Spencer's nobility, his willingness to keep his oath and
return to save Joffer, precisely because of his cultural distance:

> Why, canst thou think a stranger so remote
> Both in country and religion...
> ...and will return
> To expose all these to voluntary dangers
> For a bare verbal promise?...
> ...   Is't possible?
> Can England, so far distant, harbor such
> Noble virtues?
>
> (part II, III.iii.25–6, 30–2, 37–9)

This is, after all, exactly the sort of thing that English heroes say
about Moors in play after play and it ties in with the sense of
England as an Edenic spot of comfortable provincial ease, with its
pubs and charitable benefactions, with which the English scenes of
this play are so much involved. The point of connection with
England is not London but Plymouth and Fowey.

What really marks a collision of continents, a confrontation with
otherness, is the one practice the play types as alien, the creation of
eunuchs. Clem the Clown, whose age at the opening of part I is
carefully given as thirteen, is so keen on honour at the court in Fez

that when Mullisheg wants to honour Spencer my making him 'our chief eunuch' (part I.v.ii.93) and Bess, from justifiable self-interest, intervenes to stop it, Clem rushes forward and is taken in 'to taste the razor' (103). When Clem runs back on to the stage shouting 'No more of your honour, if you love me! Is this your Moorish preferment, to rob a man of his best jewels?' (126–7), the audience might reasonably assume that he has kept his testicles. But as part II makes clear in repeated jokes, Clem has been castrated, an action which has no significance, it seems, other than as a source for the jokes. The practice may belong to an alien culture but its significance is entirely comic.

Clem carries with him the consequence of travel, gaining experience and losing his testicles. But for others the experience of travel is gained much nearer home. For it is not always the journey itself which constitutes the structuring device. The anticipation of travel is, as we all know from bitter experience, often as time-consuming as the journey itself. For Ben Jonson, the planning becomes the device that defines structure, for the journey itself usually proves abortive. Hence a major dramatic movement running through *Every Man Out of His Humour* traces Puntarvolo's travel plans, that great speculative journey to 'the *Turkes* court in *Constantinople*'[20] accompanied by his wife and dog; when his wife becomes a justifiably reluctant traveller, his cat is unhesitatingly substituted, clearly using a transferable ticket. Puntarvolo's use of travel as speculation, his treating the journey simply as a sponsored wager, £5,000 at odds of five to one, belongs firmly to the play's argument about the connection between economic ambition and affectation. But for Puntarvolo it is tightly bound up with a fantasy of knightliness and derring-do, played out as his greeting of his wife as a wandering knight turning up at a castle. The ambiguity of travel, fantasy and economic reality, converge in the grand fantasy of the wager itself with its careful contractual clauses covering both the definition of failure ('if either of vs miscarry, the whole venter is lost...or if either of vs turne *Turke*' (IV.iii.13)) and the means of authenticating success: 'That (for testimonie of the performance) my selfe am to bring thence a *Turkes* mustachio, my dogge a *Grecian* hares lip, and my cat the traine, or taile of a *Thracian* rat' (IV.iii.39–42). It is, though, significant that the loss of cultural

identity, turning Turk, is so much at risk; it anticipates those
cultural outcasts of later plays, like Daborne's *A Christian Turn'd
Turk* (1612), where the social exclusion is defined by piracy and
religious heterodoxy and swash-buckling cannot quite provide an
adequate substitute for social marginality.

Puntarvolo's travel plans collapse when his dog is poisoned by
Macilente and 'lies giuing vp the ghost in the wood-yard' (v.iii.56–7).
The journey never takes place, need never take place, for the play's
form has depended on this structure of unrealized event, like
Fungoso's suit being as fashionable as Fastidious Briske's. This
incompletion reappears in the great journey of Sir Petronel Flash,
'your true knight venturer',[21] in Jonson's collaboration with
Chapman and Marston in that game of dramatic consequences,
Eastward Ho!. Sir Petronel may worry, as a dramatist might too, 'O
tedious voyage, whereof there is no end!' (iii.ii.182), but the journey
terminates prematurely in the shipwreck at Cuckold's Haven, that
virtuoso scene (iv.i) in which all three dramatists seem to have had a
share. As Sir Petronel tries out his bad French on some gentlemen,
convinced he is in France, only to discover that he has got no
further than the Isle of Dogs, the authentic voice of the Englishman
abroad clinging to his innate sense of cultural superiority can be heard:

SIR PET. Monsieur, plast-il d'avoir pitié de nostre grand infortunes. Je suis
          un povre chevalier d'Angleterre qui a souffri l'infortune de naufrage.
I.GENT.   Un povre chevalier d'Angleterre?
SIR PET. Oui, monsieur, il est trop vraye; mais vous scavés bien nous
          sommes toutes suject a fortune.

                                                        (iv.i.153–8)

The incomplete journey undertaken by the man of folly is used in
these two plays to provide a continuum of comic possibility. The
journey itself cannot, need not form part of the play; it lies in some
future space outside the dramatic form, a fantasy or temptation
that the drama hypothesizes only to mock as lying outside the
play's immediacy. But even where the travel is accomplished, the
educative function of the journey is not seen to be noticeably
efficacious. Thomas Heywood's *The English Traveller* (1633) is a
sustained and vicious mockery of the assumption that the observation

of that which lies out there, in some cultural other world across the channel, helps one cope with life at home.

Young Geraldine is rapturously praised by Dalavill in the first scene for having made the transition from book-learning to direct observation, praise significantly preceded by a description of a scholar's inability to steer a ship, the crucial division between theory and practice that will underpin the play:

> I haue read Ierusalem, and studied Rome,
> Can tell in what degree each City stands,
> Describe the distance of this place from that,
> All this the Scale in euery Map can teach,
> Nay, for a neede could punctually recite
> The Monuments in either; but what I
> Haue by relation onely, knowledge by trauell
> Which still makes vp a compleat Gentleman,
> Proues eminent in you.
>
> (sig. A4a)

In a clear moment of plot-anticipation, Young Geraldine reveals that while he may have seen the monuments, played the cultural tourist as efficiently as, say, Antipholus of Syracuse, he is no more ready to deal with women at home than Antipholus is to deal with women abroad, since his practice was assiduously to ignore people:

> I neuer cast on any in those parts
> A curious eye of censure, since my Trauell
> Was onely aymed at Language, and to know;
> These past me but as common objects did,
> Seene but not much regarded.
>
> (sig. B2a)

Throughout the play travel becomes a point of contrast with the increasing horror of the action, counterpointed by the fantasy of a sea-journey that, in the sub-plot, is an extravagant drunken group improvisation. Frightened and shocked by what he discovers of Dalavill and the others, Young Geraldine's only course of action is travel, offering the Renaissance equivalent of the Victorian gentleman's decision to bury himself in darkest Africa: 'I'le take my leaue, / Both of this Clime and Nation, Trauell till / Age snow vpon this Head' (sig. H2b). His father's incomprehension is also a warning; since Young Geraldine has seen so much already,

> Sonne, let me tell you, you are ill aduis'd;
> And doubly to be blam'd, by vndertaking
> Vnnecessary trauell...
> ...   Can you either better
> Your langauge or experience?
>
> (sig. I4b)

The knowledge of the objects of the other, the outside, cannot provide any structure for dealing with people who refuse to be pigeon-holed neatly according to the methods of a guidebook. *The English Traveller*, a play structured on the notion of the audience's inability to control the action, refuses to see travel as anything other than a narrowing of the mind, a culturally approved way of avoiding the comprehension of those behavioural practices which matter as causes of social disturbance, desire and its conspiracies. In the end it is Dalavill who will make the play's last journey, escaping when his adulterous relationship is revealed, becoming a traveller away from the forms of social control and punishment that the dramatic form conventionally demands and this brilliant play so cunningly resists.

For Puntarvolo, Sir Petronel and Young Geraldine the failure of travel proves therapeutic. For Peregrine, the man driven mad by the desire for travel in Brome's *The Antipodes* (1637), an imaginary journey proves to be as restorative as a real one. Peregrine's desire to peregrinate began as a child when he became obsessed with travel-books. By the time he was twenty, 'There was no voyage or foreign expedition / Be said to be in hand, but he made suit / To be made one in it'.[22] His parents' opposition and arranged marriage failed to 'call / In his extravagant thoughts' (1.ii.49–50) – Brome carefully allowing 'extravagant' its full wandering sense –

> but all prevail'd not,
> Nor stay'd him, though at home, from traveling
> So far beyond himself that now, too late,
> I wish he had gone abroad to meet his fate.
>
> (1.ii.50–3)

The travels of Peregrine, further perhaps than any since Faustus, take him to the Antipodes and all without leaving home, as the Antipodean world of 'Anti-London' (II.iv.39) is staged by Letoy and Doctor Hughball. The play solves the problems of dramatic structure by ironizing the experience of the single member of the audience for whom the show of the world upside down is staged. There is no cultural other, no continental difference to be set up, or, rather, the continent of the Antipodes is conceived of absolutely as difference and inversion, having no function other than its explicit status as inverse.

But how to get there quickly? Peregrine is persuaded that he has slept through the entire journey of 'Eight months, and some odd days' (II.iv.17) and is annoyed that he missed the trip: 'What worlds of lands and seas have I pass'd over, / Neglecting to set down my observations!' (II.iv.7–8). The seasoned traveller's responsibility to record the details in his diary can, however, be made up on the return half of the excursion. Peregrine, not surprisingly, is bemused that he has slept this long, especially when the doctor's narrative earlier in the play appears to him 'As if you had but given it me this morning' (II.iv.44), as indeed he did. The devices which had been standard components of earlier travel plays' apologias to their audiences, their awkward identifications of temporal and geographical pole-vaulting with nothing but a couplet or two to lean on, have now been compressed into poor Peregrine's psychotherapy, a psychodrama of surprisingly efficacious style. The form of the play can leap over the journey precisely because there is not one at all, the voyage explicitly both theatrically performative and imaginary, a voyage the theatre takes because it alone can provide the means for making it as a collaborative imaginative venture. In this case the problems of travelling hopefully are resolved: Peregrine arrives as smoothly as British Airways promises today.

NOTES

1 Francis Beaumont and John Fletcher, *The Works*, ed. A. R.Waller (Cambridge, 1910), IX, p. 65.
2 William Shakespeare *King Henry V*, ed. J. H.Walter (Arden Shakespeare,1954), Chorus to act II, 41–2.
3 Thomas Heywood, *The Fair Maid of the West Parts I and II*, ed. Robert K. Turner, Jr (Lincoln, NE, 1967), part I, IV. v. 1–3.
4 *Ibid.*, part I, IV. v. 3, my italics.
5 Christopher Marlowe et al., *Doctor Faustus*, eds. David Bevington and Eric Rasmussen (Manchester, 1993), B-text, III Chorus 10.

6 G. K. Hunter, 'Five-Act Structure in *Dr Faustus*', in *Dramatic Identities and Cultural Tradition* (Liverpool, 1978), pp. 335–49.

7 Thomas Heywood, *The Foure Prentises of London*, revised edition (1632), sig. E3a.

8 William Shakespeare, *Pericles*, ed. F. D. Hoeniger (Arden Shakespeare, 1963).

9 Richard Marienstras, *New Perspectives on the Shakespearean World* (Cambridge, 1985), p. 163.

10 See Samuel C. Chew's fine study of Islam and England during the Renaissance, *The Crescent and the Rose* (Oxford, 1937) and R. R. Crawley's rather disappointing books, *The Voyagers and Elizabethan Drama* (London, 1938) and *Unpathed Waters* (Princeton, 1940).

11 The shares of the collaborators have not been determined; in the course of my comments I often use 'Day' as a convenient shorthand to cover all three dramatists.

12 For the best modern account see D. W. Davies, *Elizabethans Errant* (Ithaca, NY, 1967), but also Sir E. Denison Ross, *Sir Anthony Sherley and his Persian Adventure* (London, 1933).

13 John Day, *The Works*, ed. A. H. Bullen (London, 1881), introduction to *The Travels*, p. iii.

14 Boies Penrose, *The Sherleian Odyssey* (Taunton, 1938), p. 271.

15 H. Neville Davies, '*Pericles* and the Sherley Brothers', in *Shakespeare and His Contemporaries*, ed. E. A. J. Honigmann (Manchester, 1986), pp. 106–7.

16 *Ibid.*, p. 104.

17 John Cartwright, *The Preachers Travels*, (1611), pp. 70–1.

18 [Anthony Nixon], *The Three English Brothers* (1607), sig. H4a.

19 *Ibid.*, sig. D4b.

20 Ben Jonson, *Works*, eds. C. H. Herford and P. and E. Simpson (Oxford, 1925–52), III, II. iii. 247–8.

21 George Chapman, Ben Jonson and John Marston, *Eastward Ho!*, ed. C. G. Petter (The New Mermaids, 1973), II. ii. 159.

22 Richard Brome, *The Antipodes*, ed. Ann Haaker (Lincoln, NE, 1966), I. ii. 44–6.

CHAPTER II

'Seeing things': Amazons and cannibals

Michael Hattaway

> I, when I value gold, may think upon
> The ductileness, the application,
> The wholesomeness, the ingenuity,
> From rust, from soil, from fire ever free,
> But if I love it, 'tis because 'tis made
> By our new Nature, use, the soul of trade.
>
> Donne, Elegy XVIII 'Love's Progress', 11–16

Donne, although writing about love, is here manipulating two of the commonplaces that we associate with encounters in the Renaissance between the Old and New Worlds: gold,[1] and the manner by which, when two peoples engage in trade, their natures are changed. 'Nature' in this poem is both external and internal, great creating Nature as well as that which makes up humanity.[2] 'Use' also has two meanings, 'usury' and 'cultural practice or custom'. Practice generates particular behaviour, so constituting a new 'nature' for individuals involved in that behaviour, here the process of trading. Translating this into slightly different terms, the behaviour of the market-place is a form of theatricalization.[3]

Donne may, I think, be seen here as a cultural relativist, someone who was prepared to conceive of Nature not as something transhistorical or transcultural, but as a power made by culture. We might compare Montaigne's aphorism from one of the greatest of his essays, 'Of Custom, and How a Received Law Should Not Easily be Changed': 'Custom is a violent and deceiving school-mistress...we may plainly see her upon every occasion to force the rules of Nature: *Usus efficassimus rerum omnium magister*: Use is the most effectual master of all things.'[4] Ethics might be demolished by ethnics. There were, however, few relativists before the end of the

179

seventeenth century.[5] For most writers of the period there was only one 'Nature', and Europe and the New World were seen in her terms.

That is one point of reference: for my second I want to take the title of Seamus Heaney's recent collection of verse *Seeing Things* (1991). The title proclaims a pun, obvious but unfamiliar. It reminds us that travel and voyaging may be a question of invention rather than discovery. The things a European voyager sees in America are both present and invented. In the terms of the Renaissance, they are 'fantasies', or, in the words of Florio's Montaigne, 'fashioned and masked' by their observers, 'according to the visage they saw them in'.[6] We might, by combining the Donne and the Heaney, go even further: not only does observation lead us to stereotype and 'see things', but we the observers are ourselves transformed, acquire a 'second nature' – a point made in a modern play, *The Ik* by Peter Brook.[7] It is now our task to consider not just what was seen but how it was seen, and we turn for our examples to drama.

Although Renaissance England was awash with new discoveries in physical geography, there was not, as in most periods, much attempt to separate the fabulous from the factual,[8] and little cultural curiosity compared with that evinced towards the Old World – Thomas Harriot[9] and the artist John White may exhibit more concern with specifics than most of their contemporaries, but even their 'new world' was inhabited by stereotypes and their cultural landscapes refracted through ideological commonplaces.[10] The explorers of the age, given their desire to ransack the occidental discoveries for gold, were little better than pirates. Nor was it an age of large-scale colonization – Ralph Lane complained that 'the discovery of a good mine, by the goodness of God, or a passage to the South Sea, or some way to it, and nothing else can bring this country in request to be inhabited by our nation'[11] – or of Christian imperialism – Edward Hayes (another writer anthologized by Hakluyt) lamented that no 'right way [had] been taken of planting a Christian habitation or regiment' upon the lands that lay north of the twenty-fifth parallel.[12] Plantations were simply ventures that were run abroad: there was little rumination on idealistic values of the sort that future settlers wanted to project on to the land that was to become their home.[13] The following, the digest of a young woman's 'devoir', 'an emigrant's letter to his friends at

home', in Charlotte Brontë's *The Professor* (1857), sets out commonplaces that we shall *not* find in our period:

> It opened with simplicity; some natural and graphic touches disclosed to
> the reader the scene of virgin forest and great, New-World river – barren
> of sail and flag – amidst which the epistle was supposed to be indited. The
> difficulties and dangers that attend a settler's life were hinted at; and in the
> few words said on that subject, Mdlle Henri failed not to render audible
> the voice of resolve, patience, endeavour. The disasters which had driven
> him from his native country were alluded to; stainless honour, inflexible
> independence, indestructible self-respect there took the word. Past days
> were spoken of; the grief of parting, the regrets of absence, were touched
> upon; feeling, forcible and fine, breathed eloquent in every period. At the
> close, consolation was suggested; religious faith became there the speaker,
> and she spoke well.[14]

The Renaissance was not imbued with these heroic imperialist
values; rather the New World was not seen as *different* but simply as
the 'Other',[15] the barbarous – a dystopia, or occasionally, as in the
ironic vision of a More[16] or a Montaigne,[17] a Utopia. Its customs
were seen in the light of an ethno-centred nature and not as
another culture. The cultures described in texts like Sir Walter
Ralegh's *The Discovery of Guiana* (1596), or, more fantastically, in
George Chapman's wedding masque for the Princess Elizabeth
(1612),[18] are seen almost entirely in terms of their prosperity: the
texts are a celebration of the gold that might be found in the New
World. In Ralegh's text Guiana figures also as a political prize that
might be wrested from the grasp of England's old enemy Spain.
Similarly, in Marlowe's *Doctor Faustus*, Valdes promises the hero
that the spirits shall drag 'from *America* the golden fleece / That
yearely stuffes old *Phillips* treasury'.[19]

The New World was also, interestingly, a source of evil: Ralegh
wrote: 'It is [Spain's] Indian gold that indangereth and disturbeth
all the nations of Europe: it purchaseth intelligence, creepeth into
councils, and setteth bound loyalty at liberty in the greatest
monarchies of Europe'.[20] We may be reminded of the myth of
syphilis, immediately supposed (and now proved[21]) to have crossed
into Europe when Columbus returned and, in our time, the myth
of the origins of Aids, a visitation from darkest Africa.

If money is not the root of all evil women are. In 1567 William

Painter in his *The Palace of Pleasure* wrote a chapter about the Amazons, placing them in their traditional abodes, Scythia or Libya:[22] in 1596 both Edmund Spenser and Sir Walter Ralegh, following the Spanish who had been haunted by what might lie south of the West Indies, the 'southern mysteries',[23] and who had heard of female warriors in the region, were happy to relocate them in Guiana.[24] Their soveignty over a realm of gold was to Spenser a challenge to male hegemony:

> Ioy on those warlike women, which so long
>   Can from all men so rich a kingdome hold;
> And shame on you, O men, which boast your strong
> And valiant hearts, in thoughts lesse hard and bold,
> Yet quaile in conquest of that land of gold.
> But this to you, O Britons, most pertaines,
> To whom the right thereof it self hath sold;
> The which for sparing litle cost or paines,
> Loose so immortall glory, and so endlesse gaines.
>   (FQ, iv.xi.22–30)[25]

Relationships between the sexes are one of the commonest focuses of interest in texts about the Americas,[26] and it is significant that the projection of this Amazonian myth of disorder and inversion was so central to the inventing of the New World.[27] Conversely, I think it is not too ingenious to suppose that the name 'Virginia' was not only a tribute to the Queen but suggested the possibilities for sexual adventure[28] and sexual imperialism. In *Eastward Ho!* (1605) Seagull describes how 'A whole country of English is there, bred of those that were left there in '79. They have married with she-Indians and make 'em bring forth as beautiful faces as any we have in England' (iii.iii). It may be significant that images of wealth in the New World are often the basis of bawdy: Donne's elegy to his mistress going to bed provides the obvious example. This combined concentration on wealth and the ordering of gender relationships is another point of departure and is at the centre of a play I wish to examine, Fletcher and Massinger's *The Sea-Voyage* of 1622.

Now *history* plays of the Renaissance, it is currently a truism to point out, are more profitably thought of as *political* plays. They offer refractions of what was contemporary experience. It is the same with what we might term 'geographic' plays. These plays, set in far-off places, refracted through myths like that of Atlantis, the Golden Age,[29] the isles of the blessed, or the lost tribes of Israel,[30] turn out not to be neither simple documentaries nor romances, reflections *of* other cultures, but reflections *upon* the culture inhabited by their audiences. 'Reflections upon a culture': the metaphor is, of course, misleading because 'culture' is not a tangible thing open to empirical analysis. We *construct* cultures according to pregiven categories of signification: it is impossible to escape the structures of ideology and the clutches of ethnocentricity. Indeed the relationship of 'culture' to 'history' – if we can, naively, assume that 'history' pertains to the real – may be analogous to the relationship between the perceived to the actual.

In the English Renaissance, in fact, plays that actually deal with the New World are rare: many more, Fletcher's *Island Princess* (1621) and Heywood's two-part *The Fair Maid of the West* (1604 and 1631),[31] for example, deal with Mediterranean 'Moorish' or Turkish worlds.[32] Shakespeare's *The Tempest* is, of course, not unequivocally set in the New World: it is as much Mediterranean as Caribbean. Yet it proves to be the exception that proves the rule, and is also, as we might expect, the most politically searching. It is no mere moral fable, contrasting non-Christian virtue with Christian vice, but confronts the *fact* of colonialism by testing the connections between imperialism and colonialism and deeply probing the incurable wounds of colonialism. Unusually for these narratives we catch glimpses of 'production', the work that has to be performed by both Caliban and Ferdinand. (The relationship between *The Tempest* and most other New World Renaissance texts is a bit like that between Conrad's *Heart of Darkness* and Francis Ford Coppola's movie *Apocalypse Now*.) Whereas lesser plays by their Eurocentrism *suppress* cultural difference, Shakespeare, in his depiction of Caliban and invocation of Sycorax, *stresses* difference – and he may even be considered the prototype of the post-colonial writer. Certainly *meanings* of the text in a post-colonialist age are going to be different from that of colonialist one – as myriad productions 'starring' Caliban have made clear.

Many of the Renaissance narratives of the New World involve shipwreck. Tempest is a metaphor for rebellion in the Virginia Company's pamphlet, *A True Declaration of Virginia*, one of the

principal sources for Shakespeare's play: 'the broken remainder...made a greater shipwreck in the continent of Virginia by the
tempest of dissension; every man overvaluing his own worth
would be a commander, every man underprizing another's value
denied to be commanded'.[33] The events in such narratives are
therefore likely to be read anagogically, as reflections upon divine
providence, but also, if the settlers land on a 'desert' island, they
are going to encounter another sort of monarchy, or to have to
construct an alternative variety for themselves, or establish a
republic.[34] That will highlight the difference between honours
they achieved in their native lands and the virtues they will
require: I am of course thinking of the distinction made by
Montesquieu between the monarchy 'whose operative principle is
honour and the republic whose operative principle is virtue', by
which he meant civic virtue, something rather like what is meant
today by citizenship.[35]

Fletcher and Massinger's comedy The Sea-Voyage is a text in
which honour and virtue are put to the test by adversity. This play
is interesting for four reasons: it is obviously inspired by The Tempest
as the opening scene makes clear,[36] its story offers a similar account
of 'a redemptive journey away from society in the direction of
nature',[37] it manipulates three further common tropes pertaining
to the New World, romantic space, fertile land, savage (or
treacherous) peoples,[38] and it offers an interesting if transparent
example of 'gendered racism'.

'Romantic space': as is common in travel narratives, the islands
where the play is set are empty of any 'natives'[39] – emptied we now
should say, knowing how other cultures were so often invisible to
settlers or how 'virgin' lands signified that the cultures of those who
inhabited them were ripe for the violation of colonization. There
are, however, on one island some Europeans who, having been
shipwrecked, appear to the audience to have taken on mythic roles:
it is, like so many other colonial discourses, decidedly intertextual
rather than international.

The Sea-Voyage begins with the shipwreck. Aminta, mistress to the
pirate Albert, and 'a noble French virgin', has with her lover put to
sea to find her lost brother. She appears on deck to lament her
misfortunes and is promptly clapped under hatches by the Master

of the vessel, a preliminary example of the demonization of women
that runs through the play:

> We ha' ne'er better luck
> When we ha' such stowage as these trinkets with us,
> These sweet sin-breeders. How can Heaven smile on us
> When such a burden of iniquity
> Lies tumbling, like a potion, in our ship's belly?
>
> (I.i.p. 309)

Then the Master orders that all the riches of the merchants aboard
be thrown overboard to lighten the ship: so 'order' is re-established.
The ship of state, we might imply, is threatened both by the female
and the merchant. The savages that are discovered on the
unnamed 'desert island' by those that are saved turn out to be
themselves shipwrecked Europeans and some 'Amazons'. Their
country is unplaced geographically but belongs within the Portuguese
sphere of influence.

The first point of interest is that this island is not fertile. The
shipwrecked Nicusa speaks to Sebastian his uncle:

NICUSA   Alas poor wretches!
        Had they but once experience of this island,
        They would turn their tunes to wailings.
SEBASTIAN   Nay, to curses,
        That ever they set foot on such calamities:
        Here is nothing but rocks and barrenness,
        Hunger and cold, to eat; here's no vineyards
        To cheer the heart of man, no crystal rivers,
        After his labour, to refresh his body,
        If he be feeble; nothing to restore him,
        But heavenly hopes. Nature, that made those remedies,
        Dares not come here, nor look on our distresses,
        For fear she turn wild, like the place, and barren.

                                        (I.ii.p. 310)

This recalls the descriptions of Newfoundland,[40] a poor place
compared with the parts of the east coast littoral possessed by the
Spaniards. There is also a reference to a fearful Black Lake
(II.ii.3) – could that be the pitch lake described by Ralegh?[41]

When Aminta and her shipboard companions arrive, they find

piles of gold belonging to Sebastian; their companionship, born in adversity, falls apart as they scrabble for it.

Enter, on a neighbouring and more fertile island, three Amazons,[42] Hippolyta, Crocale, and Julietta. Amazons play the role of 'natives' here; they are merely figurative savages, translations really, on whom, as is customary, can be projected images of what explorers and colonizers take to be evil. These women have established a commonwealth: it can only be evil because it repudiates and threatens to subvert the monarchy of men.[43] Halting in pursuit of a stag, they celebrate their lot:

> this place yields
> Not fauns nor satyrs, or more lustful men;
> Here we live secure,
> And have among ourselves a commonwealth,
> Which in ourselves begun, with us must end.
>
> (II.ii.p. 314)

This monstrous idealism, however, has to be revealed as an aberration: we are not surprised to hear Crocale narrating an erotic dream in which a fine young man came to her cabin. The reverie is interrupted by the appearance of Albert, washed up on the shore of their island. Their queen Rosellia appears, and urges them to have naught to do with the other sex, using an interesting argument that describes the internalization of an alien colonial power:

> The sovereignty
> Proud and imperious men usurp upon us,
> We confer on ourselves, and love those fetters
> We fasten to our freedoms.
>
> (II.ii.p. 315)

She does not, however, prevail: 'We must and will have men' (p. 316) cry the others, and Rosellia agrees to let her ladies join the shipwrecked company for a month.

This, it turns out, is the customary period of time. Sir Walter Ralegh wrote of his South American Amazons:

they which are not far from Guiana do accompany with men but once in a year, and for the time of one month. At that time all the kings of the borders assemble, and the queens of the Amazons, and after the queens have chosen the rest cast lots for their valentines. This one month, they feast, dance, and drink of their wines in abundance, and, the moon being down, they all depart to their own provinces. If they conceive and be delivered of a son, they return him to the father; if of a daughter, they nourish it and retain it, and as many as have daughters send unto the begetters a present, all being desirous to increase their own sex and kind; but that they cut off the right dug of the breast I do not find to be true. It was farther told me that, if in the wars they took any prisoners, that they used to accompany with those also at what time soever, but in the end for certain they put them to death; for they are said to be very cruel and bloodthirsty, especially to such as offer to invade their territories.[44]

And in the play the Amazons plan to kill the French after they have enjoyed them, and their anger is compounded by the fact that the Frenchmen have given them jewels that they had found on the island and which they, the ladies, had lost. It turns out, in fact, that the 'Amazons' are shipwrecked Portuguese ladies who want to revenge themselves upon the French who had forced them from their 'plantations in the Happy Islands' (v.ii). While the French are languishing in the power of the 'Amazons' there is much talk of the women's insatiable sexual appetites (IV.iii).

What makes the play of special interest is that it not only projects on to the New World the myth of Amazons but in an interesting way invokes another projection of evil, cannibalism, which, like the Amazonian state, existed only in the minds of the colonizers.[45] Now Shakespeare invoked the 'cannibals' in his Caliban – without of course inferring that his savage ate human flesh. In this play, with I take it an ironic nod to Shakespeare's text, we find that it is the shipwrecked who are tempted to indulge in cannibalism. Listen to Lamure, an 'usuring merchant', Franville, 'a vain-glorious gallant' and Morillat, 'a shallow-brained gentleman' talking about the body of the heroine, Aminta, whom they come upon sleeping:

MORILLAT She's young and tidy;
          In my conscience she'll eat delicately;
          Just like young pork, a little lean. Your opinion, surgeon?
SURGEON   I think she may be good meat; but look,
                                        We shall want salt.
FRANVILLE Tush, she needs no powdering.
SURGEON   I grant you:
          But to suck out all the humorous parts, by all means –
          Let's kill her in a chafe: she'll eat the sweeter.
                              (III.i.p. 317)

Now the would-be rape of Miranda by Shakespeare's Caliban is an early example of the mentality that generated the notion of the 'white slave': predatory sexuality is projected on to the foreigner. Here Fletcher and Massinger reverse the terms of the cultural equation, but the lubricious tone of the passage makes us sceptical of their intentions. Like the Amazons, or any alien race or nationality, Aminta attracts and repels men in equal measure.

How does it end? Well, the play is resolved in a desultory way when these Portuguese Amazons are reunited with their shipwrecked husbands and their jewels.

There is, as we have seen, precious little of the New World in this particular text: it might have made you think more of *The Pirates of Penzance* than Hakluyt or even Shakespeare. But although their natures may be constructed by the conventions of the romance plot, it is significant that on this New World island natives turn out to be foreigners, and their 'new natures' are constituted by the forms and pressures of the colonizing power, inverted in the presence of gold and an unfamiliar setting so that women are on top and gentlemen are cannibals. When we 'see things' in the theatre – or in 'new' worlds – what we are seeing are, as Hamlet reminds us, not actualities but allegories and the forms and pressures of the time; the enchanted glass of the mind reveals the invisible rather than the visible. The 'Amazons' turn out to be non-Amazons, merely disguised in the manner of a common theatrical convention. But, to end where I began, we, the audience, had gone along with the convention, had allowed ourselves to 'see things', had become part of the process of theatricalization, and had thereby acquired another 'nature'. The text serves to remind us of the way in which the textual may be surpassed by the intertextual as a source of meaning and cultural history.

NOTES

1 Gold is the first attribute of the New World, the subject of the 'Epistle to the Reader' in Ralegh's *Discovery of the... Empire of Guiana* (London, 1596), sig. A4r - ¶4v; see also George Chapman's 'De Guiana' (1596), in *Poems*, ed. Phyllis Brooks Bartlett (New York, 1941), pp. 353–7.

2 Donne is, by implication, eschewing alchemy.

3 See Jean-Christophe Agnew, *Worlds Apart: the Market and the Theater in Anglo-American Thought, 1550–1750* (Cambridge, 1986); see also Steven Mullaney, 'Brothers and Others, or the Art of Alienation', in *Cannibals, Witches, and Divorce*, ed. Marjorie Garber (Baltimore, 1987), pp. 67–89, and Stephen Greenblatt, *Marvelous Possessions* (Oxford, 1991).

4 Montaigne, 'Of Custom, and How a Received Law Should Not Easily be Changed', *Essays*, trans. J. Florio (Everyman Edition); the Latin quotation comes from Pliny, Epistle xx.

5 For the change in attitude at this time see Anthony Pagden, *The Fall of Natural Man: the American Indian and the Origins of Comparative Ethnology* (Cambridge, 1982).

6 Montaigne, 'Of the Cannibals', I, xxx, p. 218; Steven Mullaney, 'Strange Things, Gross Terms, Curious Customs: the Rehearsal of Cultures in the Late Renaissance', *Representations* 3 (1983), 40–67.

7 This play's relationships to ideas of Victor Turner and its source, Colin Turnbull's *The Mountain People* (New York, 1972), are described by Elinor Shaffer, 'The Hermeneutic Approach to Theatre and Drama', in *New Directions in Theatre*, ed. Julian Hilton (London, 1993), pp. 120–44, especially pp. 138–9.

8 See G. K. Hunter, *Dramatic Identities and Cultural Tradition* (Liverpool, 1978), p. 7; James A. Boon, 'Comparative De-Enlightenment: Paradox and Limits in the History of Ethnology', *Daedalus* 109 (1980), 73–91.

9 See Andrew Hadfield, 'Writing the "New World": more "Invisible Bullets"', *Literature and History* 2: 2 (1991), 3–19.

10 Greenblatt, *Possessions*, p. 8.

11 Ralph Lane, 'The First Virginia Colony, 1585–6', in Richard Hakluyt, *Voyages to the Virginia Colonies*, ed. A. L. Rowse (London, 1986), pp. 86–106, quote at p. 95; Harriot begins his 'Brief and true report' with a catalogue of the 'merchantable' (Hakluyt, *Voyages*, p. 109).

12 Edward Hayes, 'Sir Humphrey Gilbert's Newfoundland Voyage, 1583', in Hakluyt, *Voyages*, pp. 21-48 quote at p. 21.

13 There is a Messianic tone in a text by the Sheffield Puritan, The Revd. William Crashaw, *A Sermon Preached in London before the Right Honorable the Lord Lawarre...*(Running title, *A New Year's Gift to Virginia*) (London, 1610), but the impulse is anti-papist, 'the plantation of a church of English christians [in Virginia], and consequently the conversion of the heathen from the devil to God' (sig. C3r), a projection upon New World of English religious dissension. He also writes of the redemptive power of adversity upon the basest and worst men, 'the very excrements of a full and swelling state' (sig. E4v); the sermon is discussed by Louis B. Wright, *Religion and Empire* (Chapel Hill, NC, 1943).

14 Charlotte Brontë, *The Professor*, ed. Heather Glen (Harmondsworth, 1989), p. 177.

15 '"Of the Cannibals" is inscribed within this heterological tradition [derived from Herodotus], in which the discourse about the other is a means of constructing a discourse authorized by the other' (Michel de Certeau, *Heterologies: Discourse on the Other*, trans. Brian Massumi (Manchester, 1986), p. 68); see also Tzvetan Todorov, *The Conquest of America: the Question of the Other*, trans. R. Howard (New York, 1984); Paul Brown has demonstrated that one source of *The Tempest*'s internal complexity is the construction of the figure of Caliban as the threatening 'other'.

16 For the implications of the New World setting of the *Utopia*, see Fritz Caspari, *Humanism and the Social Order in Tudor England* (New York, 1954), p. 100.

17 'Of the Cannibals'; for Montaigne's relativism, see Tzvetan Todorov, *Nous et les autres* (Paris, 1989), pp. 51–64.

18 *The Memorable Masque of the two Honorable Houses or Inns of Court, the Middle Temple and Lincoln's Inn* (London, 1613).

19 Marlowe, *Doctor Faustus*, in *The Complete Works of Christopher Marlowe*, ed. Fredson Bowers (Cambridge, 1973), I. i. 158–9.

20 Ralegh, *Guiana*, sig.¶3v; King James also portrayed the 'barbarous Indians' as fountains of more general evils than smoking: see *A Counterblast to Tobacco* (London, 1604), *passim*; see also Karen Newman, '"And Wash the Ethiop White": Femininity and the Monstrous in *Othello*', in *Shakespeare Reproduced* eds. Jean E. Howard and Marion F. O'Connor (London, 1987), pp. 143–62.

21 See Francisco Guerra, 'The Problem of Syphilis', in *First Images of America: the Impact of the New World on the Old*, ed. Fredi Chiappelli, 2 vols. (Berkeley, 1976), II, pp. 845–52.

22 William Painter, *The Palace of Pleasure* (1567), ed. Joseph Jacobs, 3 vols. (London, 1890), II, p. 160; see also the mass of material provided by Gabriele Pearson, 'Topical Ideology: Witches, Amazons, and Shakespeare's Joan of Arc', *English Literary Renaissance* 18 (1988), 40–65, and Laura Brown, 'Amazons and Africans: Gender, Race, and Empire in Daniel Defoe', in *Women, 'Race', and Writing in the Early Modern Period*, eds. Margo Hendricks and Patricia Parker (London, 1994), pp. 118–37.

23 See Wayland D. Hand, 'The Effect of the Discovery on Ethnological and Folklore Studies in Europe', in *First Images*, ed. Chiappelli, I, p. 50.

24 Ralegh, *Guiana*, pp. 23–4.

25 This was written about the same time as the texts mentioned in note 1; Theseus' recent victory over the Amazonian Hippolyta in Shakespeare's *A Midsummer Night's Dream* might also be of topical import.

26 See Peter Hulme, 'Polytropic Man: Tropes of Sexuality and Morality in Early Colonial Discourse', in *Europe and its Others*, eds. Francis Barker et al., 2 vols. (Colchester, 1985), II, pp. 17–32.

27 Montaigne, exceptionally, writes of the 'cannibals': 'All their moral discipline containeth but these two articles; first an undismayed resolution to war, then an inviolable affection to their wives' ('Of the Cannibals', p. 222).

28 See *Fair Maid*, part I, II. ii: 'bawdy East Indian pictures worse than ever were Aretine's'. The Virginian narratives in Hakluyt, however, are notably lacking in sexual content.

29 These are alluded to at the opening of Montaigne's essay.

30 See Eric Cheyfitz, *The Poetics of Imperialism* (New York, 1991), pp. xii–xiii.

31 See Jean E. Howard, 'An English Lass Amid the Moors: Gender, Race, Sexuality, and National Identity in Heywood's *The Fair Maid of the West*', in *Women, 'Race', and Writing*, eds. Hendricks and Parker, pp. 101–17.

32 This comparative neglect of the Americas in literature was a European phenomenon (see Hunter, *Dramatic Identities*, pp. 9–10).

33 *The Tempest*, ed. Stephen Orgel (Oxford, 1987), p. 219; Spenser also uses the figure in his *View of the Present State of Ireland* / (c. 1596), p. 207.

34 The opening scenes of both *The Tempest* and *The Sea-Voyage* indicate the way that nature is a great leveller.

35 *Eclaircissement sur l'Esprit des Lois*, *Oeuvres* (Paris, 1951) II, pp. 1169, 1180–3.

36 For a recent and helpful analysis of *The Tempest* see Eric Cheyfitz, 'The Foreign Policy of Metaphor', in *The Poetics of Imperialism* (New York, 1991), ch. 2, pp. 22–40.

37 Leo Marx, *The Machine in the Garden: Technology and the Pastoral Ideal in America* (New York, 1964), p. 69.

38 I owe these concepts to a paper delivered by Professor Kenneth Parker at the *European Society for the Study of English* Conference in Norwich in 1989. They are to be found in Sir Thomas More, *Utopia*, ed. J. Rawson Lumby (London, 1885), p. 21, in the accounts of the first Virginian voyage (1584) and in Ralph Lane's *Discourse* (1585) in Hakluyt, *Voyages*, and in Michael Drayton's 'To the Virginian Voyage' (1606), reprinted in William B. Hunter ed., *The English Spenserians* (Salt Lake City, 1977).

39 For the tendency to describe the lands inhabited by Indians as vacant or virgin see J. Tompkins, '"Indians": Textualism, Morality and the Problem of History', in *'Race', Writing and Difference*, ed. H. L. Gates, (Chicago, 1986), pp. 59–77.

40 See Hakluyt, *Voyages, passim*.

41 Ralegh, *Guiana*, p. 3.

42 For an account of the play's Amazonian theme which is traced back to Spenser, see Simon Shepherd, *Amazons and Warrior Women: Varieties of Feminism in Seventeenth-Century Drama* (Brighton, 1981).

43 Compare Cheyfitz, *The Poetics of Imperialism*, p. 14.

44 Ralegh, *Guiana*, pp. 23–4.
45 For a general study of cannibalism, see Stephen Orgel, 'Shakespeare and the Cannibals', in *Cannibals, Witches and Divorce*, ed. Garber, pp. 40–66; Cheyfitz, *The Poetics of Imperialism*, pp. 41ff; and for the etymology of the word and a passage in Hakluyt where Englishmen turn cannibal, see Hadfield, 'Writing the "New World"', pp. 11–15; also relevant is Carla Freccero, 'Cannibalism, Homophobia, Women', in *Women, 'Race' and Writing*, eds. Hendricks and Parker, pp. 73–83.

CHAPTER 12

Industrious Ariel and idle Caliban

Andrew Gurr

Much attention has been given to Caliban as red man or black man, the first of Mannoni's victims of colonialism.[1] Almost none, even in the context of Stephen Greenblatt's cultural poetics, has been given to the other victim of colonialist Prospero, Ariel. Whether as man or woman (another red herring), Ariel has gained more attention from theatre directors than he has from critics.[2] Jonathan Miller for instance in his Old Vic production in 1988 matched his black Caliban with a black Ariel. When left on the island at the end of the play his Ariel took up Prospero's broken staff and put it together again in his own hands, smiling meanly at Caliban while he did so. But such hints about the post-colonial politics of the black Europeans as this suggests, the input of Wabenzi neo-colonialism, have not been very conspicuous in academic studies. So Ariel ought to be put back opposite Caliban. In the process I think that the image of Prospero as colonialist changes its colour a little, into something rather more like London blue.

The post-colonial interpretation of *The Tempest* has had a long and distinguished history by now. Octave Mannoni used the relationship between Prospero and Caliban to characterize Malagasy colonialism, in his *Psychologie de la colonisation*, as long ago as 1950.[3] When it appeared in English in 1956 it was given the name *Prospero and Caliban*. Franz Fanon intensified this post-colonial vision of the relationship, making Prospero a plainly colonialist villain, in a way that joined up curiously with the stage tradition of centring the play's pathos on Caliban that started with Beerbohm Tree at the beginning of the century. Fanon was a strong influence on the readings of anti-colonialists such as Césaire and

Ngugi wa Thiong'o.[4] Jan Kott's influential reading was planted on the same path. More recently Stephen Greenblatt brought his cultural poetics into play on the concept of Caliban as the colonized in 'Learning to Curse'.[5] A specifically Marxist reading can be found in the two influential essays of 1971 and 1986 by Robert Fernandez Retamar.[6] Between them these views seem to be the most popular way of reading *The Tempest* at present. The focus on Caliban as the signifying Other can be seen at an almost self-parodic extreme in Jan Kott who, in his essay on power in the play, says that 'there is no doubt that Prospero and Caliban are the protagonists of *The Tempest*'.[7] Without wishing to plead too strongly for a more formalist reading of the text than one which supplies it with a double protagonist, I think the focus on Caliban needs to be adjusted with a different kind of historicist context.

Kott's claim that there are two protagonists in *The Tempest*, Prospero and Caliban, standing as opposite principles, colonizer and colonized, emphasizes Prospero's function as a figure of power in the play. Mannoni's use of the play and that of those he influenced support this view. Such perspectives set up difficulties in accounting for several of the other elements in the play. The most obvious of these is Caliban's fellow-servant Ariel, and the formal patterning of the play that develops out of the contrasting relations that the two servant-slaves exhibit towards their master and magus. It is never easy to sort out the chiasmic patterning of comparability and contrast between Shakespeare's characters, but it is a sufficiently familiar feature of the plays to warrant applying it to Prospero's pair of very different colonial servants.

There are many elements in the play that emphasize the contrasting servant-roles of Caliban and Ariel, and they throw up some intriguing analogies with the 'idle and industrious apprentice' tradition. Ariel's desire for 'liberty', to be 'free / As mountain winds' (1.ii.245, 502),[8] and the shortening of his term of service, for instance, offsets Caliban's more earthbound resentment at his enforced service and the theft of his island. Their fates at the end of the play stand in similar contrast. I think that neither Caliban nor Ariel can be seen adequately in their roles in the play without some concern for the concept of service and freedom that the play flirts with. That concept has a bearing on the whole question of the post-colonial *Tempest*, since it raises questions about that favourite theme of new historicism, power.

Greenblatt, in his celebrated 1976 essay 'Learning to Curse', speaks of 'the startling encounter between a lettered and an unlettered culture' being 'heightened, almost parodied, in the relationship between a European whose entire source of power is his library and a savage who had no speech at all before the European's arrival' (p. 23). At the core of this reading is the concept of art itself as colonization. This view dextrously shifts Prospero out of the metaphor of power as colonization into the metatheatricality of art as power. Prospero is thus changed from the old image of the author as magus, playwright and presenter into a figure of power as artistic authority. This admits readings relating language to power, which again invokes what might be seen as a disproportionately logocentric attention to Caliban's power to curse. But amongst a multitude of other things it also invites a reading that lays peculiar emphasis on the play's closure, and what happens when Prospero gives up his power and the magically colonized island to return to reality. The trouble is that when the power question is laid out in these terms, whether in the colonizer or the magician-artist, it can all too easily misrepresent what is laid out in the text. The actual conditions of power in the play, and their consequences for one's view of the Prospero and Caliban relationship, call for a surer grasp than recent studies have held them in. We need to review the colonizer as a power issue and what happens to it in the closure.

Terence Hawkes in *Shakespeare's Talking Animals* was one of the first critics to take note of the presentation of the playwright as colonist. He drew attention to the problem which that image creates in the play's closure: 'Certainly the Caliban of act v is in a very real sense Prospero's creature, and the bitter justness of his retort early in the play [about language] still casts a shadow at its close. With Prospero restored to his dukedom, the match of Ferdinand and Miranda blessed, Ariel freed to the elements, and even the wind and tides of the return voyage settled, Shakespeare leaves Caliban's fate naggingly unclear. Prospero has acknowledged a bond; that is all' (p. 26).[9] I would say that Prospero's freeing of Ariel should raise questions not only about the fudging of Caliban's afterlife in the play but the comparability of Caliban's power-relation to Prospero with that of Ariel.

Ariel and what he (or she) seems to represent in the play have been called everything from 'the spirit of fancy and playfulness' (Alvin Kernan) to 'an angel and an executioner' (Jan Kott). More obviously, he is 'the instrument of [Prospero's] justice' (D. G. James). Richard Marienstras, picking up Kott's point that Ariel acts as 'agent-provocateur and the stage-manager of the performance produced by Prospero' (p. 253), calls him 'the tempter, but he is also the one who prevents illegitimate desires from being satisfied'. Germaine Greer picks up Kernan's view, claiming that he is 'the power of the collective imagination, playwright's words working on audience's faculty'. Other critics make rather more of the point about his contrast with Caliban. Kernan's is still the standard view of the two as representatives of opposing elements: 'Ariel, the light spirit of fancy, and Caliban, the creature of body and appetite' (p. 139). More relevant to my concerns, David L. Hirst writes that 'Caliban is the unwilling slave, Ariel the more pliant servant.'[10]

There of course has to be a wide variety of perspectives on the two figures who work under Prospero's magical control. Part of that variety is a large question about the radical differences in the presentation of their two servant-functions. While Caliban seeks other masters, Ariel's relationship is exclusively with his magus. We should bear in mind here that in line with his assertion that Prospero and Caliban are the protagonists, Kott dismisses any attempt to counterbalance Ariel with Caliban as 'philosophically flat and theatrically vacuous' (p. 269), precisely on the grounds that Ariel is visible only to Prospero and the audience. That, I would argue, is one of the features of difference that needs taking into account. Both Caliban and Ariel are presented as servants of sorts. The difference in the presentation of their roles is one of the factors that should modify the post-colonial readings.

Before looking into the relations of Prospero with his two servants, though, it might help to take some note of the question of colonial priority. Colonization is all about power, which is part of its fascination. But that power is usually linked, in ways not always easily identifiable, with the laws of property, or rather of prior possession. It is the last comer who is always the colonizer, if he or she is not to be merely an immigrant. Previous inhabitants are likely to have been colonizers in their turn. Colonization is almost always a layering process. The white colonizers of the Maori in New Zealand over the last century or so arrived there eight hundred years after the Maori themselves colonized the country, wiping out the Moriori who were there before them. This is an attitude to colonialism that awards ownership according to the (conceivably European-originated) 'I saw it first' rule for unclaimed objects. From what we are told of *The Tempest*'s island, before Prospero the colonizer there was Sycorax the first colonizer, black magician preceding white magician. The accident that there was nobody to colonize when Sycorax first arrived on the island gave Caliban his prime claim to it. Ariel arrived with them in the role of servant to Sycorax. As Prospero reports it (1.ii.270–3) 'Thou, my slave, / As thou report'st thyself, was then her servant', but one 'too delicate / To act her earthy and abhorred commands'. Sycorax and Caliban had the island by right of planting the first flag. Caliban, as child of the first possessor, inherited it when his mother died, and Prospero later took it from him. By the law of possession Caliban is right to say 'this island's mine'. And by the same law Prospero is doubly wrong to dispossess him and to make him a servant or slave. That raises linked questions both about Prospero's magical power and about the nature of service.

Stephen Orgel notes that Ariel is the 'unwilling servant' of both magi in the play, Sycorax and Prospero.[11] For both he works as a sorcerer's apprentice. He proved too 'delicate' for the earthiness of Sycorax, and responds better to the presumably more airy and delicate commands of Prospero. Ariel has been a servant from the outset, but now wants his freedom. He owes Prospero a debt of gratitude for releasing him from the prison Sycorax left him in, which gives a shape to his desire for freedom – Prospero's threat to him is specifically of a worse confinement. What it is that makes him call himself Prospero's slave can only be Prospero's magical power, and a combination of gratitude for the release from Sycorax's punishment and fear of its renewal. Caliban by contrast has only become a servant or slave unwillingly. He began, like any good apprentice, by living in as a member of the family. His subsequent behaviour, the failure to teach him more than language and his assault on his master's daughter Miranda, has demoted him within the patriarchy to the role of a house servant.

Orgel puts Caliban and Ariel together neatly encapsulated as an opposed pair:

In contrast to Caliban's elemental sameness, Ariel is volatile and metamorphic. He is male, the asexual boy to Caliban's libidinous man, but (in keeping with his status as a boy actor) all the roles he plays at Prospero's command are female: sea nymph, harpy, Ceres. (pp. 26–7)

Disloyal man and loyal boy, male and female. And there are other points of contrast. Politicizing the situation in relation to the context of James' noisy quarrel with Parliament in 1609–10, Donna B. Hamilton sees Caliban's coarse and cursing language of complaint as representing one aspect of the 'Commons', whereas Ariel is 'an ideally obsequious Commons such as the King himself would have preferred'. She emphasizes their joint role as servants. 'Even as Prospero speaks with the flat, impenetrable voice of the Gods, so Ariel and Caliban speak with the various voices of subjects', she says.[12] It is those distinct subject-roles that I think are most in need of re-contextualizing.

From the text it is clear that what we now prefer to read as colonialist power is verbalized as a pair of master–servant relationships. Patriarchs colonized their servants. Ariel and Caliban are both said early in the play to be servants or slaves to Prospero. At 1.ii.187 Prospero summons Ariel by the name of 'servant'. At lines 270–1 he again calls him 'servant', adding that Ariel calls himself Prospero's 'slave'. Caliban he himself calls 'slave' when he first summons him at 1.ii.315. The peculiar difference in the relationships is that in Ariel's case but not Caliban's it is not perpetual slavery but has a defined limit. Ariel insists on getting his promised freedom or 'liberty', and Prospero promises to 'abate one year' (1.ii.249–50) of his service 'before the time be out' (246). This is the language of indentured apprenticeship. The relationship is presented as if Ariel had to serve a term as his master's apprentice before reaching the journeyman or 'free' status that normally went with the completion of an apprenticeship.

The mathematics of Prospero's and Ariel's calculations of time make it rather less simple than that. In the London of the sixteenth century the youths enrolled in the major handicraft guilds normally served a seven-year apprenticeship before being 'freed' and becoming journeymen at the age of twenty-one.[13] In practice the length of the term varied – in the lists of apprentices to the printing trade, the terms served vary from six to eleven years. As late as the 1640s apprentices generally served between eight and ten years.[14] But eleven years is exceptionally long for an apprenticeship that in London would normally end when the youth reached maturity at twenty-one (twenty-four in the corporate towns).[15] The average age when apprentices started their sentence was seventeen and a half for Londoners, two years older than that for outsiders.

Both Ariel and Caliban are old for apprentices, and both are well past the threshold when they should be given their freedom.[16] When Ariel reminds Prospero of his promise to release him 'a full year' early (I.ii.243–50), he must have already been in service for most of the twelve years since Prospero's arrival on the island. He had been imprisoned in a pine by Sycorax for twelve before that, so he was older than Caliban's twenty-four. There is a symmetry in the twelve years of Ariel's imprisonment and the twelve of his service for Prospero, picked up by Prospero in his threat to imprison Ariel in an oak for another twelve (I.ii.294–6). It is tempting to maintain mathematical credibility at the expense of symmetry by giving Prospero an initial year to command his magic before he could release Ariel from Sycorax's pine, thus leaving Ariel a twelfth year to serve without the promised remission. Counting in blocks of twelve-year time-spans is more comfortable than trying to match the language of indenturing to the twelve years of Ariel's apprenticeship. But the request for freedom and the terms Prospero uses to Ariel do invoke apprenticeship, whether or not in the trade of sorcery. And Ariel, for all Jonathan Miller's device at the close, shows no special enthusiasm for the magic trade he is agent and servant in.

Nor is there anything in the play to make more specific the concept of apprenticeship in the work that either Ariel or Caliban does, or Caliban's temporary substitute the new learner and slave Ferdinand. Once Prospero has brought in Ariel in I.ii and his skills have been described, he rouses Miranda and takes her to Caliban, of whom he says 'He does make our fire, / Fetch in our wood, and serves in office / That profit us' (313–15). These are hardly the services of an Ariel, and very like the hewing of wood and drawing of water that was allocated to the sons of Ham in the Bible, a verse used in the eighteenth century to justify slavery. Whatever Ariel's work for Prospero is, Caliban's mundane duties of making the fires and fetching wood are the work of a household servant, not an apprentice. Ferdinand is given the same unskilled labour as Caliban. The other difference is that household servants, being paid for their work, unlike apprentices, and not legally bound as apprentices were, would not usually need the goal of 'freedom' at the end of their terms of service.

The most graphic and easily the most hostile description of household servants is William Harrison's, printed in the 1587 second edition of Holinshed's *Chronicles* which Shakespeare was regularly consulting through the 1590s. Holinshed thought household servants were only one step above vagrants in the English social hierarchy. He does in fact declare that they are close to being slaves, though he also makes the key differentiation that in this the English are better than less favoured races abroad. The paragraph he gives to this category of society, with whom every common player had close affinities, is a resonant statement about the region of Tudor society where patriarchal power did not lie. The relevant section of 'The Description of England', with a marginal note saying 'No slaves or bondmen in England', declares:

As for slaves and bondmen we have none, naie such is the privilege of our countrie by the especiall grace of God, and bountie of our princes, that if anie come hither from other realms, so soone as they set foot on land they become so free of condition as their masters, whereby all note of servile bondage is utterlie remooved from them, wherein we resemble (not the Germans who had slaves also, though such as in respect of the slaves of other countries might well be reputed free, but) the old Indians and the Taprobanes, who supposed it a great injurie to nature to make or suffer them to be bond, whome she in hir woonted course dooth produce and bring foorth free. This fourth and last sort of people therefore have neither voice nor authoritie in the common wealth, but are to be ruled, and not to rule other: yet they are not altogither neglected, for in cities and corporat townes, for default of yeomen they are faine to make up their inquests of such maner of people. And in villages they are commonlie made churchwardens, sidemen, aleconners, now and then constables, and manie times injoie the name of hedboroughes. Unto this sort also may our great swarmes of idle serving men be referred, of whome there runneth a proverbe; Yoong serving men old beggers, bicause service is none heritage. These men are profitable to none, for if their condition be well perused, they are enimies to their masters, to their freends, and to themselves: for by them oftentimes their masters are incouraged unto unlawfull exactions of their tenants, their freends brought unto povertie by their rents inhanced, and they themselves brought to confusion by their owne prodigalitie and errors, as men that having not wherewith of their owne to mainteine their excesses, doo search in high waies, budgets, cofers, males, and stables, which way to supplie their wants. How diverse of them also coveting to beare an high saile doo insinuate themselves with yoong gentlemen and noble men newlie come to their lands, the case is too much apparant.

Harrison gets carried away by his vision of the unproductive wastefulness of such employment. He pulls himself back from his diatribe with an image only too well fitted to a play launched by a tempest, 'But how farre have I waded in this point, or how farre may I saile in such a large sea?'[17]

The thought of Caliban also getting his freedom is never mentioned by either master or servant. Both Ariel and Caliban are servants to Prospero, but while Ariel claims a term to his service, like an apprentice, Caliban's work is that of an unskilled house servant precisely in Harrison's mould, a failed apprentice perhaps, whose teaching (Miranda's included) did not stick, so that he has no trade and no term, only a wage to supplement his board and lodging and the chancy prospect of finding new employment with passing nobles like Stephano and Trinculo. Except that Caliban on the desert island does not even have a wage (there is nothing to spend it on). With neither a contracted term of service nor a wage, his conditions actually are those of a slave.

In the complex of the play's multitude of ironic reversals, it is a nice question which is the kind of freedom at issue here, release from the bond of apprenticeship or from the bondage of an unwaged slave. The kind of freedom Ariel wants is payment for a term of faithful service, and the relation between Tudor master and apprentice does stand behind this use of the term. Apprentices lived in their master's house, receiving board and lodging, but no wage, in return for their work. They learned a skill which made them independent and eventually could make them masters in their own right.[18] House servants lived in too, earning a wage, but without the contractual bond of teaching and learning that apprentices served under. Yet considering how close the verbal links to London social conditions are, neither of these two servants in the play works at all straightforwardly in the role of student and learner to Prospero. His power is his magic, and Ariel does not try to learn it. Both Caliban and Ariel serve through the play in roles somewhere between that of bound apprentice, paid servant and unpaid slave. They take no learning and no wages. This, paradoxically, makes freedom their only reward, and returns us to the post-colonial perspective. Prospero thinks and talks much more in the mode of a London citizen-employer than as a colonialist. Like charity, it seems that Shakespeare's colonialism begins at home. But the servant role is worth chasing a little further, because behind that ambiguous, if not mixed, image of their roles looms that potent moral fable, the idle and the industrious apprentice, and that pair of folk-tale roles has a strong bearing on the play's closure.

The classic expression of the two kinds of apprentice is Hogarth's set of twelve engravings done in 1747 and published under the title 'Industry and Idleness'. These picture-stories drew on a very old morality idea with roots deep in Shakespeare's time. The specific idea for Hogarth's series, which he said was 'more for use than ornament', in fact came to him from *Eastward Ho!*. That boy-company play about apprentices became notorious at the Blackfriars playhouse four years before *The Tempest* was written under a different dispensation for the same theatre.[19] The Blackfriars was of course notable for its expensive seating and therefore its success in excluding the social ranks who filled the yard at the amphitheatres, apprentices and house servants. If *The Tempest* was, as I believe, written like *Eastward Ho!* specifically to be performed at the Blackfriars playhouse,[20] it too would have excluded the social category that both plays make use of. Shakespeare may or may not have seen *Eastward Ho!*, though he could easily have read it, and given the noise that it generated and what happened to Jonson and his co-writers over its censure in 1606 he is unlikely to have been wholly unaware of at least some accounts of its story and its satirical thrust. Quicksilver and Golding, parodic expressions of the common theme of industry and idleness presented in alchemical language, may hardly seem the most obvious precedents for Caliban and Ariel, but both sets of servant-apprentices emerged, on the same stage and within five years of one another, from the same long-running moralistic tradition that underlay all presentations of servant relationships at the time.

Eastward Ho! was written for the railing and satirical repertoire of the Blackfriars Boys. I would not suggest that it has any proximity of subject to Shakespeare's play, though it does refer to ships and Londoners bound for America (II.ii.150–1 and IV.ii.230),[21] something that the plays its title burlesques, *Westward Ho!*, and its successor *Northward Ho!*, make no mention of. Its apprentices are part of a tricksy exercise in parodying the values of both the city and the court, an exercise that probably stood to benefit from the absence of apprentices in the audience. Without directly burlesquing the popular (or at least the well-advertised) citizen values of industry and thrift that can be found in the Dick Whittington story and *The Shoemaker's Holiday*, and the translation of the prodigal son parable into a lesson in thrift,[22] it registers the alternative courses on the road to prosperity, the high road that ends in disaster and the low road that ends in prosperity. More to the point, perhaps, it upholds marrying the boss's daughter as one reward for the more industrious course. That, if nothing else, may serve to counterpoint Caliban with Ariel as servant-apprentices, and augment Ferdinand's role as temporary replacement for Caliban. Caliban's attempted rape of his master's daughter can be counterpoised against Prospero's insistence on keeping Ariel to himself, invisible most of all to Miranda. And thinking of how much more critical attention Caliban has received than Ariel, we might even find a parallel in the fact that the idle apprentice's career is always found to be more interesting than the industrious one's.

Ariel is the servant of the magus, his magic expressed in his mastery of the air and airs, his music. He is winged Mercury, antithesis of *Eastward Ho!*'s get-rich-quick Quicksilver. Caliban is not equal to the heavily worthy Golding either. The magus leaves the idle apprentice to his wanderings, keeping the industrious apprentice to himself, 'subject to no sight but mine and thine, /

Invisible to every eyeball else' (1.ii.302–3), while the idle one meets those who offer him new masters and lead him astray. Ariel is distinct in this from Subtle's servant Face, that other alchemist's assistant, who makes himself visible to every eyeball, though Ariel when he does appear to others than Prospero turns up in disguises like Face.[23] Is he an apprentice learning his master's trade (as Miller made him), or just a servant quick to obey? Ariel's loyalty to Prospero, part of his invisibility to all but his master, stands in utter contrast to Caliban's disloyalty, his readiness to serve another master. Caliban is less concerned throughout with freedom than with new servitude. Two traditions of service, Hogarth's and Manuel de Falla's, seem to converge in *The Tempest*.

Every formal feature of a play is tested by its closure. So it is necessary to test this reading by looking at the awkward question of the imbalance between the endings offered for the two servants. Stephen Orgel claims that both Ariel and Caliban get their freedom at the end of the play (p. 26). It is not so clear-cut a close as that, though. Much is made of Ariel's liberty, but Prospero's last word to Caliban is to send him with the servants of the King to his 'poor cell' to await more orders. He must presumably continue in service while his master entertains the courtly feasters and talkers before they all sail away. Whether he is expected then to continue in service and sail off with them, or whether he is left behind like Beerbohm Tree's Caliban to recolonize his island in isolation, in or out of the company of mercurial and delicate Ariel, depends on the priority you give to two things: the magical unreality of the island, and the transience of the colonialist visitors on it. Caliban's last statement, that he will 'be wise hereafter, / And seek for grace', is an act of submission worthy of a repentant prodigal and a servant-apprentice. He is a servant and needs to continue in service. One very loud contrast in his counterpointing with Ariel is his failure to think at all of freedom as a goal. So the omission of any hint that he may be freed or left behind on the island when the company sails away may be read as a reaffirmation of his servant status. The absence of any hint that he might stay when those he serves sail away also leaves him still with the status of servant. Any claim that the colonized Caliban is left free on his island at the end needs a much more positive assertion than the text supplies.

It is true of course that sympathy for Caliban and his colonized status these days is not just politically correct but an affirmation of human warmth. Prospero is not so much a colonist as a master-citizen, an indigenous and short-tempered Londoner, patriarch of his family household with its routine complement of children, apprentices and house servants, a role that is now all too easily replaced with the colonial patriarch and the hierarchy of power he represents. The power that comes from his magic conceals the power that came originally from his social source in London. To see Prospero's book and his magic as a representation of the power that came to the colonialists from superior technology, like the shadow cast by Swift's flying island of Laputa, is to read a lot of today into a text of yesterday. Colonialism in Shakespeare's time was an extension of patriarchy. Patriarchs colonized their servants. For Londoners, colonization started in London.

With all the formalist and chiasmic neatness with which one can balance the equivalent roles against one another, the differences between Ariel and Caliban are immense, and spill far beyond the rather simplistic set of oppositions between the airy and the earthy that Frances Yates and others have found.[24] Consideration of their servile relations with Prospero strengthens several features of the play that the colonialist approach obscures. They enhance, for instance, the notorious point about Prospero's bad temper. They underline his selfishness as well as the traditional London-based character of his colonialism. The duties of the two figures as servants are different even in colonial terms, the one doing only the unskilled work of the sons of Ham, fetching wood and water, while the other is empowered to enact the mage's supernatural commands. Prospero's exploitation of both of them shows in their relations with the rest of the island's occupants. Caliban is fully visible, Ariel always disguised. Miranda knows Caliban, and has helped to teach him. She never sees Ariel, being put to sleep in ii.i. before Prospero summons Ariel to appear and tells him to become invisible. The one relation is social, the other magical.

The play, of course, resists even the most politically correct readings, and offers hardly any mollification for the variety of discomforts that it so dextrously generates. I would merely claim that Prospero's magic, and the antinomy of the white magus and the black, Caliban's and Ariel's first and second parents and masters, are a mix of matters that relate to master–servant power in the play as much as to artistic or colonistic control.[25]

NOTES

1 See for instance G. Wilson Knight, 'Caliban as a Red Man', in *Shakespeare's Styles: Essays in Honour of Kenneth Muir*, eds. Philip Edwards, Inga-Stina Ewbank and G. K. Hunter (Cambridge, 1980), pp. 205–20.

2 A notable exception is David Norbrook, whose wide-ranging essay, '"What cares these roarers for the name of king?"': Language and Utopia in *The Tempest*', in *The Politics of Tragicomedy. Shakespeare and After*, eds. Gordon McMullan and Jonathan Hope (London and New York, 1992), pp. 21–54.

3 First published in 1950; translated into English in 1956 as *Prospero and Caliban: the Psychology of Colonisation*.

4 Franz Fanon, *Black Skins, White Masks*, trans. Charles Lam Markmann (Paris, 1952, New York 1967), pp. 83–108; Ngugi wa Thiong'o, *Writers in Politics* (London, 1981), p. 36. Césaire's brilliant rewrite of the play first appeared in French in 1969. See Rob Nixon, 'Caribbean and African Appropriations of *The Tempest*', *Critical Enquiry* 13 (1986–7), 557–78.

5 Originally published in *First Images of America*, ed. Fredi Chiapelli (Berkeley, 1976), pp. 561–80. It supplied the title for the book in which it was reissued, *Learning to Curse: Essays in Early Modern Culture* (New York, 1990), pp. 16–39. Quotations are from this version. Broadly similar views are expressed by Trevor R. Griffiths, '"This Island's Mine": Caliban and Colonialism', *Yearbook of English Studies* 13 (1983), 159–80; Paul Brown, '"This Thing of Darkness I Acknowledge Mine"': *The Tempest* and the Discourse of Colonialism', in *Political Shakespeare: New Essays in Cultural Materialism*, eds. Jonathan Dollimore and Alan Sinfield (Manchester, 1985), pp. 48–71; Malcolm Evans, *Signifying Nothing. Truth's True Contents in Shakespeare's Text*, second edition, (Hemel Hempstead, 1989), ch. 4; and Meredith Ann Skura, 'Discourse and the Individual: the Case of Colonialism in *The Tempest*', *Shakespeare Quarterly* 40 (1989), 42–69. See also Virginia and Alden Vaughan's *Shakespeare's Caliban. A Cultural History*, (Cambridge, 1991).

6 Reprinted in *Caliban and Other Essays* (Minneapolis, 1989).

7 Jan Kott, *Shakespeare our Contemporary*, trans. Boleslaw Taborski (London, 1965), p. 257.

8 Quotations from *The Tempest* and line references are taken from Frank Kermode's New Arden edition (1954, revised 1962).

9 Terence Hawkes, *Shakespeare's Talking Animals* (London, 1973), p. 26.
10 Alvin Kernan, *The Playwright as Magician* (New Haven, 1979), p. 136; Kott, *Shakespeare Our Contemporary*, p. 268; D. G. James, *The Dream of Prospero* (Oxford, 1967), p. 65; Richard Marienstras *New Perspectives on the Shakespearean World*, trans. Janet Lloyd (Cambridge, 1985), p. 178; Germaine Greer, *Shakespeare* (Oxford, 1986), p. 29; David L. Hirst, *The Tempest, Text and Performance* (London, 1984), p. 21.
11 Stephen Orgel, ed. *The Tempest*, New Oxford edition, p. 22.
12 Donna B. Hamilton, *Virgil and 'The Tempest'. The Politics of Imitation* (Columbus, 1990), pp. 121, 110.
13 Margaret Gay Davies, *The Enforcement of English Apprenticeship: a Study in Applied Mercantilism* (Cambridge, MA, 1956), p. 2. For an account of sixteenth-century London attitudes to work and apprentices generally, see Steve Rappaport, *Worlds Within Worlds: Structures of Life in Sixteenth-Century London* (Cambridge, 1989). His appendix 2 lists the numbers of apprentices and livery company citizens in London from 1490 to 1609, including (most pertinent for our purposes) the period 1600–9.
14 D. F. McKenzie, ed. *Stationers' Company Apprentices 1641–1700* (Oxford, 1974), records for instance Richard Alleyn binding Thomas Collins on 20 January 1640 and freeing him 1 April 1650; Francis Archer binding Edward Cleave 20 December 1633, freeing him 13 January 1642; Francis Ash binding John Jones 13 November 1637, freeing him 26 September 1646; Humphrey Robinson binding John Martyn 4 February 1635, freeing him 1 March 1643.
15 The Statute of Artificers of 1563 specified that apprentices had to be freed by the age of twenty-four.
16 Rappaport notes (*Worlds Within Worlds*, p. 295) that the average starting age was 19.5 years, and for Londoners 17.7 years (table 8.2). He also notes that only 41 per cent actually completed their apprenticeships and became 'free of the city'.
17 William Harrison, 'The Description of England,' in Raphael Holinshed, *Chronicles of England, Scotland and Ireland*, 3 vols. (1587). Both passages are in the fifth chapter of book 2 in the first volume.
18 Margaret Davies, *English Apprenticeship*, appendix 1, 'The Provisions of the Statute of Artificers Relating to Apprenticeship and its Enforcement', pp. 271–4, prints excerpts from the 1563 Statute, including Section XIX specifying the age of twenty-four as the point at which apprentices could turn into masters, Section XXIV specifying a minimum service of seven years, Section XXVI that there should be one journeyman for every three apprentices, and Section XXIX specifying that only those aged under twenty-one should be bound. Section XXXIII made special provision for the exceptional laws of London and Norwich.

19 Brian Gibbons, *Jacobean City Comedy*, second edition (Cambridge, 1980), pp. 8–11, summarises the 'idle and industrious apprentice' element in the play. His comment on its place in its time (pp. 119–20) is worth noting.

20 See '*The Tempest*'s Tempest at Blackfriars', *Shakespeare Survey* 41 (1989), 91–102.

21 Line references for *Eastward Ho!* are taken from the edition by C. G. Petter, New Mermaids (Tonbridge, 1973).

22 Laura Caroline Stevenson, *Praise and Paradox. Merchants and Craftsmen in Elizabethan Popular Literature* (Cambridge, 1984), ch. 7, makes the point that Tawney's identification of the Protestant work ethic really fits the post-1660 period. Deloney, Dekker and Heywood were more concerned to celebrate citizen spending once rich than the industrious practices that made them rich. Rappaport, *Worlds Within Worlds*, pp. 367–8, has a succinct comment on the Whittington myth.

23 Harry Levin, 'Two Magian Comedies, *The Tempest* and *The Alchemist*', *Shakespeare Survey* 22 (1971), 47–58, draws suggestive parallels between the two plays, both written in 1610 for the company playing at Blackfriars.

24 Frances A. Yates, *Shakespeare's Last Plays: a New Approach* (London, 1975).

25 By some way the most cogent essay on magic in *The Tempest* is Barbara A. Mowat's 'Prospero, Agrippa, and Hocus Pocus', *English Literary Renaissance* 11 (1981), 281–303.

CHAPTER 13

The New World in 'The Tempest'

Leo Salingar

We cannot doubt that reports about voyages to the New World in general, and about the colonization of Virginia in particular, contributed something to the production of *The Tempest* in 1611. In 1607, after the collapse of Ralegh's colonies in Virginia, a new settlement had been founded, precariously, at Jamestown. By 1609, while Spain's international power was temporarily checked, the Dutch and the French were sending expeditions to North America; and in the same year King James granted a new charter to the London Virginia Company, as a joint-stock enterprise[1] – with several of whose leaders Shakespeare was almost certainly acquainted: the Earl of Southampton, Sir Edwin Sandys, Sir Dudley Digges and possibly the Company's Secretary, William Strachey.[2] Through 1609 and the following years the Company poured out a stream of promotional sermons and pamphlets.[3] In October 1609, however, the news reached London that the flagship of an expedition which had set out in June, headed by Sir Thomas Gates and Sir George Somers, had apparently been overwhelmed, with the commanders on board, in a terrible storm; and this appeared to be confirmed – as a contemporary wrote, 'we therefore yeelded [them] as lost for many moneths together',[4] – until September 1610, when the Company's Council received the letter, or *True Reportory*, from William Strachey, recounting the wreck of Gates and Somers and their companions on the fearsome Bermudas ('the still-vex'd Bermoothes'), their amazing survival or 'redemption' there, and the sorry, though reformable, state of 'misgovernment' they found at Jamestown subsequently.[5] For a number of years the Council kept this damaging report confidential – though evidently somebody leaked it to Shakespeare, who utilized Strachey's graphic account of the storm (while drawing upon some general knowledge about seamanship as well). But meanwhile the Council embodied much of it in a propagandist pamphlet, *A True Declaration of the estate of the Colonie in Virginia*, registered for printing in November 1610; this, and an unauthorized leaflet published about the same moment by Sylvester Jourdain, were the first public notifications that Somers' party had been saved.[6]

The *True Declaration* set out to quash objectors and exhort supporters of the Company's godly, patriotic and profitable enterprise, which involves their dealings with the Indians: '[we] doe buy of them the pearles of earth, and sell to them the pearles of heaven'; (the pearls that figure in Ariel's song were a frequent item in literature of the New World).[7] And, even if they knew nothing of Strachey's letter, some of the first spectators of *The Tempest* could have noticed similarities between the play and the *True Declaration*. Thus, the pamphlet emphasizes the 'tragicall Comoedie' of the shipwreck and 'the permissive providence of God' in detaining Sir Thomas Gates on 'those infortunate (yet fortunate) Ilands', the 'hardly accessable' Bermudas, falsely reputed hitherto as 'an inchaunted pile of rockes, and a desert inhabitation for Divels'.[8] As to Virginia, a prime concern of the Company was to attract steady investment, especially from the wealthiest London merchants, who were reluctant to withdraw any of their capital from trading and risk it in a colonial plantation, with the prospect of uncertain and long-delayed returns.[9] While admitting that Jamestown was badly situated beside 'fennes', with 'unwholesome and contagious vapour' from the sea-water 'ooze', the *True Declaration* brushes aside malicious rumours about the rest of the country, so as to advertise, not for the first time, the 'temperatenesse of the Clymate' and the 'fertility of the soile' with its profusion of 'seedes of plenty and increase' – by no means 'Utopian, and legendarie fables', in spite of the misery the colonists had been reduced to before Gates' arrival, thanks to their own 'dissension', 'sedition' and 'idleness' and their 'treasons' and 'covetousness' towards the Indians.[10] The pamphlet also contains, like the play, a passing reference to Carthage.[11]

However, all this hardly makes *The Tempest* 'a veritable document of early Anglo-American history', as Sidney Lee called it, or even an 'intervention' in an 'ambivalent' colonialist 'discourse' and a 'dreamwork' of the political unconscious, in the terms (from an opposing political viewpoint) of Paul Brown and the current new historicists.[12] For one thing, as Meredith Anne Skura has pointed out, the new historicists have not been rigorously historical. A colonialist mentality was barely forming among Englishmen by 1611, though the seeds of it had already been sown in Ireland, while the idea of challenging Spain at sea commanded wide support; and any colonialist message implicit in the allusions to sea-voyages in *The Tempest* seems to have passed unnoticed at the time. Indeed, the preacher William Crashaw, an eminent spokesman for the Company, who had alleged that the actors were slandering the Virginian enterprise just before the appearance of Shakespeare's play, repeated the allegation shortly after it, and the same complaint of harmful influence due to 'the licentious vaine of stage Poets' was reiterated in a Company pamphlet of 1612.[13]

Secondly, colonialist readings of the play centre on Caliban; but there is no evidence that anyone connected Caliban with American Indians for almost three hundred years.[14] His name may suggest 'cannibal' but nothing else bears this out, and Shakespeare has surrounded him with a far-flung and ambiguous topography, since his mother has been an Algerian, though a worshipper of the demon, Setebos, of Patagonian extraction; similarly, Ariel no sooner mentions his weird mission to the 'Bermoothes' than he emphasizes the Mediterranean setting of the play's action (i.ii.226–37).[15] Vivid as it becomes for us, Caliban's island is no more a consistently identified location than the Athens inhabited by Quince and Bottom and visited simultaneously by Oberon and Puck. In any case, Caliban has been a solitary exile there rather than a representative of any tribe of aborigines; and above all, he differs extremely from Jacobean images of the natives of Virginia as men of courtesy, 'quick understanding' and 'a perfect constitution of body' (for all that they were also 'vile and cruel pagans').[16]

Further, none of the characters who have come to the island, neither Sycorax nor Prospero nor Alonso's party, have set out with a purpose that might link them with colonial venturers, such as seeking for precious metals or other commodities or discovering new sea routes or strategic bases or converting the heathen or establishing a settlement. Gonzalo's project of a 'plantation' is an invention on the spur of the moment, a reaction to circumstances, like the strange and involuntarily acquired sensations that perplex his fellow-voyagers. Strongly colonialist readings distort Prospero's project of returning to Milan, which constitutes the main plot, after all, and mask the play's affinities with other contemporary romances, whether Shakespeare's own preceding work or the scattered international romances featuring island magicians.[17]

On the other hand, Frank Kermode surely goes too far when he asserts 'that there is nothing in *The Tempest* fundamental to its structure of ideas which could not have existed had America remained undiscovered and the Bermuda voyage never taken place'.[18] It is precisely the allusions to the New World, tacit or overt, that make *The Tempest* unique. Other critics have discussed it recently in terms of 'crossing' or a dialectic between romance and history.[19] I should want to say that the topical elements in *The Tempest* set off its strangeness, that its allusive (and elusive) realism is fundamental within its structure of romance.

This turns in part upon a paradox of history. The voyages of discovery led to the rejection of some beliefs that had prevailed over the centuries, from Pliny to Mandeville.[20] But the discoveries and the spread of Renaissance learning also led to the revival of ideas and legends from the past, even though these now encountered an incipient rationalism and an intermittent readiness to question past authority. Europeans could not bring an unprejudiced consciousness to the New World. They brought their inherited culture with them, including not only their appetite for gain but their appetite for marvels. They promptly relocated the myth of a Golden Age in America;[21] or they viewed an exotic civilization in the light of romances of chivalry. Describing the Spaniards' first sight of Montezuma's capital, for instance, Bernal Diaz writes that 'These great towns...rising from the water, all made of stone, seemed like an enchanted vision from the tale of Amadis. Indeed, some of our soldiers asked whether it was not all a dream.'[22] Even the enquiring and sceptical Ralegh could persuade himself in Guiana to credit reports of headless men such as Mandeville had described, observing – much like Gonzalo after him on Prospero's island – that 'we find [Mandeville's] relations true of such things as theretofore were held incredible'.[23] William Strachey adduces 'experience' to dispose of the 'generall errour' that the Bermudas are devil-haunted; but he does it ambigously: 'Thus we shall make it appear', (he says) 'That Truth is the daughter of time, and that men ought not to deny every thing which is not subject to their senses.'[24] Paradoxically, it is incredulity, rather than excessive credulity, that he pinpoints. And he might be offering a gloss on the last act of *The Winter's Tale*.

In voyagers' comments like these a critical sense of reality entangles with a desire for wonders. A key problem for the age, the problem that not only (on one level) baffled Don Quixote but also engaged Francis Bacon's intellectual energy, was how to distinguish the untrustworthy from the credible. In a sense, the same problem was central to aesthetics. According to Tasso, for example, the prime object before the theory of epic poetry was 'how what is true to life can be joined with the marvellous'. One method Tasso recommends for 'joining these discordant qualities' is to attribute extraordinary events – or, as he says, 'miracles in ordinary speech' – to the power of God or of saints or magicians; another is to choose a subject set in remote times or remote places, such as 'the East Indies or the countries recently discovered in the vast ocean beyond the pillars of Hercules'.[25] Shakespeare was not following Tasso. But he was responding to similar imaginative demands.

The denouement of *The Winter's Tale* is said to be 'so like an old tale that the verity of it is in strong suspicion' (v.ii.28). Like that play, *The Tempest* is based on a story of enmity between two once-friendly rulers which is healed, after a storm at sea and supposed deaths, by a marriage between the rulers' children. But in *The Tempest* Shakespeare could be said to transform the conspicuous time scheme of his previous play, and similarly to invert its stagecraft. The statue Paulina theatrically unveils seems like, but is not, a work of art and seems like, but is not, a work of magic. In contrast, the shipwreck scene that opens *The Tempest* seems to the audience convincingly natural until they learn that real magic has produced it. At this point I think Shakespeare was not only utilizing Strachey's account of shipwreck followed by deliverance in the Bermudas but also activating the very recent experience in his public of dismay and then relief over news of the same event. *The Winter's Tale* ends with a shock of surprise for the audience – that

Hermione is still living. *The Tempest* opens with a more violent shock. The audience are not purely and simply detached spectators, but are drawn into the experience of the characters – which they, in turn, share with the 'amazement' of Strachey's storm-tossed companions in real life.[26] No other play by Shakespeare has adopted such shock-tactics.

Prospero assumes control from the second scene onwards. Unlike Paulina, he takes the audience into his confidence. But the effect of this is ambiguous. His art of magic, assisted by Ariel, regularly adopts the comic stage art of deception and it even produces two episodes of spectacular play-within-the-play, in the mock banquet scene and the masque; yet for much of the time the bewilderment of his victims resembles the reports of real voyagers encountering the New World. The treatment of Ferdinand in his first scene is patently stage magic, like that of Greene's Friar Bacon. But when the other members of the court party dispute about the soil and the atmosphere of the island, and hear, or profess to hear, menacing noises, they are in effect reproducing reports about the Bermudas and Virginia. Similarly, the secondary themes that run through the play, of the expectation of easy wealth, of labour as opposed to idleness, of mutiny or conspiracy, are closely akin to the records of colonization. As early as 1516, for instance, Peter Martyr had observed that 'the searchers of the newe landes, faule headlonge into ruine by theyr owne follye, consuminge them selves with civile discorde'; and the greed and indiscipline of the early English settlers in Virginia were to provoke similar complaints from Harriot and then the writer of the *True Declaration*.[27]

To all intents and purposes Prospero could be recognized and accepted by the audience as a conventional romance magician. But the reactions of the newcomers to the island were less conventional and to that extent more convincing through their resemblance to recent actualities; not least, in their uncertainty over what was monstrous on the island and what natural, what genuine and what illusory. Ralegh had convinced himself in the New World that some Mandevillian fables were reliable. Conversely, the Virginia Company was insisting, not that there was no such thing as devil-haunted islands, but that that was not the case of the Bermudas; or as a pamphlet of 1613 put it, 'our Inchanted Ilands, which is kept, as some say, with spirits, will wrong no friend or foe, but yeeld all men their expectations'.[28] The reactions of Alonso's party are closely similar to these when the spirits, or 'strange shapes', under Prospero's command set out their delusive banquet. The scoffing Sebastian is now ready to believe in unicorns and the phoenix; and Antonio agrees, with a double dose of scorn, that 'travellers ne'er did lie, / Though fools at home condemn 'em' (III.iii.26–7). Gonzalo and Alonso wonder at the unbelievable courtesy shown by the 'islanders' in spite of their 'monstrous shape' (somewhat as the unexpected courtesy of some American savages was remarked upon).[29] And Gonzalo clinches their willingness to accept the phantasmic invitation to dine with an appeal to recent and public experience:

> Faith sir, you need not fear. When we were boys
> Who would believe that there were mountaineers
> Dew-lapp'd like bulls, whose throats had hanging at 'em
> Wallets of flesh? or that there were such men
> Whose heads stood in their breasts? which now we find
> Each putter-out of five for one will bring us
> Good warrant of.

> (III.iii.43–9)

Gonzalo places Mandeville on the same footing as reports about goitre; it is typical of *The Tempest* that the unusual or the abnormal shades off into the fabulous. Here Alonso assents, only to be met by the *coup de théâtre* of Ariel's intervention as a harpy, which provides the turning-point of the play. Ariel's disguise has been borrowed from Virgil (Shakespeare has mentioned Aeneas earlier on) and his assumed role as one of the 'ministers of Fate' was probably suggested by Arcturus in Plautus' *Rudens*. But this intrusion of the marvellous, with its explosive irony, is not simply another manifestation of Prospero's magical art. It draws its full dramatic force precisely from the way the court party have just repudiated incredulity. Shakespeare pivots his dramatic use of classical myth on his allusion to actualities.

When the court party appear again, in the closing scene, their mental situation has been reversed; now it is flesh-and-blood reality that seems for a while incredible to them. For a time, they cannot recognize Prospero, even though he has met them in his once-familiar costume, 'As I was sometime Milan'. Now it is Gonzalo, the optimist, who recoils in terror:

> All torment, trouble, wonder and amazement
> Inhabits here: some heavenly power guide us
> Out of this fearful country!
>
> (v.i.104–6)

And Alonso wonders whether it has been Prospero who has embraced him, 'Or some enchanted trifle to abuse me', and whether, in this 'most strange story', he himself is now mad or sane – which Gonzalo echoes with, 'Whether this be / Or be not, I'll not swear'. Even when Prospero has revealed Ferdinand and Miranda to them, to Gonzalo's jubilation, and the ship's company have reassembled, as if 'in a dream', Alonso is still doubtful: 'there is in this business more than nature / Was ever conduct of: some oracle / Must rectify our knowledge (v.i.243–5). But in this play no oracle is needed; Prospero can reassure him :

> Do not infest your mind with beating on
> The strangeness of this business; at pick'd leisure
> Which shall be shortly single, I'll resolve you,
> Which to you shall seem probable, of every
> These happen'd accidents...
>
> (v.i.146–50)

'Strangeness' will become 'probable' (demonstrable); disenchantment will take the paradoxical course of yet another removal of disbelief.

The marvellous will be naturalized. Conjuring with appearance and reality has been frequent with Shakespeare, especially towards the end of his comedies. But here it seems to most of the characters to arise from the very nature of the island. This realm of illusion and disillusion stands for the theatre itself, but it is also an image projected from the discovery of the New World. Shakespeare attaches the half-credited, half-disavowed common belief in magic to a segment of public experience.

Moreover, the literature of discovery evidently contributed also to the political fantasies active within the play, the fantasies of wealth or dominion effortlessly acquired. Antonio and then, in parody, Stephano dream of a sudden and brutal seizure of power;

their dreams are prompted by the seemingly unpeopled condition of the island and resemble the conspiracies of colonial mutineers. They are framed, in contrast, between two other conceptions of a new society, Gonzalo's scheme of a plantation and the goddesses' promise of natural abundance in Prospero's masque. These are benign and are frankly imaginary; but they too, it seems, have been derived, in large part, from accounts of the New World and of the discovery of conditions held to reproduce the Golden Age. For example, Peter Martyr had written that the natives Columbus found in Hispaniola were living as if 'in that goulden worlde of the whiche owlde wryters speake so much', 'simplye and innocentlye, without inforcement of lawes' and likewise 'without toyle', in an ideal climate such that in places 'the Ilande enioyeth perpetuall springe tyme, and is fortunate with contynuall soomer and harvest'. And similarly Arthur Barlow had reported on the first, 1584 voyage to the 'sweet smelling' land of Virginia that

We found the people most gentle, loving, and faithful, void of all guile and treason and such as lived after the manner of the Golden Age. The earth bringeth forth all things in abundance as in the first creation, without toil or labour [30]

These reports come close to Ceres' promise in the masque of the 'foison' of unbroken harvest and spring (IV.i.110–17) and to Gonzalo's fantasy that 'Nature should bring forth, / Of it own kind, all foison, all abundance, / To feed my innocent people' (II.i.158–60) – a point not made so explicitly in Montaigne's essay 'Of the Cannibals' which no doubt was the old courtier's chief literary source. Such accounts of a golden world discovered in the Americas were plainly shaped by classical mythology although they purported to be objective descriptions of fact. Shakespeare uses them to emphasize moments of mythical thinking or wish-fulfilment. They are counterparts of the privations and the sinister illusions in the play. The dream of a new life can take various forms.

Besides drawing upon straightforward narratives of voyages Shakespeare evidently took hints from the speculative application of the discoveries to European society, as in More's *Utopia* and Montaigne's essay. To these partial sources for *The Tempest* I believe we should add Joseph Hall's satire, *Mundus Alter et Idem*, or *The Discovery of a New World*, published in Latin in about 1605 and in English in 1609. There, a voyage to the Antarctic on the good ship *Phantasia* discloses allegories of familiar home-grown vices and follies. One passage in particular makes it seem likely that Shakespeare took notice of this satire: Hall relates how the inhabitants of 'Clawback-court' are 'the strangest monsters that ever man beheld. They beare every one two faces, and speake with two tongues. . .[and] seeme to be a confused composition of Man, Ape, and Dogge' (such as may be found, the writer assures us, among some Indian people, on the 'testimonie' of Sebastian Munster). These flatterers

acknowledge no God but the man whom they make choice to serve, and him they observe with more. . .adorations than any Idoll would exact. Now all this they do with one of their mouthes onely: marry there is not a word comes out of this mouth, but the other (their dogges mouth) doth forth-with secretly retract, and disclaime.[31]

Apparently the stuff of this is refashioned in the scene where Stephano stumbles upon Caliban:

Four legs and two voices, – a most delicate monster! His forward voice, now, is to speak well of his friend; his backward voice is to utter foul speeches and to detract. (II.ii.83–6)

This leads, much as in Clawback-court, to Caliban's 'ador[ing]' Stephano as his 'God', to the accompaniment of caustic asides from Trinculo, the 'other mouth' of Stephano's imaginary 'monster'.

In more general terms, the preface to the Latin version of Hall's satire promises the reader that, 'against hope herself', he will have been 'carried,. . .not with storms nor. . .no heaving of the sea,. . .into a new world', which 'shall show forth the shape of the old', so that he will be led to 'think the two are all one'.[32] Even before the Bermuda voyage, therefore, Hall was playing upon recognized romantic or mythopoeic conceptions of the discoveries and turning them to satiric account in a pre-Swiftian fantasia. Shakespeare is not mainly writing satire, but in Hall's general statement there is at least a suggestive anticipation of Miranda's excited vision of Alonso's party as a 'brave new world', with Prospero's dispassionate comment, "Tis new to thee' (v.i.184). This is another example of that interplay between romance and actuality, fantasy and tried experience that gives *The Tempest* its distinctive yet elusive quality of a shimmering naturalism.

NOTES

1 See E. E. Rich, 'The European Nations and the Atlantic', in *The New Cambridge Modern History*, ed. J. P. Cooper (Cambridge, 1970), IV, 672–76; Wesley Frank Craven, *The Virginia Company of London, 1606–1624* (Williamsburg, VA, 1957), pp. 12–23.

2 Charles Mills Gayley, *Shakespeare and the Founders of Liberty in America* (New York, 1917), p. 81; Leslie Hotson, *I, William Shakespeare* (London, 1937), pp. 217–22; cf. Margot Heinemann, 'Rebel Lords, Popular Playwrights, and Political Culture: Notes on the Jacobean Patronage of the Earl of Southampton', *The Yearbook of English Studies* 21 (1991), 66–8.

3 Louis B. Wright, *Religion and Empire: the Alliance between Piety and Commerce in English Expansion 1558–1625* (1943, rpt. New York, 1965), pp. 89–105.

4 *The New Life of Virginia* (1612), ed. Peter Force, in *Tracts...relating principally to...the Colonies in North America* (Washington 1836), I, p. 10.

5 William Strachey, *A True Reportory of the Wracke and Redemption of Sir Thomas Gate* (1610), ed. Geoffrey Bullough, *Narrative and Dramatic Sources of Shakespeare* (London and New York, 1975), VIII, pp. 275–94; see Gayley, *Shakespeare and the Founders*, pp. 49–76, 225–9.

6 *A True Declaration of the estate of the Colonie in Virginia* ('Published by advice and direction of the councell of Virginia' (1610)), ed. Force, *Tracts* (Washington, 1844), III, no. 1, 28 pp.; Sylvester Jourdain, *A Discovery of the Bermudas, Otherwise Called the Isle of Devils* (1610), ed. Louis B. Wright, *The Elizabethans' America*, Stratford-upon-Avon Library 2 (1965), pp. 195–201; see Gayley, *Shakespeare and the Founders*, pp. 45–6, 48.

7 *True Declaration*, p. 6; for references to pearls, see, for example, Peter Martyr, *Decades of the newe worlde* (1511–16), trans. Richard Eden (1555), ed. Edward Arber, *The First Three English Books on America* (Birmingham, 1885), pp. 54, 89, 141–2, 166, 178, 180; Ralph Lane, letter to Ralegh, 1586, eds. David B. Quinn and Alison M. Quinn, *Virginia Voyages from Hakluyt* (London, 1973), pp. 26–7; Thomas Harriot, *A briefe and true report of the new found land of Virginia* (1588), *ibid*, p. 53; Jourdain, *A Discovery*, ed. Wright, *The Elizabethans' America*, p. 199.

8 *True Declaration*, pp. 10–11, 14.

9 Robert Brenner, *Merchants and Revolution: Commercial Change, Political Conflict, and London's Overseas Traders, 1550–1653* (Cambridge, 1993), pp. 92–112.

10 *True Declaration*, pp. 9, 12–17, 21; on undisciplined colonists, compare with Harriot, *A brief and true report*, eds. Quinn, *Virginia Voyages*, pp. 48–9.

11 *True Declaration*, p. 25.

12 Sidney Lee (1907), quoted, Alden T. Vaughan, 'Shakespeare's Indian: the Americanization of Caliban', *Shakespeare Quarterly* 39 (1988), 140; Paul Brown, '"This Thing of Darkness I Acknowledge Mine": *The Tempest* and the Discourse of Colonialism', in *Political Shakespeare: New Essays in Cultural Materialism*, eds. Jonathan Dollimore and Alan Sinfield (Manchester, 1985), pp. 48–71; see Russ McDonald, 'Reading *The Tempest*', *Shakespeare Survey* 43 (1991), 15–17.

13 Meredith Anne Skura, 'Discourse and the Individual : the Case of Colonialism in *The Tempest*', *Shakespeare Quarterly* 40 (1989), 42–69; compare William Crashaw, *Sermon* (1610), and the introduction to Alexander Whitaker, *Good Newes from Virginia* (1613), quoted, Wright, *Religion and Empire* pp. 101, 104; *The New Life of Virginia*, p. 4.

14 Vaughan, 'Shakespeare's Indian' 138; Skura, 'Discourse and the Individual', 47–50.

15 David Norbrook, '"What Cares these Roarers for the Name of King?"': Language and Utopia in *The Tempest*', in *The Politics of Tragicomedy: Shakespeare and After*, eds. Gordon McMullan and Jonathan Hope (London, 1992), pp. 26, 28, 39–40, 44.

16 Harriot, *A briefe and true report*, 68; John Brereton, *A Brief and True Report of the Discovery of the North Part of Virginia* (1602), ed. Wright, *The Elizabethans' America* pp. 142–4; James Rosier, *True Relation* (of Weymouth's voyage to New England: 1605), *ibid.*, pp. 148–9; George Percy, 'Observations. . .[on]. . .Virginia, 1606', *ibid.*, pp. 165, 171. See also, on John White's drawings of native Indians, John H. Elliott, 'Renaissance Europe and America: a Blunted Impact?' in *First Images of America: the Impact of the New World on the Old*, ed. Fred Chiappelli, 2 vols. (Berkeley and Los Angeles, 1976), I, p. 20; and William C. Sturtevant, 'First Visual Images of Native America', *ibid.*, pp. 417–54. Compare Lewis Hanke on Spanish opinions about the Amerindians in the sixteenth century: 'There developed. . .a kind of polarization between the two extremes – what might be called the "dirty dog" and "the noble savage" schools of thought' (*All Mankind is One*, Northern Illinois University, 1974),p. 9.

In George Chapman's *Masque of the Middle Temple and Lincoln's Inn*, contributing to the wedding festivities for Princess Elizabeth and the Elector Palatine in 1613, the principal masquers represent 'Virginian princes', sun-worshippers from a land of gold, who have come to honour the wedding (and to receive Christianity). They are dressed in silver and gold, with ornaments 'imitating Indian work', and decked out with masses of feathers, 'altogether estrangeful and Indian-like' – thus presenting an appearance utterly remote from Caliban. (Thomas Marc Parrott, ed., *The Comedies of George Chapman* (London, 1914), pp. 439–40).

17 See Bullough, *Sources* VIII, pp. 237–74; James Smith, '*The Tempest*', in *Shakespearian and Other Essays*, ed. Edward M. Wilson (Cambridge, 1974), pp. 167–72; Gary Schmidgall, '*The Tempest* and *Primaleon*: a New Source', *Shakespeare Quarterly* 37 (1986), 423–39.

18 Frank Kermode, ed., *The Tempest* (New Arden edition, 1954), pp. xxv ff. Compare Northrop Frye (1970), quoted in Charles Frey, '*The Tempest* and the New World', *Shakespeare Quarterly* 30 (1979), p. 32.

19 See Frey, *ibid.*, and Howard Felperin, 'Romance and Romanticism: Some Reflections on *The Tempest* and *Heart of Darkness*', in *Shakespeare's Romances Reconsidered*, eds. Carol McGinnis Kay and Henry E. Jacobs (Lincoln, NE, 1978), pp. 60–76.

20 *Epistle* of Maximilian Transilvane, in Antonio Pigafetta, *A Briefe Declaration of the.. Navigation Made Abowte the Worlde* (by Magellan: 1526), trans. Eden (1555), ed. Arber *The First Three English Books*, p. 248. See Elliott 'Renaissance Europe and America'; John Hale, '"A World Elsewhere": Geographical Horizons and Mental Horizons', in *The Age of the Renaissance*, ed. Denys Hay (London, 1967), pp. 317–43; Margaret T. Hodgen, *Early Anthropology in the Sixteenth and Seventeenth Centuries* (Philadelphia, 1964).

21 Hale, '"A World Elsewhere"', pp. 339–40; Robert Ralston Cawley, *Unpathed Waters: Studies in the Influence of the Voyagers on Elizabethan Literature* (Princeton, 1940), pp. 20–31; Howard Mumford Jones, *O Strange New World* (1952, rpt. London, 1965), pp. 14–20.

22 Bernal Diaz, *The Conquest of New Spain c.* 1568, ed. and trans. J. M. Cohen (Harmondsworth, 1963), p. 214; see Howard Mumford Jones, *O Strange New World*, pp. 20–7.

23 Ralegh, *The Discovery of Guiana* (1596), in *Selected Writings*, ed. Gerald Hammond (Harmondsworth, 1984), p. 111; see Hale, '"A World Elsewhere"', p. 338.

24 Strachey, *True Reportory*, ed. Bullough *Narrative and Dramatic Sources*, p. 280.

25 Torquato Tasso, *Discourses on the Heroic Poem* (1594) ed. and trans. Allan H. Gilbert, *Literary Criticism: Plato to Dryden* (1940, rpt. Detroit, 1962), pp. 480–1, 488.

26 Strachey, *True Reportory*, pp. 276, 279.

27 Peter Martyr, *Second Decade* (1516), in Arber *The First Three English Books*, p. 115; Harriot, *A briefe and true report; True Declaration*, pp. 15–17 (extracts in Bullough, *Sources* VIII, pp. 297–8).

28 *A Plaine Description of the Bermudas* (1613), ed. Force, *Tracts*, III, no. 3, pp. 22; compare *True Declaration*, p. 10.

29 See Brereton *A briefe and True Report* and Rosier, *True Relation*; cf.

William Strachey, *History of Travel into Virginia Britannia* c. 1612, ed. Wright, *The Elizabethans' America*, p. 215.

30 Peter Martyr, *Decades* (1511–16), in Arber *The First Three English Books*, pp. 71, 78, 167–8; Arthur Barlow, *Report* (in Hakluyt, *Principall Navigations* 1589), ed. Wright, *The Elizabethans' America*, pp. 104, 109; cf. n. 21, above.

31 Joseph Hall, *The Discovery of a New World*, ed. Huntington Brown (Cambridge, Mass., 1937), pp. 106–8.

32 *Ibid.*, appendix B, p. 141.

CHAPTER 14

'What's past is prologue': metatheatrical memory and transculturation in 'The Tempest'

Günter Walch

The Tempest has occasioned an astounding dialogue across times and continents. In particular, Caliban has made an amazing career through the ages. In the course of that career, during which he managed to become Prospero's serious rival for critical attention, he graduated from Renaissance wild or primitive man, savage and slave[1] to lecherous drunk, cannibal and savage monster reflecting European fears of the non-European world, but also noble being in the eighteenth century; to a victim of oppression from 1838, when the modern Caliban seems to have been born, ape and Darwin's missing link,[2] downtrodden peasant and Saxon serf;[3] to the 'Americanist Caliban' since 1898;[4] Fritz or the Boche at the end of the First World War and finally colonialized black nationalist and Irish peasant.[5]

We know from Montaigne, of course, writing in 1588[6] that Renaissance Europe had become curious about the newly discovered exotic 'Other'. Also we have known about the travel literature Shakespeare may have used for *The Tempest* since Malone,[7] and we know about Frobisher bringing home strange kinds of people in 1576 whom he described as wild beasts as did Hakluyt,[8] and that Indians began to appear in masques from 1613.[9] Yet we also know that the 'Americanist Caliban' remained invisible for three centuries, and that we have a hard time trying to detect actual Indian traits in Caliban. What, then, makes Caliban, in the words of Meredith Anne Skura, a 'walking screen for projection'?[10]

The opaqueness and the openness of Shakespeare's plays have moved very much into the foreground of contemporary Shakespeare criticism. Gone seem the times of critical claims to a single valid interpretation. Instead, Shakespeare's play-texts have begun to be considered the ground for many simultaneous readings, all legitimate even if frequently mutually exclusive. *The Tempest*'s remarkable resistance to interpretative closure, it seems, has begun to be respected.

Even critics who have achieved seminal thematic readings of Shakespeare's plays have at times shown signs of unease. Northrop Frye defines 'the action' of *The Tempest* as 'a transformation within nature'. But, he says, '[t]here are times when we wonder, as we wonder at the end of *The Winter's Tale*, whether that is really all that is going on'. And he then points out contradictions in some of the songs and speeches. Harold F. Brooks speaks of an 'ever-expanding and formless vapour'.[11] There are at the moment a number of approaches to what seems to be a new heuristic situation. Cedric Watts, for instance, in his introduction to *Hamlet*, tries to work out an answer to the venerable *Hamlet* mystery, but not by adding another closed interpretation to the long series started by that essay presumably by Thomas Hanmer in 1736.[12] Instead of solving the *Hamlet* mystery once again, he attempts to explain the 'mysteriousness' of the text, to try and understand, in other words, which textual qualities are responsible for the generation of that inordinate number of readings. These he sees in a high degree of coordination of textual elements feigning a non-existent textual unity and harmony, in conflict with a 'muddle', a high degree of lack of co-ordination, of contradiction and confusion. From this interaction emerges 'a central interrogative principle through productive friction and complexity'.[13]

I will argue that we cannot hope to understand this phenomenon in terms *just* of *mimesis*, looking for the 'imitation' of the actual historical world. Of course the power struggle in Renaissance Milan, its continuation and – presumably – temporary termination on the 'vninhabited Island' form the backbone of the play and are thus indispensable for us to grasp what is happening on the stage. But for a proper understanding of what the play does, and how it is doing it, we should, I suggest, turn to *poiesis*, to the making of a fictional world, to a construction whose similarities with the historical world are founded on structural analogies, specifically encoded. In other words we should look for the world that

Shakespeare's play builds with its specific dramatic means and devices, its forms and the discourses represented in it, to look for at least some of the ways in which *The Tempest* forms its own system of reference.

What has so far been hinted at concerning textual activity, the co-operation of, and struggle between, discourses enabling texts and contexts constituting a play, relates, of course, to drama (and narrative) generally. But Shakespeare's plays, and, incidentally, his other works, owe their exceptional vitality to an unusual degree of such dynamic poietic codification. And Shakespeare himself is offering us a highly relevant and stimulating metaphor referring to what the play of his theatrical discourses causes to happen in our minds by referring to it as 'the quick forge and working-house of thought...' (*King Henry V*, v. Chorus. 23).[14] I wish to expand and transfer the metaphor: what happens in our imagination is stimulated by the theatrical activities inside that 'wooden O' (I. Chorus. 13) in which the King's Men generated meaning using the software provided for them by their leading playwright. That makes the 'wooden O' itself a highly productive poietic 'working-house of thought'.

I have tried elsewhere[15] to demonstrate an aspect of that process in *King Henry V* by isolating the Chorus in that play, the speaker of those famous words, and analysing his dramatic function in a play parading, even flaunting, the orthodox ideology represented in it in a way highly unusual for Shakespeare. I tried to show how positive as well as negative reactions to the text have, encouraged by the Chorus, usually been occasioned by identifying both the central character and the play as a whole with the ideologemes represented in it; but that the Chorus is made to play with the audience's conventional expectations in a number of intricate ways by raising, in the role as it were of court 'historiographer',[16] expectations which are then, in the play's action, fulfilled grudgingly or not at all; that much of the information provided by the Chorus is either superfluous or unreliable. This used to be explained by the hypothesis of the Chorus being a later, hasty addition; but the Chorus is, on the contrary, an integral part of his play *because* he is unreliable and apparently blind to certain goings-on on the stage, thus directing our attention to those discrepancies and contradictions in the text, and the suspicious gaps in that ancient stage device's text.

If the Chorus thus strongly influences the hermeneutics of *King Henry V*, what informs, directs and controls the hermeneutics of *The Tempest*? In the critical situation in the early seventeenth century we certainly have, to use Bakhtinian language, generally a sharpened dialogic relationship among concepts and values from which new meanings emerge. In *The Tempest* we have an assortment of heterogeneous materials and styles, a rich mixture of represented discourses, obviously of the discourse of power, of common sailors, of grotesqueness, of magic, of overseas travel and adventure, of alterity or the Other, and transculturation and, above all, of the theatre. The discourse mentioned last, that of the theatre itself, is very important for my discussion of *The Tempest* in terms of a 'working-house of thought', as an epistemological tool to think, imagine and judge with. And there is yet another discourse represented in *The Tempest* not mentioned so far, the discourse of memory which, although occasionally mentioned has not attracted the attention it deserves. I shall point out some of the ways in which these two discourses function in the play, in which they work together in 'the quick forge' of the imagination, and a few of the consequences this has for the dramatic uses the other discourses initially mentioned are put to, principally the discourse of alterity, of the colonial Other, travel and transculturation. As far as the discourse of alterity is concerned, the focus will be shifted from the consequences for the colonized which have been covered so well during the last two decades, to the potential consequence to the colonizers themselves structurally opened by the play.

First, then, the theatre. Owing to the massive representation of the discourse of the theatre in the play, *The Tempest* has rightly been called Shakespeare's 'most consistently metatheatrical play'[17] although obviously so many of the dramatist's plays, *Hamlet* for instance, are also highly metatheatrical. *The Tempest*'s metatheatricality 'destroys the illusion of immediacy and, *regardless of its subject*, offers constant interpretation of the medium in which this subject is meditated upon. . .'[18] Self-referential interpretation enhances the epistomological function of the medium. This involves sceptical self-questioning as explicitly in the epilogue when Prospero acknowledges that the final result of the performance depends on the audience at least as much as on the creator:

> Gentle breath of yours my sails
> Must fill, or else my project fails...
>
> (11–12)

Prospero does indeed address the audience as a creator at the end of the play. Emphasizing the play's metatheatricality, Northrop Frye defines its subject succinctly as 'the producing of a play', 'put on by the chief character'.[19] That is what we see most clearly as happening on the stage: Prospero giving 'my instructions' (*The Tempest*, III.iii.85)[20] to '[t]hese our actors' (IV.i.148) and to 'my meaner ministers' (III.iii.88); praising one of them: 'Bravely the figure of this Harpy hast thou / Performed, my Ariel...' (III.iii.83–4); and referring to his project as 'Our revels' (IV.i.148) or, to the masque within the play, as 'some vanity of mine Art' (IV.i.41) or 'this insubstantial pageant' (IV.i.155). What Fry does not say is that this is Prospero's play that is not identical with the larger play, *The Tempest*, which contains, controls, contradicts but also confirms it.

These are only a few instances of the play's metatheatricality, but they suggest why Prospero, *the* creator, should have been traditionally identified with Shakespeare, *his* creator, not least because of the theatre magician's reference to 'the great globe itself' (IV.i.153). This seemingly harmless romantic biographical fallacy has, in spite of modern critical resistance, become too deeply entrenched in our cultural memory to be easily deleted.[21] Yet that fallacy impedes activity in the 'working-house of thought', for Prospero inhabits the house, its chief actor and instrument, not its creator. If Prospero were Shakespeare, then his views would be those of Shakespeare, and Prospero's views would be identified with those of the play, much in the way in which the Chorus' views have for so long been identified with those of *King Henry V*, the history play.

The Tempest tells us through its metatheatricality how aware it is of what it is doing. The play, as Stanley Wells tells us, begins at the end of its story.[22] We are also told so directly when Antonio in his *Macbeth*-like conspiracy with Sebastian suggests that they

> perform an act
> whereof what's past is prologue; what to come,
> In yours and my discharge.
>
> $\qquad$ (III.247–9)

Perform, act, prologue, discharge, – the passage is studded with stage terminology, and it reminds us of the unusual way in which we have been told about events before, Milan's past political history, the kind of power struggle so well rehearsed in the histories and tragedies, and even in the comedies. It is indeed, in the words of Wilson Knight, 'a summation' of Shakespeare's previous work, although not so much, I think, in order to outline 'a myth of the national soul',[23] but to put Machiavellian politics once again to the test, this time under conditions of perfect control exercised by art using magic as a theatrical device. The working-house, in other words, is used as a theatrical laboratory to conduct a crucial test under isolated island conditions, thereby presenting 'a fantasy about controlling other people's minds',[24] but finally showing ambiguous results. The method has further consequences. The themes are displayed, not evolved.[25] The method also bestows on the characters the curiously abstract quality frequently noted before. There is a remarkable achievement here. While it does not seem, rather surprisingly, to diminish audiences' pleasure in them, it creates a particularly rich potential for associations and hence interpretations. It contributes to the play's productive openness.

'What's past is prologue', yet I find it hard to think of any other play so haunted by the past. That is why memory is so dominantly important to *The Tempest*. We are, of course, made familiar with the past after its representatives have been stormily summoned to the scene. The characters are frequently bidden to remember the past, and so are we. Paradoxically, the result is 'a more consistent and deeper consciousness of the effects of time than in plays in which a wider time-span is directly presented'.[26] Ironically, Antonio refers to Gonzalo as

> this lord of weak remembrance, this,
> Who shall be of as little memory
> When he is earth'd...
>
> $\qquad$ (II.i.227–9)

But the memory scene that first comes to mind is the one in I.ii, and is of the kind Dr Johnson so strongly disapproved of: 'Narration in dramatic poetry is naturally tedious, as it is unanimated and inactive, and obstructs the progress of the action.' Well, the *coup d'état* Prospero tells Miranda about also provides the plot of the history play unperformed in *The Tempest*. We witness more, though, than 'the incident imperfectly [told] in many words, which might have been more plainly delivered in few'.[27] In this 'long, technically rather clumsy scene', as Frye seems to agree,[28] Miranda apparently has to be perpetually reminded to 'ope thine ear / Obey, and be attentive' (i.ii.37–8): 'Dost thou attend me?' (78), 'Thou attend'st not' (87), 'Dost thou hear?' (105). Is it true then, as Rose A. Zimbardo contends, that we're dealing with an 'almost completely inattentive Miranda'?[29] I believe that her reactions, the one to the last admonition, for instance, tell a different story: 'Your tale, sir, would cure deafness' (106). The dramatist seems concerned about reactions by the audience off stage rather than on stage. And the audience is also shown that the magus is apparently very nervous, acting under considerable pressure.

What we witness is more than the necessary transmission of mere facts. The magus had to select most carefully the most propitious moment for imparting the story to his daughter, recipient of a private aristocratic education, but ignorant of the past. We witness the magus equipping his daughter with a new identity by building a surrogate memory into her. The way he does that seems to me to be very important. Miranda, having remembered 'Four or five women...that tended me', is asked insistently, 'What seest thou else / In the dark backward and abysm of time'. 'How thou cam'st here', for example. 'But that I do not' (47; 49–50; 52), Miranda replies, and her father has to impart the information to her the hard and 'tedious' or 'clumsy' way, the narrative way. And this tells us that Prospero, although revealed to be a magician, cannot rely on his magic powers in this particular situation. He has of course taken off his magic robe for the occasion, making it visible. Although the 'Four or five women' remembered sound suspiciously like the 'images' in a 'place' used in the Art of Memory, we are shown that Prospero is not using occult memory art, that he cannot impart the memory storage of 'artificial memory', for example, but has to rely on 'natural memory' like a common mortal. Obviously Prospero would have no problem remembering. But the text also seems to show him labouring over (re)constructing the past. There is no short cut for even the magus in imparting the contents of his mind to Miranda's memory. We do not know how impressed Shakespeare was by the more sinister medieval, Catholic and Hermetic associations that had made the Art of Memory, widely spread throughout the fifteenth and sixteenth centuries in Italy, France and England, and increasingly used as the mnemonic part of practical rhetoric, suspect to English Protestants.[30] I'll stick my neck out: it seems to me that the verbal architecture of Sonnet 55 bears the marks of 'artificial memory', the transformation of the mnemonic memory system from a carrier of multiple information to one exclusive image being another witty expression of the all-importance of its subject safely stored till after Doomsday. It is another aspect of overdetermination in the Sonnets: the young aristocrat is of such supreme value to the speaker that only a whole memory frame, normally the storage-drum of complicated, and occasionally pretty obscure, masses of information, is deemed adequate to hold this one item secure.[31] But having a veritable magician on the stage is different. The play may remain ambiguous about magic, but in that scene Prospero has been shown to rely on natural memory. He is powerful, but in terms of his own culture dangerous only to his evil enemies.

Memories are shown then, to be supremely important to the play, but not only the memories themselves. Amazingly what is also shown is the technique of managing, storing and recalling memories, a dramatic device designed also to emphasize the importance of memories to the world of the play. That world is very clearly defined physically. It is another 'O', not surrounded by wooden planks but by the sea, a magic circle, and just as densely structured to encourage the working of thought, and of course ultimately contained and authorized by the playhouse. Immediately after the apparent shipwreck of the Neapolitan royal seafarers and their party the audience learns from Miranda in the very first lines of the second scene (I.ii.1–2) that this isolated world is ruled by a very superior male European who owns a 'magic garment' (line 23) which enables him to perform impressive feats on a large scale.

Later in this scene the audience will partake of Prospero's overwhelming memories of that *coup d'état* in Milan, secretly nurtured for twelve long years, and will understand how Prospero is setting the scene for his long-awaited revenge. The audience will then in effect see the quintessential Renaissance play about power and revenge. But even that part of *The Tempest* is different from essentially the same kind of plot in the history plays, and the tragedies, and the comedies.

It is the phenomenon of exotic travel that changes everything fundamentally. Having travelled a long way the Italians first find the accustomed order and degree suspended as meaningless in the midst of the raging tempest, then have their automatic Machiavellian responses magically frustrated with such ease that the play later has to make an effort to show the limits to the usefulness of Prospero's art. It takes another kind of magic, the charm of the charismatic Harry, to get somewhere near the magical efficiency of Prospero's isle, but even there the effort it costs the King and the transience of his achievement are all too palpable. But the island is much more, and something much more innovative, than a battlefield for courtly revenge and restitution, although it definitely is that, too. The island also sets a space for contact with the New World, and immediately, as has been noted so often throughout the 1980s, the discourse of colonialism is constituted. In this respect our time has caught up with the play, it might be said. Prospero's harsh treatment of his 'salvage and deformed slave' has been at the centre of this debate. And indeed the Duke is never at a loss for fresh contributions to the textual production of the Other. To him, 'all the subjects' that he has, Caliban, on whom he depends for his labour, is 'filth' (I.ii.348), 'hag-seed' (I.ii.367), 'a born devil' (IV.i.188) and so forth. The island and its inhabitant are encoded as in need of rational European domination. Prospero operates as an early colonizer using some of the classic tools of colonizing. An early traveller, however involuntary, he also anticipates the famous eighteenth- and nineteenth-century geographers, botanists and zoologists by his colonizing use of science, one of the most conspicuous instruments of European expansion. His white magic rests on the study of the forces of nature which allows him to dominate them. And his possession of the books on which he depends for his proto-science makes him a bringer of the print culture indispensable for the creation and imposition of a European order. The production of a non-European subject for an English audience also involves the codification of cultural difference in terms of the critical difference between Caliban's lust and the young aristocratic couple's well regulated sexuality. But the culture transfer involves not only moral norms, of course, but everything that constitutes 'culture', the only culture recognizable to Europeans, their own. Therefore Miranda has taught him 'each hour / One thing or other' (I.ii.355–6), her motive in her own words significantly being pity (355: 'I pitied thee'), a very early touch of sentiment foreshadowing what will begin happening in eighteenth-century travel literature. In the same passage it is again Miranda[32] who reminds the ungrateful savage of his previous cultural deficiency, his lack of language. The point here is not simply that Miranda has acted as a benevolent instructress in a language foreign to the student. The non-European subject is constructed as having had no language at all:

> when thou didst not, savage,
> Know thine own meaning, but wouldst gabble like
> A thing most brutish, I endow'd thy purposes
> With words that made them known.
>
> (I.ii.356–60)

The ability or inability to produce meaning itself, not merely the command of another language, is made an integral part of the construction of cultural difference. The play seems to comply with this assumption, initially supplying the definition of 'The Scene: an vn-inhabited Island'. The island is uninhabited because Caliban is culturally non-existent. He becomes codified as a person exclusively in relation to European aspirations and needs. What we have here, then, is an early encoding of the European habit of representing other parts of the world as having no history of their own.

That encoding follows basic rules of any production of meaning. According to Niklas Luhmann[33] any such production invariably involves the reduction of world complexity. This applies very much to the discourse of alterity. The narratives developed by western societies particularly see the Other as less complex, much simpler and far more static than the Self. This seems to apply to Caliban's construction by *The Tempest* as a non-European subject briefly sketched out above, and to a large extent it does. But the various discourses co-operating and competing in *The Tempest*'s working-house of thought also create openings through which the audience may glimpse other aspects of that fascinating creation. The remarkably poetic quality of Caliban's language has long been noticed. It certainly acts to resist the reduction of the Other in the discourse of alterity. Yet following through our argument it would not only mean that we are faced with that rare phenomenon, a user of a language not his mother tongue putting the medium to poetic use, an oral Joseph Conrad. What it would mean over and beyond this is that that feat is performed by someone with no previous linguistic competence at all, by someone only gabbling 'like a thing most brutish' and consequently not knowing his 'own meaning'. The latter is a very apt way of putting it. It implies both the lack of language and the consequent inability to make sense of one's own existence, in other words, to narrate one's history. Yet Caliban is not devoid of memory. He knows the history of his descent just as well as the Europeans know that of their Renaissance dynasties. It would not perhaps be appropriate to the way Shakespearean drama works to pursue the formal logic of this situation to the conclusion that Caliban must have learnt his history together with his language from his teacher Miranda. Rather, I would argue that we have here reached a point where the play through its theatrical activity is deconstructing its own text, thus opening a gap for the stimulation of audience activity. Quite clearly Caliban has digested the implications of his history. He is bitterly aware of having been fashioned by linguistic transculturation, having achieved a knowledge of 'how to curse' (i.ii.366). And obviously Caliban vigorously resists the social engineering and discipline brought on by the Renaissance colonizers.

Miranda having made Caliban a person, although irrevocably a transcultural European subject, the various aesthetic and historical discourses of the play co-operate to make him even more of one, most interestingly, perhaps, in contexts where this is not so obvious. The masque, generally recognized to be of central importance to *The Tempest*, but interpreted in many different ways, is a crucially important instance. Shakespeare's inclusion of the masque in his play represents a mimetic act obviously of significance very much in accordance with the politics of the play. Aristocratic transactions of power having been successfully effected, what better way to celebrate the betrothal at the fictitious court in the same way as was customary at the real court? There seems to have been a growing fashion among audiences at the Globe and at the Blackfriars for such spectacle. It appeared to be new from the court, but was also already a part of cultural memory. As a part of cultural memory, which in literature and the arts is significantly generic memory, the masque imports its own rules of production into its dramatic host. Consequently, we see a conventional masque with a classical cast and classical motifs. In so far as we can speak of *auto*poiesis, the appropriated genre is reproducing itself according to its specific rules and conventions.

But this is of course only true up to a point. What had been a dramatic tendency under the Tudors and was fast becoming a conventional masque form under James is severely upset in *The Tempest*. In the 'real' Jacobean masque we have, as Stephen Orgel has shown us,[34] a movement from conflict to harmony, from the initial disturbance of the anti-masque, often grotesque, to a resolution of the conflict by the mere appearance of aristocratic actors, finally merging in the important stately dancing which is joined by the court audience. In *The Tempest* we have no initial anti-masque to the masque proper, nor do we have any revelation of the masquers except for an unorthodox magic one (the actors are revealed to have been spirits), and the dancing cannot involve the stage audience because it is suddenly and disharmoniously interrupted by the famous 'strange, hollow, and confused noise', 'after which' the dancers, 'certain Reapers' and 'the Nymphs' 'heavily vanish' (IV.i.38 ff.). *The Tempest* has therefore been generally likened to a masque, with the play providing anti-masques in the shape of the opening storm and the harpies' banquet, with 'the figure of Iris...an appropriate exorcist for both'.[35]

Yet the mimetic appropriation of the masque seems to serve the function primarily of refreshing the Jacobean audience's cultural memory of the genre in order to make the changes stand out very clearly. This play-within-the-play represents an astonishing conflu-

ence of the conventional masque discourse traditionally associated
with power, with the discourses of magic and, also, of alterity. What
happens then in fact amounts to a violent inversion of the court
theatre convention by Caliban's appearance at precisely the point
at which the newly regained harmony and peace should be
celebrated. Caliban is, of course, not to be seen anywhere on stage
at this point. The troublemaker appears not on the stage, but
significantly in Prospero's mind. We are told in this strange scene
that Prospero is 'in some passion / That works him strongly'
(143–4). He is terribly 'vex'd', his 'old brain is troubled' (158–9)
enormously. Setting 'divers Spirits, in shape of dogs and hounds'
(254) on the 'varlets' (170) later, towards the end of act IV, comes too
late from the point of view of the masque form to eliminate the
problem. What the poietic inversion of the masque tells us is that
the superior prince and magician can control the forces of nature
with elegance and his enemies up to a point, but that there is
something else, this curious creature Caliban, whom in the end he
cannot control, whom he even finds it impossible to banish from his
memory. There is a future implied in this text, a future of violence.
That is another reason why the discourse of memory is important
to *The Tempest*: what happens in the protagonist's memory apparently
has a greater danger potential than what happens in the visible
world of the stage.

The inversion of the masque seems to be the single most
dramatic poietic move of the play creating the protean character of
Caliban, Caliban as a poietic 'projecting screen'. Since the culture
transfer is shown to be unilateral, Caliban's transculturation also
seems unilateral. But memory, that subject introduced so prominently, at least for Renaissance audiences, provides the medium for
a potential bilateralism. Travel to the remote island populated
through the Europeans by an act, not of biology but of culture, has
brought Prospero into contact with the native who has presently
been inscribed by the European discourses carried in sixteenth-
and seventeenth-century transoceanic travellers' baggage as a
slave, servant, native subject by Prospero, as a monster and slave by
the jester and the drunken butler. But the process is not quite as
one-sided as it has always seemed to critics. Caliban bothering
Prospero not by his presence but through the magus' memory

shows that his physical and cultural existence has been interiorized by the Duke. Travelling back to Milan, Caliban will accompany him as a troublesome memory. That seems to be the reason, or at least one reason, for the play to leave Caliban behind on the island. The consequences of this in terms of the play's activity are different and graver than an alternative fulfilment of European dreams like Trinculo's of exhibiting Caliban to holiday fools for 'a piece of silver' (ii.ii.29–30) or Stephano's of selling him to the highest bidder (ii.ii.78–80).

In conclusion, a brief glance at the German play by Jakob Ayrer of Nuremberg, *Die Comedia von der schönen Sidea, wie es ihr biss zu ihrer Verheuratung ergangen*[36] (The Comedy of the Beautiful Sidea, how She Fared till her Marriage) will convey an impression of the two vastly diverging versions of probably the same ancient story in the background. (The play dates before 1605, the year of Ayrer's death, and was possibly played by English comedians.) The contrast in quality between the two texts is due to the contrast between provincial Germany and rapidly developing England just beginning to reach out into the world, to get excited by exotic travel and to think of empire. The plot analogies are indeed amazing. There are a few minor differences and one major difference. Thus we have not one, but two princes each accompanied by a daughter who are banished from their respective realms. Very significantly, they escape into the deep woods, not an island like the one suggested to Shakespeare by absorbing contemporary reports. As for the rest, the stories are more or less identical, down to the princes' using magic against their enemies and taking their enemy's son prisoner, and even to Sidea's helping the young prince her admirer to carry logs. But the major difference is provided by Caliban's counterpart, a character called Jahn Molitor, the Latin name suggesting a mischievous managing type, an operator. But he is hardly more than a fairly provincial low-class good-for-nothing, a corn-stealing miller, who refuses to support his illegitimate children, dresses up like an old woman and makes the devil dance to his whistle. Caliban's 'I'll be wise hereafter, / And seek for grace' (v.i.294–5) is paralleled, but given greater emphasis by being placed in an epilogue given to Molitor. There is little in this provincial German character that equals that fascinating figure of the Other created by the English theatre when England was just beginning to think of empire and embarking on an intercontinental dialogue and transculturation. It is that fascination by, and discourse of, far-away lands and strange people that made Caliban, and *The Tempest* as it now stands, with its poietic openness and textual productivity, possible.

NOTES

1 Trevor R. Griffiths, '"This Island's Mine": Caliban and Colonialism', *Yearbook of English Studies. Colonial and Imperial Themes.* Special number, 13 (1983), 169.

2 Virginia Mason Vaughan, '"Something Rich and Strange": Caliban's Theatrical Metamorphoses', *Shakespeare Quarterly*, 36 (1985), no. 4, 392.

3 Griffiths, '"This Island's Mine"', p. 169.

4 Aldent T. Vaughan, 'Shakespeare's Indian: the Americanization of Caliban', *Shakespeare Quarterly* 39 (1988), no. 2, 139.

5 Paul Brown, '"This Thing of Darkness I Acknowledge Mine": *The Tempest* and the Discourse of Colonialism', in *Political Shakespeare: New Essays in Cultural Materialism*, eds. Jonathan Dollimore and Alan Sinfield (Manchester, 1985), pp. 57 ff.

6 Richard Marienstras, *New Perspectives on the Shakespearean World* (Cambridge, 1985), p. 160.

7 William Aldis Wright, ed., *Shakespeare: Select Plays, The Tempest* (Oxford, 1986), p. vi.

8 Marienstras, *New Perspectives*, p. 233.

9 Meredith Anne Skura, 'Discourse and the Individual: the Case of Colonialism in *The Tempest*', in *Shakespeare Quarterly* 40 (Spring 1989), no. 1, 57.

10 Skura, 'Discourse and the Individual', p. 60.

11 Harold F. Brooks, 'Annual Shakespeare Lecture: *The Tempest*, What Sort of Play', given 27 April 1978, in *Proceedings of the British Academy*, (1978), LXIV, p. 43.

12 Anon., *Some Remarks on the Tragedy of Hamlet Prince of Denmark* (London, 1736).

13 Cedric Watts, '*Hamlet': Harvester New Critical Introduction to Shakespeare* (London, 1988).

14 References to John H. Walter, *King Henry V*, The Arden Shakespeare (London, 1977).

15 Günter Walch, '*Henry V* as Working-House of Ideology', *Shakespeare Survey* 40 (1988), 63–8.

16 The term is Eamon Grennan's in: '"This Story Shall the Good Man

Teach his Son": *Henry V* and the Art of History', *Papers on Language and Literature* 15 (1979), 370–82.

17 Karol Berger, 'Prospero's Art', *Shakespeare Studies* 10 (1977), p. 235.

18 *Ibid.*, my italics.

19 *On Shakespeare*, p. 172.

20 References to Frank Kermode, ed., *William Shakespeare, The Tempest*. The Arden Shakespeare (London, 1976).

21 'Cultural memory' is my first use of 'memory', the recent term signifying a long-term memory of cultural objectivations in contrast to 'communicative memory' reaching back three to four generations at the most. See Jan Assmann, 'Kollektives Gedächtnis und kulturelle Identität', in *Kultur und Gedächtnis*, eds. Jan Assmann and Tonio Hölscher (Frankfurt-on-Main, 1988), pp. 9–19.

22 Stanley Wells, 'Shakespeare and Romance', in *Later Shakespeare*, eds. John Russell Brown and Bernard Harris, Stratford-upon-Avon Studies 8 (London, 1966), p. 70.

23 G. Wilson Knight, *The Crown of Life* (London, 1977), p. 255.

24 Stephen Orgel, ed., *William Shakespeare, The Tempest*, The Oxford Shakespeare (Oxford, 1987), p. 51.

25 See Rose A. Zimbardo, 'Form and Disorder in *The Tempest*', *Shakespeare Quarterly* 14 (1963), p. 49.

26 Stanley Wells, 'Shakespeare and Romance', p. 71.

27 Samuel Johnson, 'Preface to Shakespeare', in A. J. Valpy, ed., *The Plays and Poems of Shakespeare* (London), p. 69.

28 Northrop Frye, *On Shakespeare*, p. 176.

29 Rose A. Zimbardo, 'Form and Disorder in *The Tempest*', p. 55.

30 Frances Yates' *The Art of Memory* (London, 1966) remains the standard work on the subject. See also William E. Engel, 'Mnemonic Criticism and Renaissance Literature: a Manifesto', *Connotations: a Journal for Critical Debate* 1 (1991), 12–33.

31 Günter Walch, 'Shakespeares Sonettdichtung als Gedächtniskunst', in *Shakespeares Sonette in Europäischen Perspektiven*, eds. Dieter Mehl and Wolfgang Weiß (Münster, Hamburg, 1993).

32 It is itself culturally most significant that Dryden and Theobald would rather give I. ii. 353–64 to Prospero thus supplementing the conventional construction of the female gender as inadequate to the cultural task at hand conspicuously absent from *The Tempest*.

33 Niklas Luhmann, *Soziale Systeme: Grundriss einer allgemeinen Theorie* (Frankfurt, 1984).

34 Stephen Orgel, *The Illusion of Power: Political Theater in the English Renaissance* (Berkeley, 1975).

35 *Ibid.*, p. 47.

36 Adelbert von Keller, ed., *Jakob Ayrers Dramen*, 4 vols. (Tübingen, 1865), IV.

CHAPTER 15

Lope de Vega and Shakespeare

Kenneth Muir

In a recent article[1] I pointed out that two of the contributors of verses on Shakespeare to the First Folio were distinguished Hispanists: James Mabbe, the translator of *Celestina* and Leonard Digges who was responsible for the first comparison of Lope with Shakespeare.[2] He lived near Stratford, where his stepfather was to become the overseer of Shakespeare's will. I suggested further that Shakespeare would have appreciated the sustained irony of Lope's verse address to the Madrid Academy, *The New Art of Writing Comedies*, as he too had been badgered by critics who regarded popular plays with disdain. Lope had pretended to lament that his plays were not modelled on those of Plautus and Terence. In only six of his 483 plays did he not sin against art:

> Yet I defend what I have written. Though,
> If I had striven for a stricter style,
> The plays might have been better, yet I know
> My faithful patrons would have run a mile.
> Their principles, alas, are so debased,
> My very lapses satisfy their taste.

There was no British Academy in Shakespeare's day; but he and his fellow-dramatists were haunted by the ghost of Sir Philip Sidney whose justifiable strictures on the drama of his time were written before the advent of the University Wits. He ridiculed the plays written for the professional stage because they flouted the Unities; and the one modern play he could bring himself to praise was *Gorboduc*, written in the Senecan style by two aristocratic amateurs. It was natural that his devoted sister, the Countess of Pembroke, should encourage a group of poets to follow his

239

precepts. Kyd and Lodge, like the Countess herself, translated plays by French Senecan dramatists, and Daniel and Greville wrote plays on the same model. The dramatists who wrote for a living knew that this was not the way to attract audiences, but some of them felt vaguely guilty. Webster, for example, blamed the defects of *The White Devil* on the 'uncapable multitude'; and he wrote this without Lope's saving irony.

It is no part of my argument that Shakespeare had read Lope's poem or, indeed, any of his plays. Nevertheless it is difficult to doubt that Digges, who loved both dramatists, would have discussed Lope with Shakespeare and made him realize that they had certain affinities.

It was not accidental that one of Shakespeare's earliest comedies was based on two plays by Plautus, but the imitation was far from slavish. He doubled the confusion by giving Dromio a twin; he turned a farce into a comedy by putting it in a romantic framework, taken from the old tale of Apollonius; and he transformed the debate on marriage by setting the play in the Christian era at Ephesus, a town known to the audience from the journeys of St Paul and his discussion on marital duties in the Epistle to the Ephesians.

Near the end of his career, Shakespeare again obeyed the Unities by putting into Prospero's mouth his long account to Miranda of the conspiracy that brought them to the island. Yet in the other plays of his last period, Shakespeare jettisoned the Unities. The action ranges from country to country; and in *Pericles* and *The Winter's Tale*, in defiance of Sidney's ridicule, we follow Marina and Perdita from birth to marriage. The dramatist calls attention to what he is doing by having Time tell the audience not to impute it a crime that Sidney's precepts were being ignored.

There is some evidence that Shakespeare had read *The Defence of Poesy* at the time he was writing (or re-writing) *Hamlet*.[3] Sidney's claim, for example, that one of the functions of tragedy was to show forth the ulcers that are covered with tissue was the probable origin of the iterative image of the play. Before writing *Macbeth* for the new monarch Shakespeare seems to have undergone a refresher course on the plays of Seneca, partly in the Tudor translations and partly in the original. There are echoes of *Hercules Furens*, *Medea* and *Agamemnon*.[4] He may have intended to adopt a more classical style,

but without obeying the unities. *Macbeth* and *King Lear* both cover
several months and the voyage from Venice to Cyprus destroys the
unities of *Othello*.

In the tragedies from *Julius Caesar* to *Coriolanus*, all the heroes
(except Macbeth who has to have his head chopped off) die on
stage; in *Hamlet* four of the main characters die in the last scene, and
Polonius has been slain earlier. Although Duncan is murdered off
stage, we are not spared the slaughter of Macduff's family.
Shakespeare took from Seneca what he regarded as useful, but he
refused to copy those characteristics that would have reduced the
excitement of his plays, such as the moralizing chorus beloved by
Senecans everywhere. When he needed a choric comment, as he
often did, he used one of the regular characters. In *King Lear*, for
example, the Fool, Kent and Edgar all have choric functions, and
after the blinding of Gloucester, Cornwall's surviving servants
guide the responses of the audience;

SECOND SERV.   I'll never care what wickedness I do,
                 If this man come to good.
THIRD SERV.   If she live long
    And in the end meet the old course of death
    Women will all prove monsters.
                          (III.vii.97–100)[5]

Shakespeare and Lope agreed with all sensible dramatists on the
necessity of pleasing their audiences. *As You Like It* and *What You
Will* were not sarcastic comments on their depraved taste. His
purpose, as expressed in the epilogue to *The Tempest* was to please;
but, like Lope, he believed that the taste, even of the groundlings,
was pretty good. It is the princely snob, Hamlet, who declares that
they were capable of nothing but dumb shows and noise. Shakespeare
knew better; after all, *Hamlet* was the most popular play of its time.

Shakespeare and Lope had another thing in common. Nearly all
their major plays are open to widely different interpretations. No
two critics agree about the so-called 'problem plays'. Is *Troilus and
Cressida* a comedy, a tragedy, a satire, a comical satire or a tragical
satire? Is *Measure for Measure* Shakespeare's most Christian play, or a
satire on Christian beliefs? But the ambivalences are not confined
to the problem plays, and one is tempted to say that all the plays are

problem plays. There is no generally accepted interpretation of *Hamlet*. *Othello* is a long-continued battleground fought between the followers of Leavis and Helen Gardner, and more recently between male and female critics. *King Lear* is described by some as a Christian play in a pagan setting, by others as a forerunner of the theatre of the absurd, even as a coded message to atheists in an age of theists. I hope to show in the remainder of this paper that in several of Lope's best-known plays there is a similar ambivalence. I have limited my discussion to one comedy, two tragi-comedies and one tragedy. I have made use of previous translations[6] but I have sometimes had to substitute my own.

The Dog in the Manger is a light-hearted comedy about the Countess Diana, who falls in love with her handsome secretary, Teodoro. She confesses in soliloquy that she would dearly like to marry him, but that his lowly birth makes this impossible. She is jealous of Marcela, one of her maids with whom Teodoro has been flirting; and it is her knowledge of this that has kindled her own passion. She confesses her love by getting Teodoro to correct a poem she pretends she has written for a friend. She disparages Marcela and keeps wavering between love and anger. Teodoro remonstrates with her, calling her a dog in the manger. She attacks him furiously and makes his nose bleed. Later, in remorse, she asks for his blood-stained handkerchief and gives him two thousand gold coins. This is the position at the end of the second act. Then a happy ending is engineered by Tristan, Teodoro's witty and unscrupulous servant, who persuades Count Lodovico that Teodoro is his missing son, who had been captured by pirates and sold to slavery. Teodoro, however, is honest enough to confess to Diana that the story is a fabrication. She decides, nevertheless, to marry him. Provided that other people believe that Teodoro is of noble blood, honour is satisfied. Before this, when she thought that Teodoro was lost to her, Diana had cried:

> Honour, I curse your name!
> You are the cause of endless misery
> In banning all our natural inclinations.
> Who invented you? Although, 'tis true
> Your bridle curbs much vice.
>
> (act III, my translation)

Pring-Mill pointed out that the recognition of his son by Count Lodovico is a wonderful parody of traditional happy endings.[7] But that, in addition, since honour in one sense can be satisfied by a sham, Lope offers 'a witty and ambiguous comment' on how much such honour is worth. Another comment on honour is implied in the sub-plot when Diana's rejected suitors – noble both – bribe the disguised Tristan to murder Teodoro. Nobility of birth is not always matched with nobility of conduct. Lope's scornful treatment of honour goes beyond the criticisms offered by Calderón.[8]

Peribañez and *Fuenteovejuna* are two tragi-comedies which continue with Lope's analysis of honour. In both plays the honour of peasants is contrasted with the dishonourable conduct of the lords they kill. In both plays they are pardoned by their respective Kings in much the same way as the King pardons the Mayor of Zalamea in Calderón's play.

Fuenteovejuna is probably the most famous of Lope's plays in English-speaking countries. The title is the name of a village which revolts against an evil overlord who has raped the wives and daughters of the peasants. Inspired by one of his victims, they kill him and his pimps and underlings. When the villagers are arrested and tortured, they all say 'Fuenteovejuna did it.' The play has often been performed by left-wing groups in England because it was thought to have a revolutionary message. This has led to protests from scholars who point out that no dramatist of the period could have believed in democracy; that Fernando disgraced his rank by his conduct; that the rebellious peasants, a century before Lope's birth, had been pardoned by the King of that time; and that the play is essentially royalist in tone.[9] It should be noted, however, that the sole reason why the King pardons the villagers for what he calls their 'dreadful crime' is the lack of evidence, a lack due entirely to the bravery, endurance and solidarity of the whole community. Lawrencia, the victim, is heroic figure, and every audience today admires her for inciting the rebellion. It must surely have been the same when the play was first performed, although the audience might not have agreed that rebellion against intolerable tyranny is justifiable. Lope, moreover, ensured that we should regard the torturing of women, boys and old men to extract confessions as barbarous. Portia in *The Merchant of Venice* tells

Bassanio that men upon the rack would confess anything. Lope could not have been happy with the methods of the Inquisition, any more than Shakespeare was with the methods of the Elizabethan Security Services. That popular reactions to Lope's play conflict with the arguments of learned critics seems to suggest that the play may be legitimately interpreted in more than one way, and that the ambivalence is built into the whole structure. The strongest argument in favour of the royalist critics is that the rebels, before they are arrested, compose a song in praise of King Fernando and Queen Isabella, even as they bear aloft the head of the tyrant impaled on a lance.

The same considerations apply to *Peribañez*. The hero is a prosperous farmer who kills the local overlord who is trying to rape his wife, Casilda. He and Casilda travel to the court, so that she can claim the reward for bringing him to justice. The King, a more sympathetic figure than his counterpart in the other play, does not merely give Casilda her reward, but he makes Peribañez a captain in the army. The play, however, is much more complex than this summary would suggest. The rapist, Don Fadrique, is a brave and successful soldier. After an accident he recovers consciousness in Peribañez' house on the day of his wedding. He beholds the beautiful bride and imagines that he is in heaven, and that she is an angel. Later he follows the cynical advice of his servant, Lugan, on the arts of seduction. He puts Peribañez in charge of a detachment of soldiers on active service so that he will be away from home and his wife will be more vulnerable. Peribañez returns and kills the would-be rapist, who, as he dies, confesses that the wronged husband was fully justified in his deed. This recovers some sympathy for the repentant Fadrique, especially as we know that the murder had been carefully planned. Peribañez had persuaded Don Fadrique to dub him a knight, so that he was entitled to avenge his honour. He had become violently jealous when he saw the portrait of Casilda commissioned by Don Fadrique. He realized why he had been given a commission, and in a long soliloquy he repeats four times the proverbial maxim '*Mal haya el humilde, amen que busca mujer hermosa*' (Woe betide the poor man who wants a pretty wife) – a saying that has been associated with Iago's mysterious line, 'A fellow almost damned in a fair wife'.

It is not surprising that Lope spoke enthusiastically of Honour as a suitable dramatic topic, for it was one in which social *mores* and Christian teaching were bound to conflict. There is a similar reason for the popularity of Elizabethan Revenge Tragedy. However much divines and philosophers condemned vengeance, the ordinary gentleman, the ordinary man in the street, the ordinary playgoer, could not help feeling that if he was unable to get redress by legal means, it was right to avenge himself. Lope, like Calderón, was a priest and he objected particularly to murders that did not give the victims the opportunity of receiving absolution. The Ghost in *Hamlet* complained bitterly of this:

> Cut off even in the blossoms of my sin,
> Unhousel'd, disappointed, unanel'd.
>
> (I.v.76–77)

Later in the play, however, the Prince contrives that Rosencrantz and Guildenstern should be executed, 'not shriving time allowed'. Hamlet's complacency about this visibly shocks Horatio.

The King in Lope's play expresses surprise that 'a peasant should so cherish his good name'. Peribañez, indeed, boasts to the King that his blood is pure, with no trace of Moorish or Jewish blood, and that he had been Mayor for six years. So he clearly subscribes to both meanings of Honour. As James Lloyd points out in his excellent edition, it was often argued that country people were more virtuous, more honourable than town people: 'Whereas in a village a good man is honoured for his goodness and a bad man is condemned as bad, at court nobody is regarded for his inner integrity, but for what his possessions are worth.'[10] Everything in the play bears this out. The beautiful love-duet between Peribañez and his bride in the first scene of the play, expressed in imagery appropriate to countryfolk, radiates a purity of feeling which remains with us throughout the play.[11] Here I depart from Lloyd's translation, because I think that formal blank verse gives a misleading impression:

> Casilda, so long as you cannot
> Outdo my affection, my sweet,
> You may not outdo me in speeches.
> I'd like to place at your feet

The town of Ocana, the land
Beside the river that reaches
From here to the Portuguese frontier,
Then enters the Spanish main;
For you are lovelier, my dear,
Than olive-groves laden with fruit,
Than meadows covered with flowers
Trodden by none but the feet
Of Dawn in the month of May.
Not all the things that I love,
Sweet-smelling red apples (I say),
Olive oil, golden-bright,
Gleaming in earthenware jars
Can give me as much delight,
For your lips are sweeter far
Than the scent of sweet white wine
Laid down for some forty years –
To Lords the rose smells sweet,
To peasants the scent of wine.
The grapes when newly pressed
In October; refreshing May showers;
Stooks in the August fields,
The vine-shoots that I uproot
In winter, all these are fine;
But far and away the best
Of my joys is to see you, my bride,
Here in my house beside me,
A splendid protection for us
From the winter's numbing cold
And the burning summer heat.

I turn lastly to one of Lope's greatest tragedies, *El Castigo sin Venganza*. The ambivalence of this play may be suggested by the objection of many readers to the title. Instead of *Justice without Revenge*, it might be entitled *Revenge without Justice* – unless we can suspect that Lope's original title was ironical. On the one hand it is argued that under the honour code a husband is entitled to murder his wife and her lover, and he would have an additional motive if the lover is his own bastard. Moreover, the clever trick by which he gets Federico to murder Cassandra, and to have him executed for the murder, restores his own 'honour' by exonerating his wife. The fact that this solution involves lying and deception on a grand scale

Date due: 9/23/2013,23:59
Item ID: 30301000893988
Title: TRAVEL AND DRAMA
IN SHAKESPEARE'S TIME
Date charged: 9/4/2013,17:
23

RENEWAL
DATE_____
RENEW ONLINE WITH YOUR
CARD AT
www.parkridgelibrary.org
OR CALL 847-590-8706

is neither here nor there. It is true that the Duke has been a whoremonger who has treated his wife abominably, but there are some slight indications that, like many worn-out libertines, he intends to turn over a new leaf. To which the obvious retort is that Federico is a much more attractive figure than his brutal father. He is civilized, courteous and loveable; he falls in love at first sight with his stepmother before he knows her identity; he struggles hard not to confess a love which he knows to be sinful, and when he is induced by Cassandra to admit that he loves her, he realizes that he has taken a fatal step. It is clear that Cassandra admires him and that inevitably she contrasts his virtues with her husband's vices. The love of the young couple is passionate and profound, and, one is tempted to add, pure. If the story of Paolo and Francesca makes Dante the narrator faint away with compassion, so the story of Federico and Cassandra evokes pity and sympathy, even if they are damned.

Soon after their first meeting, their dialogue shows how quickly they have fallen in love:

> CAS.　　　　　I cannot rate too highly
> The pleasure I receive in meeting you.
> All the praises I have had of you
> Seem but meagre now that we have met.
> 　　　　　...
>
> 　　　　　From this day,
> Count Federico, I will be your mother.
> So think of me and I will be delighted.
> My soul rejoices to possess the treasure
> Of having such a son, more than for the title
> Of Duchess of Ferrara.
>
> FED.　　　　　Beauteous lady,
> I know not how to answer. I'm confused
> By such great honour. This day the Duke divides
> My very being. If my body alone
> Was born before, my soul – my greater part –
> Is brought to birth by you.

(act i)

In an article on the use of the sonnet in Lope's plays, Peter Dunn shows[12] that Federico's sonnet later in the play is an epitome of the

theme and that, like many of Lope's non-dramatic sonnets, it takes
the form of a debate between himself and his thoughts:[13]

> Impossible thought! What do you seek of me?
> Barbarous prompter, what would you have me do?
> Why, without reason, would you slay me so,
> Soaring beyond the wind's authority?
> O cease your wandering activity!
> You seek the death of both of us. I claim
> Some little respite: do not let me see
> So dire an end to such a noble aim.
> There is no thought that's so corruptible
> Can be indulged without a hoped-for prize;
> And yet that hope must surely be the door
> To sin. For lovers all is possible;
> But what was kindled when we first changed eyes
> Must be impossible for evermore.
>
> (act I)

Peter Dunn goes on to claim that this sonnet is immediately
followed by Cassandra's seduction of Federico. This is questionable.
Cassandra knows, of course, that Federico is in love with her, as she
with him, and she induces him to confess by telling the story of how
the love of Antiochus for his stepmother was discovered. The
seduction, if that is the appropriate word, is mutual. It is important
to realize that, although Cassandra speaks of avenging herself on
her evil husband, this is because she wants an excuse for her
incestuous desires, as she similarly clutches at the thought that as
she has no blood-relationship with Federico, she is less guilty than
brothers and sisters, or fathers and daughters, who commit incest.

In many of her phrases Cassandra echoes Federico's sonnet. In
bewailing the power of imagination, she complains that it conjures
up impossible worlds in which all things are possible. She declares
that her hopes choke her honour in seeking to feed on things
impossible. When pressed by Cassandra, Federico admits that he
does not love Aurora, who is only the pale light of dawn compared
with the sun. Cassandra advises him to confess his feelings to the
woman he loves, and not go to the grave in silence. Then under the
guise of a story about the hunting of pelicans by surrounding them
with a ring of fire, Federico argues that silence is best:

My thoughts which are the children of my love
Kept in a nest of silence are consumed.
The flames are fanned now by the wings of love,
Which burns what it intends to liberate.
You deceive me, and I burn; you urge me
And I am lost; you cheer me and I'm fearful;
You encourage me, I'm troubled; you set me free,
And I am caught; you point me out the way,
And I'm confused—for I am in such peril.
That I believe less evil would ensue
(Since everything at last must end in death)
Were I to die and never break my silence.

(act ii)

In the next meeting with Cassandra he does break his silence.
The lovers confess that they are lost for ever; that they are bereft of
God and seized by a madness that can only lead to death. The
second act ends with an eight-fold tolling of the word for death
(*muerto*). The whole scene is written in stanza form, rhyming ababa
(*quintillas*). This is worth pointing out, as translations in prose or
blank verse give a totally misleading impression. The characters
are not exchanging disjointed exclamations of passion and horror.
They are engaged in a duet far removed from ordinary speech in
which the rhyme sweeps them into a headlong rush to destruction.
It is more like a libretto than a conversation piece:

CAS.   Leave me, Federico.
         Fare you well.
FED. [*aside*]   This is treason.
CAS.   'Tis best for you to go,
         Although the voice of reason
         Warns me that through the hand
         Poison may reach the head,
         Making us understand
         That we shall soon be dead.
FED.   Cassandra, your siren-song
         Drowns me full-fathom-five,
         And death will not be long.
CAS.   I shall be lost! O, strive
         Honour! O Fame, resist!
FED.   My forces now are spent.
CAS.   My soul is in a mist!

FED.   What strange bewilderment!
CAS.   I die for you.
FED.   My breath
        Is at this moment fled.
CAS.   Count, you will be my death!
FED.   But even though I'm dead,
        And you are lost to me,
        Rejoice! The dateless lease,
        Of immortality
        Is guarantee
        Our love need never cease.

                          (end of act II)

Of course they have to die: they know they have damned themselves. At this point they are not thinking of earthly retribution. But, at the end of the play, the Duke's obscene plot ensures that the audience sympathizes with the lovers.

When I was editing *Macbeth* some forty-five years ago, I called Shakespeare 'Poet for the Defence', by which I meant that by the poetry he was able to arouse our understanding, and to some extent, our sympathy, for a murderer; and can make us recognize that if we had been so tempted by wife and supernatural soliciting, we too might have fallen.[14] John Donne, warning us of the sin of premature judgement, remarked 'Thou knowest this man's fall, but thou knowest not his wrestling, which perchance was such that almost his very fall is justified and accepted of God.'[15] What I am suggesting is that Lope was another 'Poet for the Defence', and that his clients included Federico and Cassandra. We certainly observe their wrestling with temptation before their fall.

Nevertheless, we must remind ourselves of another characteristic Shakespeare and Lope have in common. We cannot deduce the meaning of their plays by quoting the remarks of their dramatis personae. In spite of the absurdity involved, dozens of critics from Swinburne to Kott have assured us that the keynote of *King Lear* was to be found in Gloucester's words, spoken after his savage blinding and his realization that he has been duped by Edmund's lies about Edgar:

        As flies to wanton boys are we to the gods:
        They kill us for their sport.

                          (IV.i.36–7)

The assurance of these critics conveniently ignores the fact that later in the same act Gloucester prays to the gods whom he calls ever-gentle. Both speeches are appropriate to the speaker at different moments in the play; but as Gloucester is depicted as superstitious, foolish and credulous, it is impossible to believe that Shakespeare would have chosen him to enunciate the keynote of his play. Lope and Shakespeare were dramatists to their finger tips. Their creations speak not for their creators but for themselves. Even the supposedly choric characters disagree among themselves.

This is one of the causes of the ambivalence of many of their plays, and of the difficulty of ascertaining the private opinions of the authors, especially if their religious professions conflict with their belief in the holiness of the heart's affections and the truth of the imagination.[16] As interpreters of Shakespeare we continue to believe that the meaning of the plays is not beyond all conjecture; and we assume that the same thing holds true for Lope's plays. We have to consider the views of all the characters and the deliberately conflicting impressions we are given by the dramatist. It is safe to assume that the authorial viewpoint is more likely to be expressed by the more sympathetic characters than by those who are depicted as evil. We should trust Kent rather than Oswald, Cordelia rather than Regan, Federico rather than his father. What the characters do is more important than what they say. The poetry, moreover, often modifies, and sometimes contradicts the prose paraphrase of a speech. A famous example is the soliloquy in which Macbeth decides not to murder Duncan for purely prudential reasons – that the deed would damage his reputation and lead to reprisals; but it is clear from the imagery that his real motive for not killing the King is quite different. He shrinks from the crime because his conscience is outraged.[17]

> Besides, this Duncan
> Hath borne his faculties so meek, hath been
> So clear in his great office, that his virtues
> Will plead like angels, trumpet-tongued, against
> The deep damnation of his taking-off;
> And Pity, like a naked new-born babe,
> Striding the blast, or heaven's cherubin, hors'd

> Upon the sightless couriers of the air,
> Shall blow the horrid deed in every eye,
> That tears shall drown the wind.
>
> (i.vii.16–25)

There is no doubt that Lope sometimes uses poetry with a similar function, as in some of the scenes we have been discussing.

We can speculate whether the text or the sub-text expresses the poet's own views, while realizing that both or neither may do so; and there is always the danger of our trying to saddle the poet with our own convictions and prejudices.

Keats praised Shakespeare for something that Dr Johnson regarded as a serious weakness, his refusal to be didactic. This refusal is linked to what Keats described as Negative Capability, his willingness to be in 'uncertainties, doubts and fears, without any irritable reaching after fact and reason'. We may suspect that Lope, too, despite his religious convictions, possessed something of the same negative capability. Living in an age in which, we are told, 'the best lack all conviction', we might be tempted to salute the lack of conviction in poets of past ages. But we should be wrong for two reasons: it would exhibit a total misunderstanding of Keats, and it would be based on Dr Johnson's strange belief that Shakespeare wrote without any moral purpose.

Keats certainly objected to poets who had a palpable design on their readers, to the egotistical sublime of Wordsworth's poems, and to the blinkered party spirit of Dilke, since he believed that 'the mind should be a thoroughfare for all thoughts'. Yet he himself had strong convictions and he had absorbed Moneta's lesson – that to be a great poet, rather than a dreamer, one had to be on the side of suffering humanity.[18]

Shakespeare's didactic purpose was to be a truth-teller. He did not believe in 'gilding the harsh realities of life with innocent illusions', for which Washington Irving absurdly praised him. Eighteenth-century critics who complained of Shakespeare's failure to satisfy the demands of poetic justice really wanted him to rig the evidence, in order to prove that the world was providentially governed, and that the good ended happily and the bad unhappily. That, said Miss Prism, was what fiction means. Shakespeare's fiction was not of this kind.[19]

NOTES

1 *Bulletin of Hispanic Studies* (1992), 91–6.
2 See Paul Morgan "Our Will Shakespeare' and Lope de Vega: An Unrecorded Contemporary Document', *Shakespeare Survey* 16 (1963), 118–20.
3 See A. Thaler, *Shakespeare and Sir Philip Sidney* (Cambridge, Mass., 1947).
4 See editions of *Macbeth* by J. D. Wilson (Cambridge,1947) and Kenneth Muir (London,1951, rpt. 1984).
5 Omitted from the Folio text, but audiences need this expression of their outrage. The lines are included in nearly all editions of *King Lear* and in the edition of the Quarto text included in *The Oxford Shakespeare*, ed. Stanley Wells *et al.* (Oxford, 1987).
6 For example, Roy Campbell, James Lloyd, Jill Booty. Roy Campbell's version of *Fuenteovejuna* was published in *The Classic Theatre*, ed. Eric Bentley (New York, 1959), III. Booty's are listed in n. 7 and Lloyd's in n. 10. In *Literature and Translation* (1992), 104–11, I have argued that it is desirable to use rhyme in some scenes of Golden Age plays, although this involves less literal accuracy.
7 In the preface to Jill Booty's *Five Plays* (New York, 1961), p. xxviii.
8 See, for example, the lines in *No siempre lo peor es cierto* in *Four Comedies*, tran. Kenneth Muir (Lexington, KY,1980), p. 170:

> Woe to the first who made so harsh a law,
> A contract so unjust, a tie so impious,
> Which deals unequally to man and woman,
> And links our honor to another's whim.

9 Geoffrey Ribbans, *Bulletin of Hispanic Studies* 31 (1954), 150–70, shows that the monarchy was the rock on which society rested, the aristocracy being the greatest potential cause of trouble. More controversially, he argues that Lope disapproved of Lawrencia's 'vehemence, lack of control and violent language'. The later revelation that she had fought off the rapist was a dramatic necessity if the audience was to accept the possibility of her marriage. Attempted rape surely justifies violent language.
10 Lloyd in his edition of the play (Warminster, 1990), p. 45, quotes from Antonio de Guevara. Similar views were expressed by Wordsworth and Thomas Hardy.
11 E. M. Wilson, 'Images et structure dans *Peribañez*', *Bulletin Hispanique*, 51 (1949), 125–59.
12 *Bulletin of Hispanic Studies* 34 (1957), 213–22.
13 I am indebted to Ann L. Mackenzie for assistance with this translation.
14 *Macbeth*, p. xliv.

15 Peter Alexander applied Donne's words to Macbeth.
16 John Keats, *Letters*, ed. H. E. Rollins (Cambridge, Mass., 1958), I, p. 184.
17 Kenneth Muir, *Shakespeare the Professional* (Liverpool, 1973), p. 137.
18 Keats, *Letters* ed. Rollins, I, pp. 224, 387, II, p. 213.
19 Kenneth Muir, *Shakespeare's Didactic Art*, Pratt Lecture, Memorial University of St John's (Newfoundland, 1984), *passim*. Reprinted in *Shakespeare : Contrasts and Controversies* (Brighton, 1985).

Index